JEWELRY MAKING
Techniques for Metal

JEWELRY MAKING
Techniques for Metal

Tim McCreight

Dover Publications, Inc.
Mineola, New York

Acknowledgments

Putting this book together has been a pleasure for me largely because of the help that I've received from many sources. I'm grateful to a lot of folks: to my colleagues and students at the Craft Center, who encouraged me with their questions; to Chuck Evans, Curtis LaFollette, and Will Earley, who read, questioned, and contributed; and to my wife, whose many hours of typing and reading are of little importance compared to the support that she's given me throughout the entire project. That's why this book is **for Jay**

Copyright

Copyright © 1979 by Tim McCreight

Bibliographical Note

This Dover edition, first published in 2005, is an unabridged republication of the work originally published as *Metalworking for Jewelry: Tools, Materials, Techniques* by Van Nostrand Reinhold Company, New York, in 1979. The color plates of the original edition have been rendered in black and white for the present edition and appear between pages 58 and 59; the plates appear in color on the covers. Unless otherwise stated, the drawings and artwork are by the author, and the photographs by John I. Russell.

Library of Congress Cataloging-in-Publication Data

McCreight, Tim.
    Jewelry making : techniques for metal / Tim McCreight.
        p. cm.
    Reprint. Originally published: New York : Van Nostrand Reinhold, 1979.
    ISBN 0-486-44043-5 (pbk.)
     1. Jewelry making. 2. Metal-work. I. Title.

TT212.M385 2005
739—dc22

2004061819

Manufactured in the United States of America
Dover Publications, Inc., 31 East 2nd Street, Mineola, N.Y. 11501

Contents

Introduction

Each of us comes to craftwork in a different way. Some approach it as a business. For others it can be a social activity. For all of us it is to some degree a form of therapy. It is our chance to stare the world in the eye and say, "I made this." Whether we're holding a masterpiece or a crude first attempt, the value lies not in the object itself but in the fact that we made it. Since this showdown with the universe can be a bit scary, it's natural to want to arm yourself with some information that will make the creative work a little less chancy and the results a bit more valuable. And that is the reason for this book.

It contains nothing magical. In it you'll find procedures and gimmicks that have been invented or discovered by ordinary people over the past several thousand years. If you had the time, you might also be able to come up with some of them. But in the interest of efficiency I've collected the tricks and techniques that seem most useful to me and tried to explain them.

Jewelry making is a particularly enjoyable craft to teach because it is made up of more or less independent components. The techniques described here are like building blocks. With just one or two you'll be able to make a piece of jewelry. With the time and interest you can acquire more skills and increase your versatility. Though I am writing for the beginner, I have not limited the scope of this book only to the basics. No particular procedure is impossibly complicated, but I think you'll find the sophisticated techniques of raising, mokumé, wire inlay, and casting challenging enough to keep any metalworker occupied for a while.

This book is designed to be a reference volume that will come in handy for a long time after your initial reading. I have tried to include formulas, recipes, and tables that will make your work faster and technically correct. As your involvement in jewelry making deepens, you may want to complement this book with others on the history of metalwork, contemporary jewelry making, and design.

Any craft involves an interplay of materials, tools, and techniques. After describing the metals most commonly used in jewelry work I present a sampling of the tools that are needed. My attempt is not to equip the professional shop but to give the average crafter an idea of what is available and what it looks like. The next chapter describes the basic techniques of this craft. Since these procedures are repeated in almost every piece that you make, they are laid out as clearly and in as much detail as possible. The chapter on finishing provides enough information for you to complete a piece of jewelry. With just these four chapters you should be able to make several jewelry pieces and have an overview of the methods involved. Subsequent chapters describe methods for altering the shape or surface of the metal in increasingly sophisticated ways. The final chapter deals with the possibilities of making a living from the sale of handcrafted jewelry. This is not meant to be a guide to starting a business but is included to answer some important questions in the minds of those readers who want to become professionally involved in crafts. The appendices at the back of the book provide addresses of suppliers, tables and charts, and information on buying stones and precious metals.

I have tried in the illustrations to offer as clear a presentation as possible of the idea at hand. The photographs represent not only work by professional craftspeople but pieces made by students. Care was taken to select work that showed a single technique as clearly as possible in an effort to give a succinct account of what it can accomplish.

I didn't learn to make jewelry so that I could write a book. I didn't even learn so that I could make a living at it. I make jewelry because it's fun and because it answers a basic need. It is my response to a universe that says, "Who are you?" I hope that you can find the same kind of enjoyment and fulfillment in the craft.

1. The Metals

A number of factors comprise a finished piece of craftwork: the skill of the maker, the materials used, the function of the item, and the tools available. Any handcrafted item can be analyzed in terms of these factors and others like them, but the enjoyment is not found in that kind of analysis. The pleasure of a handmade article lies in a response to the material and to the hand that shaped it. For metalworkers the material makes this appeal almost by itself. It is bright and shiny, can take on a range of colors, and will yield an endless supply of forms and textures.

Though the metals usually used for jewelry are not cheap, any hesitation about the cost should be tempered with the knowledge that every scrap can be refined and reused. On a small scale scraps are often used as decoration or to provide small bits for melting. If a greater volume is involved, special trays are mounted under the workbench to catch scraps and filings (called *lemel*) so that nothing is lost. These can be reshaped into a usable form in the workshop, but many jewelers find it more economical to send the scraps to a refiner, who will exchange them for standard material.

Precious metal is available in the form of sheets, wires, and small ingots or pebbles called *casting grain.* The thickness of sheet and wire is measured in terms of a scale called the *Brown and Sharpe (B & S) gauge system.* It consists of a series of numbers running from 0 at the thickest (about ¼″ or 6mm) to 36 (finer than a human hair) at the thinnest. Though the system includes all the digits from 0 to 36, only the even-numbered sizes are readily available, and they provide a sufficient choice for almost all jewelry needs.

Precious metals are usually sold by the *troy ounce,* a unit of weight slightly greater than the common avoirdupois ounce. Details on purchasing metals and addresses of metal suppliers are found at the back of the book.

In order to describe the materials most frequently used in jewelry making, it is necessary to know a few terms that deal with the properties of metal. When combined with air, most metals have a tendency to *oxidize,* or to combine with oxygen along their surface. This produces a scale or film; on steel it is called *rust;* on silver, *tarnish.* The ability of a metal to resist oxidation is an important factor in determining its use. Tin, for example, oxidizes just enough to produce a film that is oxide-resistant. This makes it useful for food vessels and explains why copper cookware is usually tin-lined. Pure silver oxidizes very little and is suited for use under transparent enamels. Pewter, on the other hand, oxidizes slowly and develops a rich *patina,* or surface color, that adds to its beauty. It is generally true that the rate of oxidation increases as heat is applied; and, since an oxide layer inhibits the flow of solder, metals that oxidize rapidly are usually more difficult to join.

Another important property of metal for jewelry purposes is its tendency to harden as it is stressed. This is called *work hardening* and is the result of the compaction of an orderly crystalline structure by external forces—such as the blow of a hammer or the force needed to twist a wire. Some metals (such as silver and copper) can withstand more stress than others—these are said to be more *malleable*—but every metal has its breaking point. It would be impossible to make some shapes if it weren't for the ability of metal to *anneal,* or to be returned to a malleable state when heated. As it is heated, the crystalline structure recreates its normal alignment, bringing the metal back to its original malleability. This process can be repeated as often as needed, allowing flat shapes to be hammered into deep vessels or stretched into thin wires. Sterling and gold are supplied in the annealed state (technically called *dead soft*), while copper and brass are available in either hardened or annealed form, depending on the source.

The Noble Metals
Gold

Gold has always been one of the most prized of all metals; this is one of the few constants that link cultures that developed independently, separated by time and geography. Gold was probably the second metal to be fashioned by man, following copper, which, like gold, is found in nature as nuggets. Gold is notable for its extreme malleability, resistance to corrosion, warm shine, and alloying response—that is to say, it can be shaped easily, doesn't tarnish, polishes well, and can be mixed to yield a wide range of properties. Its melting point varies from 1515°F to 2300°F (815°C to 1247°C).

The amount of pure gold in an alloy is called its *karat* (K)—not to be confused with *carat,* which is a

alloy	% gold	% silver	% copper	% other	melting point (approx.)	
18K yellow	75	10-20	5-15		1660°F	903°C
14K yellow	58	4-28	14-28		1565	843
10K yellow	42	20-30	28-38	16-19	1515	815
14K white	58		16-19	nickel	1690	920
18K green	75	25			1770	965
14K green	58	42			1600	862
18K rose (pink)	75		25		1600	862
14K rose (pink)	58.3		41.7		1670	911
platinum gold	60			40 platinum	2300	1247
dark red	50		50		1832	1000
blue	75		25 iron		2129	1165

unit of weight used in measuring gems. The karat is the numerator of a fraction in which the denominator is 24 and refers to the amount of pure gold in an alloy—18K gold, therefore, is 18/24 pure gold. Two other common alloys are 14K, which is 58% gold, and 10K, which is 42% pure. Alloys containing less than 10 karats cannot legally be called gold.

By changing the ingredients and proportions of an alloy gold may be changed in color from its natural yellow. Pure gold is extremely malleable and any additive makes it harder, but this can be controlled to create an alloy that is relatively hard for some uses, such as teeth, and relatively soft for other needs, as for hammering and stretching. The chart (left) lists some of the common alloys of gold.

Though it is of only minor importance to craftspeople, an explanation of gold-coated metal is relevant here. Any karat of gold may be plated, or deposited on an item made of cheaper metal. The thickness of the coating is important, since a thin layer will wear off sooner than a thick one. The term *plate* refers to a thin layer of gold, the karat of which should be plainly stated, as in "24K gold-plated." The term *gold-filled* refers to a thicker layer and actually means external gold that is filled with another metal. A common deposit is 1/20 the total thickness of the item; it is designated as 18K 1/20 GF. This means that the piece is covered with a layer of 18K gold that makes up 5% of the total thickness. The metal underneath may be silver, brass, or any other metal: it need not be identified. Gold-filled wire is commercially available from some jewelry-supply companies, but its use is limited, since any filing or cutting will reveal the base metal.

Silver

Silver is a white-colored metal that takes on a bright shine when polished. In its unalloyed state it is too soft for most decorative uses, but it has a high resistance to corrosion that makes it valuable for electrical contact points and medical implants, including tooth fillings. It occasionally occurs independently in nature but is most commonly obtained as a by-product of the refining of gold, lead, copper, and zinc ores. In jewelry work fine or pure silver is used in connection with transparent enamels, in which the oxidation of other metals would cloud the color, and in making *bezels,* the rims of metal that encircle gemstones and hold them in place; fine silver is especially appropriate, because its softness allows the metal to be safely pressed against the stone. The melting point of silver is 1761°F (961°C).

Sterling Silver

Many years ago it was found that, if small amounts of copper were mixed with silver, the resulting alloy retained the characteristic bright shine but was much stronger. Over the years it was determined that a mixture of 92½% silver to 7½% copper was the best all-around blend. This alloy came to be known as *sterling silver,* and its use is so common that the terms "silver" and "sterling" are now almost synonymous.

Because of its strength and shine sterling has many uses, from buttons to trophies. The copper content in the alloy, which makes it so versatile, does not come without a price. Unlike its parent metal, sterling combines with air to form a gray surface coating (tarnish) that hides its luster. The alloy also has a tendency to break down at the high temperatures needed for annealing and soldering, forming a gray oxide layer called *fire scale,* which can greatly mar the beauty of a piece. The melting point of sterling is 1640°F (893°C).

A variation of the sterling alloy, called *coin silver,* contains between 80% and 90% silver, with the balance copper. The 90% variety was used in American coinage until 1966. Coin silver has a slightly higher melting point than sterling but is generally worked in the same way and with the same solders. It polishes to about the same degree of shine as sterling but tarnishes more quickly, taking on a dull gray finish. This alloy is frequently used for jewelry construction in non-English-speaking countries and accounts for the familiar gray color of much imported work. Items made of coin silver bear a mark reading 800 or 900, indicating the parts of silver per thousand.

Platinum

Platinum is a very hard, silver-colored metal that is slightly more costly than gold. Because of its extreme hardness it is commonly used if groupings of expensive stones are to be set. It can be cast, hammered, and soldered (using special platinum solders), but because of its cost it is not often used by handcrafters. Platinum has a high resistance to corrosion; and, since it is malleable enough to be formed into thin sheets, it is used as leaf if a bright silver color is desired. A residue of platinum ore, called *rhodium,* is similarly tarnish-resistant and is used in the jewelry industry as a plating on sterling articles to prevent tarnishing during shipping, storage, and display. This is a *flash,* or very thin plating, that wears off quickly as the piece is worn. The melting point of platinum is 3225°F (1775°C).

Copper and its Alloys
Copper

Copper is familiar to everyone from its use in pennies; and, having seen enough of these, we all know that copper can take a bright, red-orange shine when polished but quickly tarnishes into a dull brown. Copper is similar in hardness to sterling and can be used to practice techniques before working them on the more expensive metal. Its cost has been going up over the last few years, but it is still relatively inexpensive—a piece the size of a penny costs about a penny. Copper can be sawn, bent, and formed in the same manner as sterling and may be joined with silver solders (which will leave a silver-colored line). Though copper can be cast, it is less desirable than other jewelry metals because of the large amount of *slag,* or waste material, that is produced in melting.

Because of its industrial uses there are many forms of copper available. Many craftspeople buy their copper directly from jewelry-supply companies. From these sources it can be bought in small, regular pieces, such as disks and squares of common B & S gauges. Copper is available commercially in hot- or cold-rolled sheets. These terms refer, not unexpectedly, to the temperature at which the metal is pressed through rollers to make it into sheet. *Hot-rolled* copper is the softer of the two but has a rougher surface texture. For this reason most craftspeople prefer to buy *cold-rolled* stock and to anneal it themselves. When buying from industrial suppliers, be prepared to order thickness by the thousandth of an inch and feel free to explain your needs, since there are many alloys available. The melting point of copper is 1981°F (1083°C).

Brass

Brass is basically an alloy of copper and zinc, but modern technology has created a vast assortment of brasses that confuses all but the professional metallurgist. Simply stated, brass can be divided into *low-zinc* alloys, which contain less than 30% zinc, and *high-zinc* mixtures, which contain more than 30%. The high-zinc metals are very strong and are used to make screws, fittings, and nozzles. The low-zinc brasses are of greater interest to jewelers, since they are more easily worked and more closely resemble gold in color. A mix of 90% copper and 10% zinc, known as *commercial bronze* (though it's not a bronze at all), is readily available and works well for jewelry. Another common alloy contains 88% copper and 12% zinc. It was developed in Victorian times as a substitute for gold and was then called Pinchbeck metal. Today it can be bought as Nu-Gold, Red Brass, or Jewelry Bronze #226. The melting point of brass is approximately 1600°-2000°F (860°-1090°C).

Bronze

In ancient cultures *bronze,* which is an alloy of copper and tin, was widely used for art objects and utilitarian implements. Very little pure bronze is manufactured today: small amounts of other metals are usually added to create an alloy that is especially appropriate for industrial needs. The most common is *phosphor* bronze (94.65% copper, 5% tin, 0.35% phosphor), which is very hard and inappropriate for most jewelry work. The melting point of bronze is 2822°-3420°F (1550°-1900°C).

Nickel (German) Silver

Nickel (German) silver is a confusing term, since this alloy contains no silver at all. It is similar in color to silver and is often used as a base upon which silver is plated. A common variety contains 62% copper, 33% nickel, and 5% zinc. It is sold by some craft suppliers and sometimes used by beginners who are hesitant about starting out with a precious metal. It is harder to bend than sterling and demands higher temperatures for soldering and fusing. These factors, together with the fact that the finished product does not have the warm shine characteristic of sterling, lead me to recommend that beginners swallow their fears and start with the more precious metal. The melting point of nickel is 1960°F (1060°C).

White Metals
Lead

Lead is a gray metal that is soft enough to be scratched with a fingernail. It is one of the oldest metals known to man, since it occurs near the earth's surface and can be reduced from its ore with a normal fire. Because it is so soft, it is almost never used in jewelry. Its softness, however, does make it useful as a piece of jewelry-making equipment, and it is discussed in this context elsewhere in the book. It is important that lead not be left on a piece of silver or gold that is to be soldered, since it will burn holes into the precious metals when heated to soldering temperatures. The melting point of lead is 621°F (327°C).

Tin

Tin is a soft white metal that is rarely used by itself but is common in alloys and as a plating. It is resistant to acids and air and is used as a coating to make vessels such as cans safe for food. It is combined with copper to make bronze and is important in the production of soft solder, an alloy of tin and lead. The melting point of tin is 450°F (232°C).

Pewter

Pewter was originally an alloy of lead and tin that was widely used in the Orient and throughout the Roman Empire. It is traditionally associated with colonial America, where a mixture of 20% lead and 80% tin was very popular. Because of the danger of lead poisoning modern pewter, more correctly called *brittania metal,* is composed of 91% tin, 7% antimony, and 2% copper. It is more silvery in color than old pewter, stronger, keeps its luster longer, and, because it contains no lead, is much safer. Pewter is very soft and does not harden when it is worked. It may be sawn, bent, and raised in the same way as harder metals but must be joined with tin-base solders. The melting point of pewter (brittania) is 471°F (244°C).

All these metals are traditionally associated with precious objects and are those most commonly used today, but the enterprising jeweler should not feel limited to them. Contemporary craftspeople are experimenting with aluminum, steel, stainless steel, and new alloys using precious metals. And there is plenty of room for newcomers.

2. The Tools

It has been said that a craftsman is no better than his tools, and, though I think that this is slightly overstating the case, there is no question that a unique and intimate bond can be formed between a worker and his or her tools. As a hobby jewelry making is no more expensive than many others and can in fact be cheaper. For the cost of a set of golf clubs, for instance, a very adequate shop can be set up; and, while golf continues to cost (fees, rubbing alcohol), an investment in jewelry stands a good chance of paying for itself as you sell your work.

There is a great advantage in having a permanent workbench set up and ready to go. Not only can you leave your work out while in progress, which saves a lot of time, but you can mentally shift gears and get into the proper frame of mind more quickly when a specific corner of the universe is devoted just to you and your work.

You need some sort of sturdy table or workbench. In some parts of the world metalsmiths sit on the ground and work at low tables. Most professional jewelers in the West prefer a small, high bench that puts the work at eye level. Many people start out on a desk or kitchen table. Your own situation determines the type of bench that you have, and this in turn affects your shop layout and working pattern. There are no absolutes, but a few commonsense ideas are in order. The layout should be compact

enough so that most of your tools can be reached without getting up. Clean activities (drawing, sawing, bending) should be kept separate from dirty ones (buffing, soldering). The space must be well lit and should provide adequate ventilation. You should have a comfortable chair and a handy source of water.

Before spending any money on tools take a look around the house, since you might already have some of the basic equipment. You need some pens and pencils, paper, string, masking tape, a good small ruler (preferably steel), a compass, epoxy, and a few old toothbrushes. A pair of heavy-duty (or kitchen) scissors comes in handy, as does an assortment of small jars and dishes. A Pyrex dish and a hot plate are needed; and, while you're in the kitchen, pick up some baking soda and laundry borax powder. From the toolbox you can use a lightweight tack hammer, a ball-peen hammer, any old files that you can find, pliers, wire snips, and perhaps an adjustable wrench. If you run across a drill, this puts you ahead of the game, and you'll also find uses for an assortment of large nails and lengths of dowel. Not all these tools are used on the jewelry itself but are needed for general shop operation. When you've spirited these things away, you're ready to invest some money in the specialty tools used in jewelry making.

At the back of this book there is a list of several major supply companies. You can also check the Yellow Pages for local craft-supply stores. Most large companies go to great expense to print carefully detailed catalogs, and it is a good idea to send away for a few. A good catalog is more than just a list of available items and should be read periodically as a textbook. Instead of trying to photograph individual tools here I have left this rather costly chore to the distributors and suggest that you consult their catalogs for details on equipment.

Like buying clothes or books, purchasing tools is a personal activity; and, though many sources can give you hints, in the end your own intuition plays a big role in determining what you buy. Many tools come in several sizes and often in several quality ranges. Although it is sometimes important to pay a bit more to get the best, in other cases the cheaper product will serve your needs just as well. My own choices are given here with this note: any jeweler you talk to has his or her own ideas of what is a good buy or a necessary tool and of what is overpriced or extravagant.

I have divided the tools into six categories according to metal treatment. My intention is not to provide a comprehensive list of all the tools that are made for a given purpose but rather to describe the equipment most commonly used by practicing craftspeople. The tools are described in sufficient detail to purchase them, but their use is explained in subsequent chapters. The topic of tools can overwhelm a beginning student, so a list of important tools is included at the end of the chapter. Some suppliers offer a starter kit containing many of these items, and in some cases it can be a good buy. Only the basic tools are discussed here—more specialized equipment is described in the appropriate technique chapters.

Measuring and Marking

The most expensive piece of measuring and marking equipment is the *troy-weight scale,* and it becomes important only when dealing with a large volume or with a lot of gold scraps. Both the *degree* gauge and the *gauge wheel* are used to determine thickness and are most frequently used when doing commissions or repairs that involve matching an existing piece. Most jewelry items, including precious stones, are measured on the metric system, so it is a good idea to have a *metric ruler.* Transparent-plastic *templates* are convenient for drawing exact ovals, hexagons, and other shapes. At a few dollars each they are not essentials but timesaving luxuries. They can be bought at an art-supply store. Though you should be careful about making scratches in sheet metal, a sharp *scribe* leaves a clean line that shows up through soldering heat. I especially recommend it for marking lines with a ruler. Keep the scribe point sharp by sanding it as necessary.

Cutting and Bending

This category is the most essential, and top-quality buying is recommended across the board. The most confusing item in this group is probably the *pliers,* since a range of shapes, sizes, and prices is available. The three shapes that I find most useful are *chain-nose* (flat, pointed jaws), *round-nose* (cone-shaped jaws), and *flat-nose* (flat, wide jaws). Beyond these, each type has a specific function that can make it handy to an advanced worker, but the beginner need not invest in more than these three. The average length of jeweler's pliers is about 5″ (13cm), which is small enough even for delicate hands. Beware of the term "watchmaker's" in connection with any handtool: it indicates a miniature version that is too frail for jewelry construction. Almost all pliers are available in either box- or parallel-jaw construction. A box joint opens like a scissors but is especially designed to keep the two halves from separating sideways. A parallel-jaw opening is slightly more bulky in the hand but has the advantage of providing more grip along the piece that is held.

Wires are cut with a plierlike tool called a *snips.* It is available in two varieties: *side cutters* are more versatile than the slightly broader *end cutters.* These tools can be bought in a local hardware store or through a jewelry supplier. Too large a snips is awk-

Measuring and marking equipment: (1) steel rulers (with metric scale), (2) gauge plate, (3) degree gauge, (4) masking tape, (5) steel scribe, (6) templates, (7) troy-weight scale.

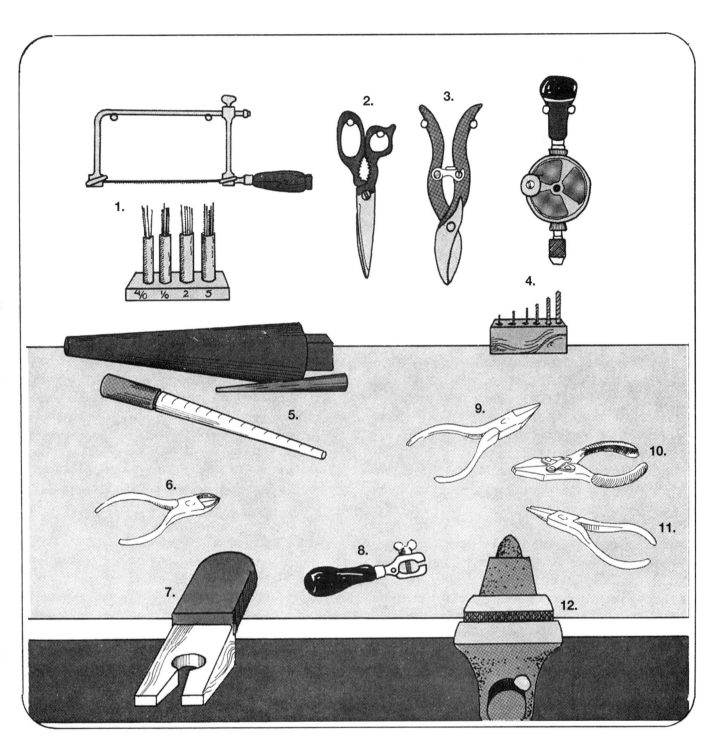

Cutting and bending equipment: (1) saw frame and assorted blades, (2) kitchen shears, (3) aviation shears, (4) eggbeater-type drill and assorted bits, (5) mandrel (ring, bezel, and bracelet), (6) snips (side cutters), (7) combination bench pin and surface plate, (8) hand vise, (9) chain-nose pliers, (10) flat-nose pliers (parallel-jaw construction), (11) round-nose pliers, (12) bench vise.

ward to use, but the smallest styles do not stand up to long use: a middle range, in both price and size, is recommended.

Thin sheet up to 20-gauge can be cut with *kitchen shears*. If you plan to work with heavier stock, you should invest in *aviation shears,* which are heavy-duty scissors that look like garden shears. They are available in a wide price range from a hardware store or jewelry supplier; the more you can spend, the better tool you will get, but even a cheap model should last for several years.

Any rod used as a guide and support for forming is called a *mandrel.* The three most common varieties are *bezel, ring,* and *bracelet.* Because commercial mandrels are made of accurately machined, good-quality steel, they are not cheap. Money spent here is a good investment, since mandrels never wear out if they are used properly, but the shoestring hobbyist can get by with substitutes until the capital is forthcoming. A sawn-off baseball bat works well as a bracelet mandrel (ask the local team for one of their broken bats), and a ring mandrel can be made of wood. It can be turned on a lathe if you have access to a woodworking shop, or the tapered rung of an old chair (check the dump) can be used. A machinist's tool called a *drift pin* makes an excellent bezel mandrel; a good-size hardware store carries it. Commercial mandrels are available in both round and oval shapes, but I have never found the more expensive oval type to be necessary. Mandrels are not machines that automatically form the metal to a given size but curved supports against which the metal is shaped. By sliding the work along the mandrel and turning it in your hand you can bend any curved shape on a round mandrel.

As simple as it is, the *bench pin* is the focal point of the jeweler's bench. It is a block of hardwood that projects from the workbench to provide support while sawing, bending, or setting stones. Some benches are made with a slot that allows the pin to be inserted into the tabletop itself. A cast-iron flange can be bought and screwed onto the front of the bench to hold the work, or a board can be simply clamped onto the bench in the correct position with a C-clamp. The bench-pin holder shown in the diagram, which seems to be a good investment, is a variation that provides a holding flange with a surface plate that can be used for hammering.

In just about any cutting or bending operation it is important that the work be securely held. The best device for this is the hand, but it must sometimes be aided by tools. The most versatile holding device is a large *vise.* It is used more to hold tools than the metal itself and is almost like having an apprentice around to help. A heavy vise (around 20 pounds) is worth the investment, even if you have to wait a while to get a good one. It should be bolted to a sturdy table and equipped with copper, plastic, or aluminum jaw covers to protect soft metal from scarring. A much smaller vise that is held against the bench pin when in use is called a *hand vise.* Several models are available, and any one of them seems to do the trick.

Next to pliers the most frequently used piece of equipment in the metal shop is the *saw frame.* It is priced between $4 and $14; I would not recommend spending less than $8. Cheap frames fail to hold saw blades tightly, causing frustration and wasting time. Frames are sold by the depth of cut possible, or the distance from the blade to the back of the saw. Small frames are lighter and easier to control than large ones: a 4″ size should be adequate for most jewelers.

Soldering

Light soldering can be done right at a jeweler's bench; but, if space permits, it's a good idea to prepare a separate area. The soldering bench should be covered with asbestos board, called *transite* (available from a lumberyard), well ventilated, and dimly lit. Ventilation is a good idea, since fluxes and pickle give off nasty fumes, and low lighting allows better perception of the color changes in metal as it is heated.

The *torch* shown in the drawing uses disposable cylinders of *propane* and can be bought at a hardware or discount store for about $12. It has a few drawbacks—it is awkward to use, for example—but for the price it is hard to beat. If funds permit, a Prest-o-lite unit is the next step up. It oper-

Soldering tools: (1) propane torch with disposable cylinder, (2) iron binding wire, (3) tripod with steel mesh, (4) solder (cut), (5) firebrick, (6) soldering probe, (7) copper tongs, (8) transite, (9) 6″ soldering and cross-lock tweezers, (10) pumice pan.

ates on a tank of acetylene gas, which is mixed with atmospheric air at the tip. Several brands are available from a plumbing or welding supplier. The gas tanks are purchased full and swapped when empty. Not shown but perhaps worth investigation are torches that use solid pellets to produce oxygen. They provide a hotter flame than single-gas torches but are usually equipped with a tip that is too large for jewelry use. The best choice, and one that is used by many professionals, is an oxygen-acetylene torch with a microtip. It produces a very hot, precise flame that is difficult for a beginner to manage but quite versatile in the right hands.

Soldering can take place on a number of surfaces, each of which has advantages and disadvantages. Many craftspeople are concerned about the use of asbestos, since its fibers, once inhaled, can cause respiratory harm. Soft, flaky asbestos *millboard* is especially troublesome and is not recommended. An asbestos paper that is rolled into a coil and set in a small, flat dish seems slightly less harmful and makes a flat soldering surface. The best surface is probably *firebrick*, which is used to build kilns. A soft variety is handy, since pins can be pushed into it to hold work while soldering. For holding work that does not have to lie flat, pebble-size pieces of *pumice* are commonly used. A smaller grain, made of Carborundum, is used in the same way and is sometimes preferred for more delicate holding. Pans made to hold this grain can be found through jewelry suppliers, but a standard round cake pan can also be used. It is advantageous for the dish to pivot so that heat can be spread evenly. To accomplish this, a penny can be taped onto the underside of the pan in the center, or a bump may be hammered with a nail or punch from the inside center to form a raised knob that allows the pan to revolve.

Many aspects of soldering differ according to specific needs and preferences. I like to keep solder cut and ready to use; any shallow container can be used to hold it. For those who prefer a wire solder a small handle called a *pin vise* is handy for holding short lengths; a *hemostat*, available from the family doctor, is another good holder. I like to keep two pairs of soldering *tweezers* on the bench, since they tend to heat up as they are used. You can switch back and forth between the two and save an occasional burned finger. The *probe,* which is used to carry solder into the flame and to manipulate work while it is hot, can be bought as a scribe or improvised from an old needle file or a piece of coathanger wire. A *striker,* used to light the torch, can be bought at a hardware store or replaced by a disposable cigarette lighter.

Hammering

Of top priority in this category are the *mallet,* planishing *hammer,* and smooth *surface plate.* A small plate is sufficient for most jewelry needs—which is fortunate, since the larger sizes are expensive. The *anvil, stake holder,* and *stake* shown are used in raising and heavy forging and are not essential for most beginning jewelers.

Be careful to distinguish between hammers used on soft metals (copper, gold, sterling) and hammers used to drive nails or strike punches. It is important that the face of any hammer used to strike the jewelry metal be free of nicks. Any scratches will be transmitted to the metal with each blow, resulting in a scarred shape that will need filing. Marks accidentally made in a hammer face should be removed with fine sandpaper. The same rule of smoothness applies to the surface plate and anvil; it is a good idea to make a wooden cover for these pieces to protect them from accidental scarring. If the wood is saturated with mineral or linseed oil, the covers will also prevent rust.

Hammers can be bought from local sources, such as antique, junk, or hardware stores, but specific shapes are available only from a jewelry-supply company. Except for the cheapest models, which are obviously inferior, I have found good-quality hammers from each source. It is not uncommon to buy old heads, file out all the scars, and equip them with new handles. Before proceeding, however, test the hammer face to ensure that it is hard enough to retain a smooth finish. Slide a file across the head. If

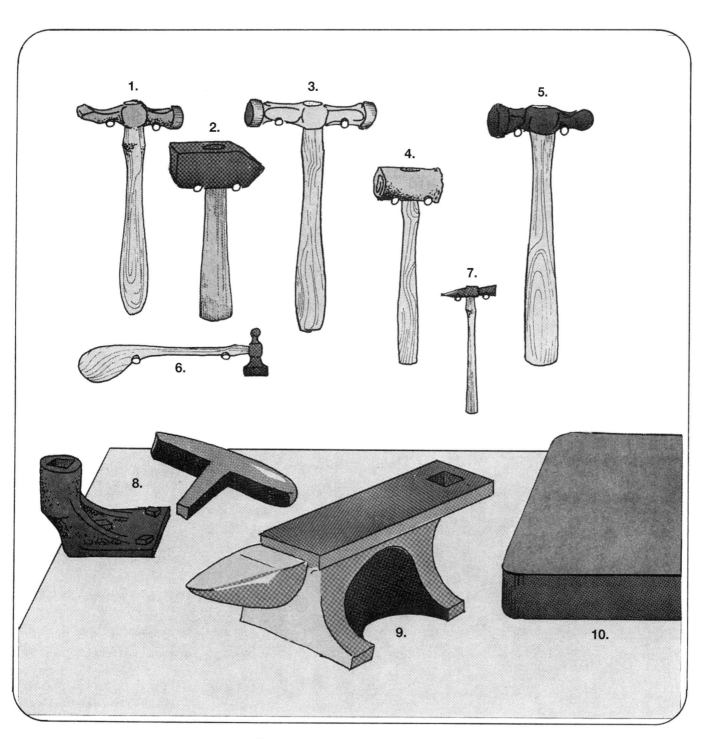

Hammering equipment: (1) raising hammer, (2) forging hammer, (3) planishing hammer, (4) rawhide mallet, (5) ball-peen hammer, (6) chasing hammer, (7) riveting hammer (8) stake holder and T-stake, (9) anvil, (10) surface plate.

it makes a high-pitched, scratchy noise but does not cut in, the hammer is tempered and worth refinishing. If the file cuts into the head, it is made of mild steel and is good only for hitting punches. To secure the head onto a handle, pound hardwood wedges into a sawn slot and hold in place with glue.

For any hitting operation the hammer needs to be heavy enough to do the job but light enough to be controlled. The weights given below are appropriate for people with an average build; adjust your needs accordingly. One word to the wise, however—a light hammer means only that you have to work harder, not that you are being kind to yourself. I prefer an 8- or 10-ounce *planishing hammer* and a slightly heavier *forging hammer* if much work on thick stock is planned. For hitting short steel punches you need a *chasing hammer* or a light *ball-peen hammer*—around 8 ounces. A *cross-peen,* or *raising, hammer* should weigh between 8 and 12 ounces. All these hammers are made of steel and will dent or flatten precious metals. To form soft metal without distorting its thickness, a mallet made of rawhide, wood, rubber, or plastic is used. The rawhide type is the most common. A 10-ounce head is preferred.

Filing and Polishing

Most people recognize that a chisel must have a precise edge and would be willing to pay more for top quality. If you think of a *file* as a collection of hundreds of tiny chisels, the importance of buying a good file becomes apparent. Files found at a discount store tend to be made under less exacting controls than are expensive files and wear out quickly. If you find yourself replacing files every six months, you should perhaps consider the meaning of the phrase "false economy."

Hand files are sold according to the length of the toothed section and may be furnished with or without handles. I find a small file just as easy to use without as with a handle, but the larger sizes can do more cutting for the push if they are lengthened by adding a handle. Hand files can be bought at a hardware store. A number of systems are used to describe the coarseness of files; since most catalogs are careful to describe their terms, I refer you to them. As a rule I prefer a coarse or medium-coarse grit, leaving finer work to sandpaper. The most commonly preferred shapes are half-round, triangular, and hand. One of the small sides of the hand file, which is rectangular in section, should be a safe edge—that is, without teeth.

Needle files are precision tools used to work in tight places. The same rule about cheap materials pertains here. Needle files are sold according to their overall length, about a third of which is a round-knurled shank: 6¼" (15cm) is a standard size. The handiest shapes are half-round, equaling (flat), round, triangular, crossing (double-curve), and square. A similar tool that is slightly thinner and about twice as wide as the equaling file, called an *ignition-point file,* is available from auto-supply dealers.

If you intend to do much work with pewter, you should keep a separate set of files for it. Files appropriate for precious metals clog quickly if used on a soft material such as pewter, and the filings will contaminate silver or gold. Wide-tooth, self-clearing files, often with teeth that run in parallel lines, are made to be used on pewter, plastic, or wood and are worth the cost if much work with such soft materials is anticipated.

Riffler files have a specialized use and are not a necessity to the beginning craftsperson. They are about the same size as needle files but have teeth only along the tip. They are handy for mechanically precise work; but, as is true of any file, care must be taken that they are used only if needed and that a larger file is substituted when possible.

Also shown here is the *buffing machine,* which is discussed in chapter 4. You should not try to use the machine until you have read the appropriate section, since there are some safety precautions that can save time, trouble, and perhaps pain.

Casting

Casting is discussed in chapter 8, which starts with a list of definitions that makes these tools and their uses more comprehensible to the beginning

Finishing equipment: (1) hand files, (2) file card, (3) needle files, (4) sanding sticks, (5) buffing machine.

Casting equipment: (1) rubber bases, (2) pouring crucible, (3) flasks, (4) vibrator, (5) plastic sleeves, (6) assorted hard and soft wax, (7) alcohol lamp, (8) biology needle and dental tool, (9) centrifugal casting machine.

student. A great deal of casting equipment can be bought secondhand from a dental laboratory or improvised from other materials. A common waxworking tool is a *biology needle,* which can be bought wherever scientific supplies are sold (such as a college bookstore) or, as a *clay needle,* from a ceramics supplier. Fine *chisels* for carving can often be picked up from a dentist.

Shop Equipment

All the tools mentioned so far can be grouped under the general heading of bench tools, since that's where they are kept. As a rule, they are frequently used items that should be owned by every jewelry worker. Described here are some larger pieces of equipment that are used in common by many people—for instance, in a class or production shop. Some of them are motorized and stationary. They are all expensive: from $50 to $200. Most of them do work that can also be done by hand, but they do it more quickly and often more neatly. I mention them here so that the reader is aware of their possibilities and so that a student who has access to them is familiar with their function. They are all available from large jewelry suppliers, and comparative shopping is recommended, since prices can vary considerably.

Flexible-shaft Machine

The *flexible-shaft machine* is the most versatile of the shop tools and the first that I would encourage the budding professional to buy. It consists of a small precision motor, a variable-speed foot pedal (as on a sewing machine), a springlike shaft encased in a rubber hose about a yard long, and a handpiece that fits at the end of the shaft to hold tools. The tools are small steel shanks, called *mandrels,* which can be fitted with any number of attachments: fabric buffs, abrasive grinding wheels, or rotary files, for instance.

The flexible shaft can be used with any tool that turns and is employed in all phases of jewelry construction, from preliminary carving to final polishing. Its advantages lie in the range of speed available and in the shaft arrangement, which allows the tool to be brought to the work instead of the other way around. The flexible shaft can be assembled from component parts or bought as a package, which often includes a set of the most commonly used burs. A number of handpieces are available; I prefer to use a *Jacobs chuck* (the standard three-jaw attachment that requires a key for tightening). It takes a bit longer to adjust when changing burs but allows great versatility, since anything from nails to Q-tips can be gripped. The machine requires very little maintenance—oil regularly and don't overload the motor by putting a strain on it.

Like any other tool, the flexible shaft has great advantages when used properly but can create problems when misused. Because it is so versatile and comfortable to use, it is not uncommon for students to substitute the power tool for hand filing and sanding. Be warned that, as handy as miniature tools can be, they result in an unattractive wavy surface if they are pushed beyond the job that they are meant to do. As a rule of thumb, do as much as you can with a large tool and use the flexible shaft only when nothing else can do the job.

Rolling Mill

The *rolling mill* is used to flatten sheet or wire by forcing it between cylindrical steel rollers. It is a heavy-duty piece of equipment; and, since it must be machined to precise specifications, it is quite expensive. It should be used only with nonferrous metals. Any material passing through the mill should be carefully cleaned and dried, since impurities and moisture might cause the rollers to corrode. The only precaution that must be taken with the rolling mill is to avoid stressing the gear wheels by trying to reduce thickness too quickly. To thin a piece of metal, the rollers should be adjusted so that they are slightly closer together than the thickness of the existing sheet. The sheet is then passed through by turning the handle; and, after it is removed, the rollers are brought closer together. If the rollers are closed too quickly, a tooth might be broken off the gear wheels that hold them in place. Maintenance

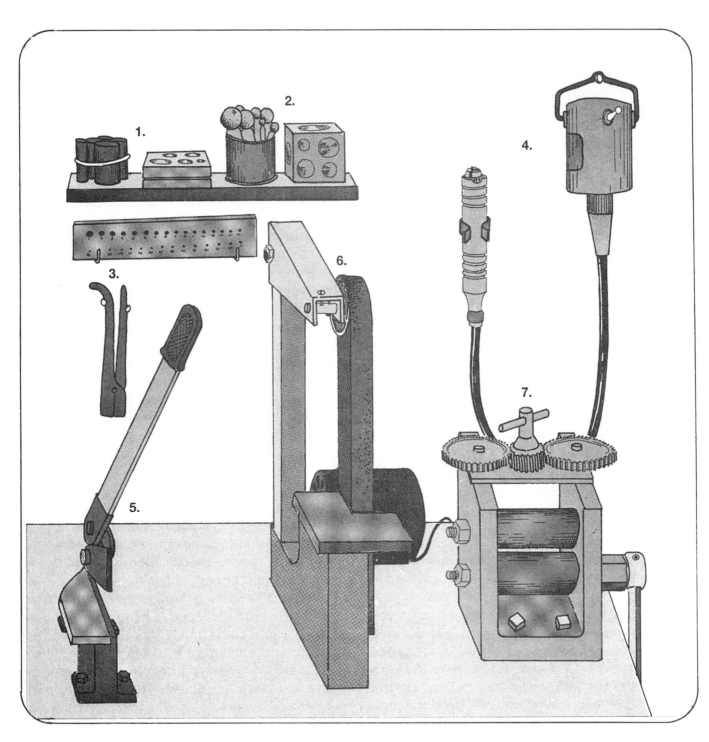

Shop equipment: (1) disk cutter with dies, (2) dapping block
and punches, (3) drawplate and drawtongs, (4) flexible-shaft
machine, (5) bench shears, (6) band sander, (7) rolling mill.

includes keeping the machine clean and protecting the rollers with vaseline or oil when in storage.

Band Sander

The *band sander* is a motorized unit that includes a band of sandpaper that is 42″ (just over 1m) long and 1″ (2.5cm) wide. Because the strip is so narrow, the tool has many applications for jewelry work. It generally replaces a file when working on large, open areas and is useful for fast cutting of soft materials. In addition to its use on jewelry itself the band sander is handy for sharpening drill bits and chisels, removing scratches from hammer faces, shaping plastics or bone, and many other jobs. It is available in bench and freestanding models and can be bought from a jewelry-supply, hardware, or lumber store. When buying belts for this machine, specify that you want those made for metal, since the type made for wood breaks easily. When using the band sander, always wear goggles and respirator, tie back loose clothing or long hair, and keep your mind on what you're doing.

Bench Shears

The *bench shears* is a handy cutting tool that in many ways resembles a paper cutter. It consists of a thick steel blade that is attached to a long handle for leverage. Like a paper cutter, it does a rough job on curves but cuts a straight line easily. The expensive part of the machine is the cutting edge, and care should be taken not to chip it. Only copper, brass, gold, or sterling should be cut, since steel will damage the blade.

Drawplate

The *drawplate* is a steel plate that can be used to make wire smaller and at the same time can change its cross-section shape. It is a very straightforward tool, as it contains no moving parts; but, because it must be of the highest grade of tool steel, it is rather expensive. When buying this, you should also purchase a pair of drawtongs, a sort of heavy-duty pliers with a serrated gripping jaw. The drawplate should be lightly oiled or coated with vaseline when stored for a long time and should always be handled with care so that it doesn't bend or chip. The plate is used only for nonferrous metals such as sterling, gold, copper, or brass.

Disk Cutter

The *disk cutter* is a die arrangement that cuts disks by hammering a cylindrical punch through a matching hole. Most suppliers sell two sizes: one has an assortment of small holes and the other ranges from ½″ to 1″ (12mm to 24mm). The effectiveness of the tool is proportional to its fit: if the punch and die are not perfectly true, the disk will be ragged if it can be cut at all. A problem arises when the punches are mistakenly hit on both ends. Since the hitting flares the end, the punch will no longer fit. I suggest that the top ends be clearly marked. Again, it is crucial that rust be avoided. It is a good idea to make a wooden box to hold the tool and to saturate it with linseed oil, which forms a moisture seal.

Dapping Block and Punches

The *dapping block* is also a die and is often used in conjunction with the disk cutter. It is a steel cube into which are cut hemispheres of graduated sizes. They are matched up with *punches* that look like a steel marble attached to the end of a thick rod. To make a dome, a disk of metal is laid into a depression larger than its circumference, and a punch that fits the depression is hammered down onto the metal, sandwiching it into place. The process can be repeated into depressions of decreasing size to increase the curve of the dome. Dapping punches are handy tools to own and can be used for the techniques of repoussé and die forming, which are discussed in chapter 6.

Handtool Checklist

For the beginning student the following list of handtools essential for jewelry making is offered. Each jeweler has his or her own ideas: let intuition and experience help you as you buy.

1. Saw frame and at least a dozen blades, size 1/0
2. Heavy-duty scissors (kitchen type)
3. Bench pin and holder, with built-in surface plate
4. Chain-, round-, and flat-nose pliers
5. Rawhide mallet—10-ounce
6. Planishing hammer—8- or 10-ounce
7. Small ball-peen hammer—for chasing, rivet-The total cost, if you are buying all of the above new, is about $100.
8. Propane torch and striker
9. Cake pan filled with pumice pebbles
10. Soldering tweezers, fine tweezers, and copper tongs
11. Pyrex dish for pickle
12. Hand (flat), triangular, and half-round files
13. Assorted needle files
14. Assorted sandpaper grades
15. 6″ ruler with millimeter scale
16. Assorted drawing tools

The total cost, if you are buying all of the above new, is about $100.

3. The Basic Techniques

Bending

From auto bodies to paper clips, one of the most obvious things to do to a piece of metal is to *bend* it. This holds for jewelry construction as well, and a few commonsense rules are all you need to get started.

Before you can do any bending, you have to cut off a piece of metal to work with. Wires are cut with *snips,* which can be bought separately or as part of a pliers. The snips always leave a pointed end on the tip of the wire, which gives a rough look and a shape that cannot be easily soldered. It's a standard practice to square off the end with a file; when you pick up one tool, you might as well start looking for the other. Sheet metal of up to 20-gauge thickness can be cut with shears. They are fast but curl the edge slightly and should be replaced by a saw if a smooth or detailed piece is to be cut.

While you are bending a wire, it is necessary to finish the ends. Filing them square is better than

Marion K. LaFollette. Sterling pin, 2″ high. The piece was made, just as it would appear, by bending a single piece of metal. The folds were filed to allow easy bending and soldered for strength afterward. The frosted finish is the result of careful stroking with sandpaper after all forming was completed.

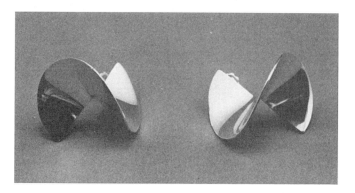

Patricia J. Daunis-Dunning. Sterling earrings, 1½″ diameter. These graceful shapes were made by cutting into a simple form and distorting it slightly with the fingers.

leaving the snipped points, but there are better methods. One possibility is to file the end to a graceful taper; this is especially suitable for a design that includes scroll curves. A common decorative end is made by drawing a bead on the end of a wire. The wire is held vertically in soldering tweezers, and the tip of the torch is directed at its lower end. The metal will redden, become shiny, and form a blob that will crawl up the wire. The torch should be slowly withdrawn, leaving a smooth-surfaced ball attached to the end of the wire. It may be left round or hammered flat into a miniature lollipop shape.

When bending a right-angled corner in light wire, it's a good idea to work over a wooden edge such as the end of the workbench. Complete as much of the bend as possible with pliers and then true the angle with a few taps of the rawhide mallet. On thick sheets of metal it helps to scratch a deep line on the inside of the bend, using a sharp scribe and a steel ruler for sheet. For heavy sheets—say, over 20-gauge—deepen the scratched line with a square or triangular needle file, cutting about two-thirds of the way through the metal. By bending over a sharp edge and hitting it a few times with a mallet a sharp corner should result. If a sharp corner is going to take much stress, it is a good idea to solder the bend closed after forming it.

When a design calls for duplicate bent shapes, such as a pair of wire earrings or several bracelet links, a jig might be used to make the work faster and more consistent. It can be as simple as a few nails pounded into a board or more elaborate and versatile. When using nails, drive them deep enough to give access to the bending area and cut off the heads so that the finished project slides off. To make a more sophisticated jig, you can saw a shape out of a piece of wood (Masonite works well) and glue it to a base. This jig can also be used in conjunction with nails. A handy jig can be made by drilling holes into a board and matching them up with short pieces of doweling. The jig shown here uses both ⅛" and ¼" holes (3mm and 6mm). The entire piece was rubbed with linseed oil to keep it from warping.

Perhaps because it is so obvious, some people overlook the possibilities of bending. Bent wires can be twisted, tied, or soldered together. They can be used in a complex tangled pattern or in a simple configuration of predominantly straight pieces. Further diversification is possible by combining round, square, and half-round wires.

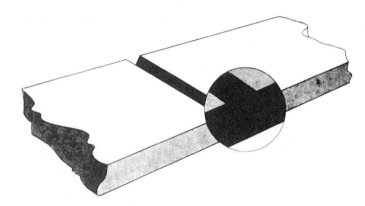

To make a neat, sharp-angled bend, the line of the fold should be scored, or cut away. On thin stock this can be done by scraping with a scribe. On heavier stock such as this the line should be started with a scribe and deepened with a square or triangular file.

Patricia J. Daunis-Dunning. Pewter napkin rings, 1½" in diameter.

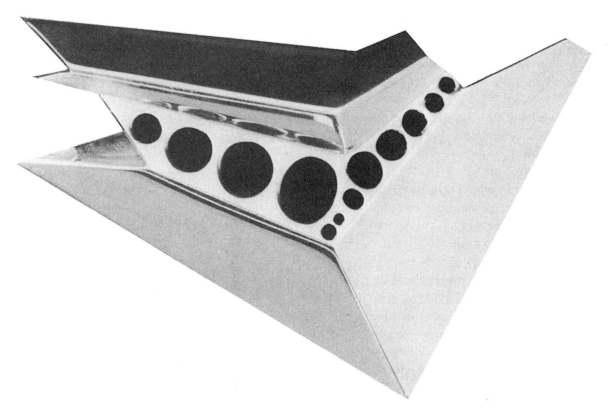

Curtis K. LaFollette. *City Scape #3* (sterling pin), 3″ across. The clean lines of this piece were made by scoring each bend until the fold line was paper-thin. In this way the sheet can be bent with the fingers, avoiding the use of pliers, which would scar the metal. The join was then soldered on the back to strengthen it.

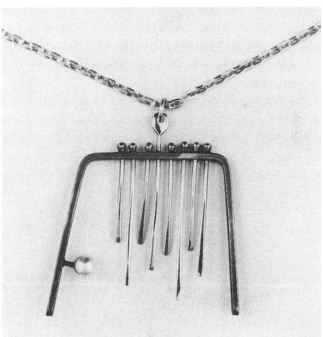

Jay W. Tuttle. Pendant, sterling with 14K yellow gold dangles and pearl, 1½″ high.

Twisting

One specific variation on bent wire is the *twist,* which can be used by itself to make rings, earrings, or bracelets or as a decorative element in more complicated pieces. This photo shows some of the effects that can be achieved by twisting, and wires of different metals may be used to increase the range of possibilities. The idea can be expanded upon by braiding, weaving, or knitting wires in techniques traditionally associated with fibers.

Though twisting can be done entirely by hand, it is faster and more even if a hand drill is used. In some cases the drill must be supplemented by a hand vise or vise-grip pliers. To make a simple twist, cut a piece of wire 2½ times the length of the desired result. Any twisting process scars the ends of the wire, so plan for this by allowing a little extra. Folding the wire in half, grip the two ends in a vise and clamp down hard. The resulting loop can then be gripped in a hand vise (especially good for heavy wires) or caught up in a hook held in the chuck of a hand drill. A cup hook or a bit of bent coat-hanger wire can be used. The wire is then twisted by operating the drill, keeping a slight backward pressure on the tool as you do so to prevent the wire from buckling. The twisting may be wound as tightly as desired; but, if the going seems hard, it may be necessary to stop midway and anneal.

The hook obviously cannot be used if the wire doesn't have a loop, as in the case of twisting wires of different metals. The drill can be used by omitting the hook and gripping the ends of the wires directly in the chuck, or a hand vise can be substituted.

When working with wires of different thicknesses, either tool will be unable to grip the thinner piece. To solve this problem, the larger wire should be flattened on its tip by hitting it with a hammer until it is about the same thickness as the thinnest piece. It is usually a good idea to complete a twist by soldering the wires together; this is especially important if the twist is to be flattened. Flattening can be done with a planishing hammer on a surface plate or by passing the twist through the rolling mill.

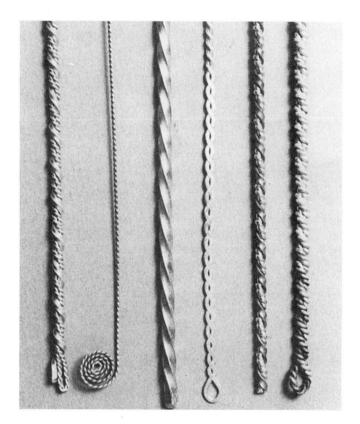

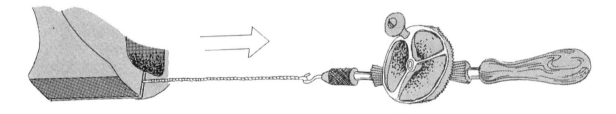

The fastest way to twist a wire is to use a hand drill and a vise as shown. If different wires are used, the hook can be omitted and the wire gripped directly in the jaw of the drill. Note the light backward tension, which keeps the twist from buckling.

Jump Rings

The building block of many shapes is the *jump ring,* which is any small circle of wire. It is easily made and may even be purchased ready-to-use if you are in a hurry. To make round rings, wire of any size that looks appropriate to the need at hand is coiled around a round stick. I keep a collection of nails and short pieces of dowel handy for this purpose. The wrapping is easier if about 1″ (2.5cm) of wire is left unwound and sticking out from the rod to act as a grip for the thumb. The remaining wire is then coiled neatly around the nail and pulled tight, being careful that each circle of wire lies snugly against the previous one. The springlike coil may then be slid off the post and held in the fingers, which are in turn supported against the bench pin. A single cut is made through the coil with the saw to release the jump rings. The sawing process feels awkward at first, but with a little perseverance it produces results quickly. Some people prefer to use a rod with a groove cut in the tip, which allows the coil to be sawn while in place. Either method becomes easier if the saw is held at such an angle that it cuts into three rings at once so that, when one falls off, the blade is already seated in a groove on the next ring. A third method is to cut through the coil with a separating disk held in the flexible shaft. The coil can be left on or taken off the rod.

Oval jump rings can be made by wrapping wire around two round sticks held together. If one of the sticks is larger in diameter than the other, the result will be an egg-shaped ring. When dealing with loops that are other than round, the wire has a tendency to clamp onto the rod, sometimes making it difficult to slide the coil off. To avoid this problem, the rods can be wrapped with a double layer of masking tape. After winding the rod is sufficiently heated with the torch to burn the tape, allowing clearance for the coil to slide off. To make rectangular loops, which are especially good for chains, the wire is wrapped around a strip of heavy-gauge copper or brass. The strip is sawn out, filed to remove burs, and wrapped with masking tape as above.

When opening jump rings, do not straighten the wire, which will expand the loop. A neater job will result if the ring is opened and closed by pushing the ends off to the side. In this way the circle (or other form) is left open but evenly shaped. Whether or not to solder a jump ring closed depends on several factors, such as the wear that the piece is likely to receive, your personal standards of craftsmanship, and the ratio between the size of the ring and the thickness of the wire used to make it, called *hoop stress.* A loop ¼″ (6mm) across made of 22-gauge wire, for instance, would be frail. A jump ring of the same diameter made with 14-gauge wire would require pliers to open it and would be sturdy enough for most jewelry uses without being soldered. If you don't want to solder a ring closed, be sure to use wire that is sufficiently thick.

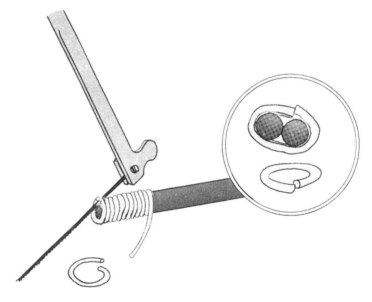

Sawing

One of the most versatile tools in the metal shop is the jeweler's *saw frame*. Frames are sold according to depth, or the distance from the blade to the back of the saw. A depth of about 4" (10cm) is the easiest to control and is usually used in jewelry work, but larger frames might be needed for a big sheet of metal. A good-quality frame is important: it is unwise economy to skimp here, since a cheap frame breaks blades, wasting time and money.

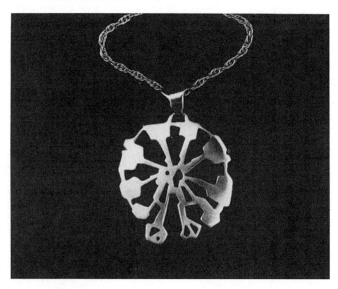

Pendant, sterling, 2½" in diameter. This piece was made with only a saw. It was cut from 18-gauge stock and finished with a wire brush.

Heather Sommers Sussman, Sterling earrings, 1½" high.

All frames use the same blades. They are 6" (15cm) long and available in 17 sizes, from 8/0, the smallest, through 7/0, 6/0, and so on to 0, and up to 8, the largest. Most people prefer the 1/0 size for everyday work. Smaller blades break more easily and are somewhat flimsy, making them more difficult to control. The larger sizes do not turn corners well and are wasteful, since they cut a wider kerf. There is an ideal ratio between the blade size and the metal being cut: three teeth should be on the metal at all times. This becomes particularly important when cutting designs in thin sheet, where a blade that is too large will snag on the metal and give an uneven cut. The teeth of the saw blade should always point toward the handle of the frame. If you can't see the teeth to determine the direction in which they point, slide the blade across your clothing: it catches only in the direction toward which the teeth are pointing.

Probably the most common sawing problem for beginners is a loose blade. A loose blade requires more effort to control, leaves a rough edge, and is likely to break sooner than a tight one. These two methods are standard ways of tightening the blade in the saw frame; everybody develops his or her own variation with a little experience.

1. With the blade clamped at one end, adjust the length of the frame so that the loose tip of the blade just reaches the other clamping plate and tighten the set screw on top of the frame so that the length does not change. Rest the front tip of the frame on the edge of the workbench and lean into it, compressing it until the blade slides into the clamping plate. While still leaning, tighten the screw down on the blade. When the pressure is removed, the frame springs back, putting tension on the blade.

2. Fasten the blade at both ends, keeping the length-adjusting screw loose. Grip the frame ends with each hand and spread them apart, tightening the blade. Hold the frame in its extended position by placing your thumb on the sliding bar while you tighten the top screw. With either method test the tautness of the blade by plucking it with a fingernail. A melodic ping should result.

The jeweler's saw is designed to work in an up-and-down motion, cutting on the downward stroke. It works most efficiently when used with a bench pin. In order to provide maximum support for a piece of metal while it is being sawn, many jewelers cut a V-shaped notch in the pin, and some prefer to have a large hole drilled at the top of the notch. The pin should be located at about mid-chest height. This allows the most natural and relaxed position of the arm for sawing. When preparing to saw, sit slightly to the left of the pin (for right-handers) so that it is in line with the shoulder of the sawing hand. This also allows greater comfort and control. Sawing, when done correctly, is a very relaxing activity—and when it is relaxing, it's probably being done correctly. I've noticed that, if I concentrate on keeping the little finger of my sawing hand unclenched, I get a better result and break fewer blades. If the pinky is relaxed, the hand is relaxed; the whole arm is moving loosely, which is what you want. Very little effort is needed to make the blade travel forward; in fact, it seems to pull itself along naturally. When sawing a sharp angle, it is necessary to hold the blade back—that is, to keep it from moving forward while turning the corner. The blade is simultaneously moved up and down and turned in a motion similar to running in place. It usually takes five or six strokes to turn a right-angled corner.

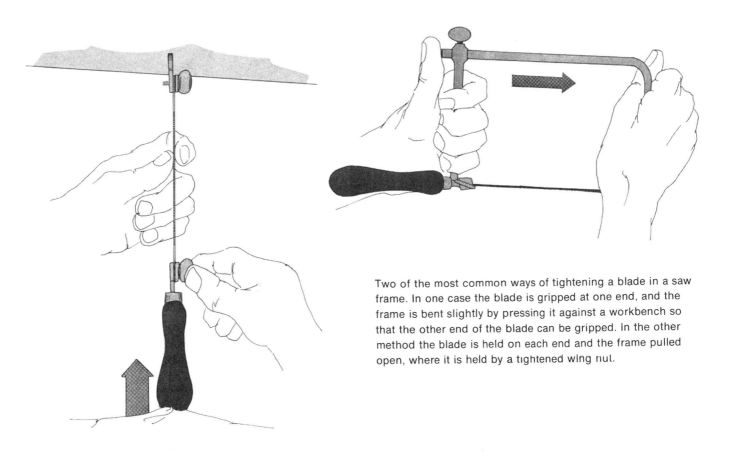

Two of the most common ways of tightening a blade in a saw frame. In one case the blade is gripped at one end, and the frame is bent slightly by pressing it against a workbench so that the other end of the blade can be gripped. In the other method the blade is held on each end and the frame pulled open, where it is held by a tightened wing nut.

It is important to have a clearly visible line to follow when sawing. It's a common mistake to think that you can rough out the shape and then true it up with a file. It is actually much easier and yields a better result to draw and saw meticulously from the outset. Following are three methods for transferring a design.

1. A clear black line may be drawn on sheet metal with a fine-line india-ink pen tip, such as a crow quill, or with a Rapid-o-graph-type pen. When using wet ink, it's a good idea to let it dry for a minute before sawing. Otherwise the filings stick to the ink and tend to obscure the line.

2. You can coat the metal with Chinese white, a solid pigment available from a jewelry-supply house, or with white tempera paint, which is similar. It can be painted on with a brush or rubbed on with a finger; and, if spread thin, dries quickly to a bright white surface that shows pen and pencil marks clearly. The paint can be washed off with water after the sawing is completed.

3. If less precision is needed, you can stick masking tape or glue paper onto the metal and saw through the sheet, paper and all. An advantage here is that pencil marks can be easily erased.

About the only thing that you should avoid in transferring a design is to scratch into the metal with a scribe. This does produce a sharp line and is convenient for ruled lines or for tracing around a hard object, but for freehand drawing or for tracing a paper form I don't recommend it. If you slip or change your mind while sawing, you'll be left with scratch marks that must be sanded and polished out.

If areas of the design are to be *pierced*—that is, removed from within the piece—they should usually be cut before sawing the outside shape. This allows extra metal around the work area to improve your grip. The first step in piercing is to drill a small hole for each area to be removed to allow the saw blade to enter—a larger hole is all right but wasteful. (Drilling is discussed in the next section.) The blade is then inserted and tightened, and sawing proceeds as previously described. After the shape is sawn out but

Curtis K. LaFollette. *City Scape #1* (pin), sterling with agate, 3″ in diameter.

Pendant, sterling, 2″ high. This technique, called overlay, uses two sheets of metal. The top sheet is pierced and refined with files, a saw blade, or sandpaper. It is then soldered onto a back plate that will support weak areas while providing a surface that can be oxidized (blackened) to emphasize the design. For a piece of conventional size I usually use 20-gauge for the top piece and 22- for the back.

before the blade is removed, it's a good idea to use the blade as a file and to trim off any minor irregularities. To do this, slide the blade along the edge of the metal so that it cuts without biting into the sheet. When the edge looks good, loosen one end of the blade and remove it. After all the piercing is done, the overall shape of the piece can be cut out. To do this, determine the method that leaves the most metal attached to the sheet to serve as a handle while sawing. With a little thought and a practiced eye even tiny, involved shapes can be sawn out without much trouble.

Saw blades are frail creatures—you should not become too attached to any particular one. They're bound to break sooner or later, mostly sooner. Blades cut because of the *set* of the teeth—that is, the way in which each tooth is bent slightly out to the side. Even if a loyal blade resists breaking for weeks, the set may wear off, and the blade must be abandoned. Most suppliers stock two qualities of blades: *Swiss* and *German.* The Swiss type is slightly more expensive, and it's my experience that you get what you pay for. The cheaper blades do the job, but they tend to wear out or to break a bit faster than do the more expensive ones. When a blade breaks, it is possible to adjust the frame to a shorter length and to keep using it, but shortened blades tend to break more easily than do whole ones, making your thriftiness a waste of time. When a blade breaks, it sometimes leaves a tiny end stuck out of sight behind the gripping plate of the saw frame. Unless it is removed by sharply rapping the frame on the bench, the next blade will not grip firmly and might break prematurely.

Drilling

There are many occasions when a jeweler needs to make a hole in metal. A simple method is to puncture the metal by striking a scribe with a hammer, but this is at best sloppy and at worst uncontrollable. It is better to use a *drill bit,* which yields a clean hole exactly the right size and exactly where you want it.

Several types of drills are available to the craftsperson. The cheapest and most easily obtainable is the *eggbeater-type* drill, which can be bought at a local hardware or discount store. Even if you avoid the cheapest model, which is likely to jam or to have an undependable gripping mechanism, it should cost only about $7. The *push-type* drill, which often doubles as a screwdriver, is to be avoided, because the force needed to make it work will break small bits. A tool of ancient origin is the *jeweler's bow* drill, which converts an up-and-down movement into a twist as a leather thong wraps and unwraps around a vertical pole. The advantage of this

Pendant, copper, 2″ high. Though a saw was used to shape the outside edge, this piece was made primarily with a drill. The design was carefully measured with a compass, cut out, sanded, and bent over. This formed the back piece as well as a loop for the cord to pass through.

tool is that its operation requires only one hand, leaving the other free to initiate the twisting and to hold the metal. A disadvantage is that it takes some finesse to keep the bit turning at a regular speed.

The next step up is an *electric hand drill.* It might be a bit clumsy for precise work, but its rugged construction and versatility make it a good investment. A ¼" (6mm) variable-speed drill can usually be bought for between $15 and $20, so it isn't a staggering investment. A tool that is as much more versatile as it is more expensive is the *flexible-shaft machine* described in the section on shop equipment in chapter 2. The top of the line and the best device for drilling is the *drill press.* This machine holds the bit steady and at a perfect right angle to the work. It is an expensive piece of equipment, however, and not necessary for the one-person shop.

Finding the right size bit is the next order of business, and it can be a little involved. Most hardware stores carry bits as small as 1/16" (1.5mm); but, since this is too large for most jewelry needs, you'll probably have to go to an industrial- or jewelry-supply house. Large bits are sold by the fraction of an inch,

but this system is rarely used for the small bits that you need. Some companies describe the diameter of the bit in thousandths of an inch as a three-digit number. Another system uses numbers ranging from 1, the largest, to 80, the smallest. Appendix 2 renders these sizes in a more recognizable form. I suggest that you buy sizes that match common wire dimensions, which makes life easier when doing rivets, inlay, or hinges. Some common sizes are 67, which is equal to 20-gauge B & S, 60 (18-gauge), and 55 (16-gauge).

No matter what kind of drill you are using, the bit should be gripped into the chuck as far as possible to prevent wobbling and breaking. In some cases it might be necessary to break off part of the shank in order to allow only about ¼" (6mm) to protrude from the drill. This can be done by gripping the bit in a vise, with the "extra" part of the shank extended. A hard blow with a metal hammer will snap the bit off squarely. Even in a drill press the bit has a tendency to wander, and in hand-held drills this can be a serious problem. The solution is to make a dent, called a *centerpunch,* exactly at the point at which the hole is to be drilled. This is done by striking a centerpunching tool with a hammer.

Whenever possible, do all the necessary drilling before sawing, since small shapes are difficult to hold. If this is impractical, glue the pieces onto a board with fast-setting epoxy, drill, and pry or burn the pieces loose. When using any power drill, it's a good idea to lubricate the tip of the bit with oil or wax to keep it cool and therefore hardened. Goggles should be worn when drilling, since chips of metal will fly off to the side.

A small drill bit can be improvised from a sewing needle as shown. Though a bit tedious, it's a handy trick to know about in a pinch. The eye of the needle is easily broken off by gripping it in pliers and twisting. The shaping can be done with sandpaper but is much faster if a grinding wheel is used in the flexible-shaft machine. The top is flat-ground and smooth-sided. It is then pointed at a 45° angle as shown. Clearance faces are cut at about a 12° angle, one from each side. The angles and cutting procedure are the same for resharpening a dull bit.

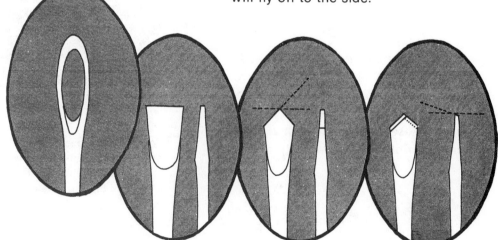

Fusing

Fire is an important part of the metalsmith's art. The history of almost all cultures has been shaped by their use of metals, and this was in turn dependent on their ability to control fire. Heat is used to soften the material, to form it into ingots, to texture it, and to join it.

Fusing is a process of melting metal. If a bit of nonferrous metal is laid on the soldering block and melted with the torch, it will draw itself into a sphere, called *shot.* The resulting ball will have a smoother surface if the mass is allowed to cool slowly, preventing uneven contraction. To do this, slowly lift the torch away from the bead just as it draws into a ball. Shot made on a soldering pad has a flat underside, which is handy if the pieces are to be soldered onto something, since it keeps it from rolling away. If the flat bottom is not wanted, a depression can be pressed into a charcoal block with any rounded object, and the shot melted in the depression.

Fusing can be used to join pieces of metal together in a connection that is as strong as the metal itself. It has the disadvantage of a lack of control but can result in rich textures and organic forms that would be difficult to obtain with any other process. Sterling and gold fuse nicely, but copper and brass are somewhat less responsive. Any metals may be fused together, but the results will be cleanest when components with similar melting points are used. Wire and sheet may be combined, or either may be fused by itself.

The pieces to be joined are laid on the soldering block and coated with *flux,* a chemical preparation that prevents the metal from forming a scale on its surface during heating, which would inhibit joining of the molten metal. (Fluxes are discussed in more detail in the next section.) If a thick piece is to be joined to a thin one, the thicker (or larger) piece should be laid down first and preheated. When all the pieces are positioned, the torch is moved over them, taking care that they all reach the same temperature simultaneously. This is indicated by the colors that the metal acquires as it is heated. Small units pick up heat that is thrown off from the larger

Fused ring, sterling. The ring was started by laying small pieces of 16-gauge wire across two longer strips of the same wire. After fluxing the metal was heated until it started to melt and run together. At this point the flame was carefully tilted and moved to control the flow of the molten metal. Where the wire melted apart, additional bits were set into place and fused to cover the gap.

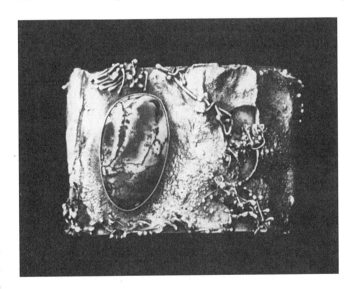

Carol S. Kestler. *Black Mesa* (bracelet), fused silver with moss agate, 2″ wide. Most of the work on the bracelet was done with the metal flat on the soldering block. After fusing the shape was curved, and the bezel that holds the stone was soldered into place. To emphasize the texture, the bracelet was oxidized and polished. Photo by John F. Martin.

ones, so the torch is aimed only at the latter so that all the elements turn the same color at the same time. As the entire assemblage becomes bright red, the torch can be directed at specific connecting points to bring them to the *molten* stage, at which joining occurs. When adjacent pieces become molten, they have a tendency to flow together and to bond. This may be encouraged by poking the melt with a steel probe. As each join is completed, the flame is moved to the next area, and the fusing continues. It is possible that an attractive accident can be damaged by overheating in an attempt to fuse another section onto a fused piece. In such cases it would be better to switch to the more controlled process of soldering, which, when done correctly, does not run the risk of melting (and therefore losing) existing shapes.

Soldering

Soldering is probably the single most important technique in small-scale metalwork, and I shall try to describe it in the detail that it deserves. No matter what else you do to a piece of metal in the way of bending, sawing, or forming, there's a good chance that you'll want to attach it to something or something to it, and this almost always involves soldering. The process is the same for gold, sterling, copper, and brass, and the information given here applies equally to whatever torch is used.

Metals characteristically tend to combine with oxygen in the air, which forms a scale on the surface. Scale formation is accelerated by heating, which means that the process of soldering inherently causes a surface scale on most metals (one exception is pure gold). This scale prohibits solder from flowing and prevents a strong joint from being formed. It is therefore crucial to keep the surface protected throughout the soldering operation. This is usually done with a chemical substance called a *flux,* which coats the metal and keeps the oxide layer from forming, allowing the solder to flow. (The root of the word "flux" is from the Latin term meaning "flow.")

Soft Solder

There are two distinct families of solder that should not be confused. *Soft solder* is a low-melting material that is usually an alloy of lead and tin. *Hard solder* consists of silver or gold mixed with zinc or copper in exact proportions to achieve a distinct melting point. Soft solder melts at around 450°F (230°C) and is probably familiar from its applications in electronics and plumbing. A recent variation that contains no lead was developed by the silverware industry to secure stainless-steel knife blades into sterling handles. It is sometimes sold as silver solder because of its color, but it is a soft solder and should not be confused with real silver-based solder. Soft solder is not very strong and has limited use for the jewelry crafter. It can be used to fasten findings onto jewelry (as cufflink backs to coins), but a demanding craftsperson tries to avoid this. Besides its lack of strength and unattractive dull gray color soft solder cannot be overheated without causing serious damage to silver and gold, which means that a piece that has been soft-soldered is difficult to repair. When lead is heated to the high temperatures needed for hard soldering, it eats holes in precious metals; for this reason it's a good idea to keep lead away from the soldering area altogether.

Soft solder is usually purchased in the form of thick wire wound on a spool and is available through hardware dealers. It is used with a flux that resembles petroleum jelly or a liquid called tinner's flux, which can be bought along with the solder. The flux is generously dabbed on with a stick or brush, and the solder is fed into the joint as heat is applied. A torch may be used, but an electric soldering gun has the advantage of a more appropriate heating range. When using a torch, it is easy to overheat the work and burn the flux, which prevents it from keeping the metal clean. If the flux turns black, it is overheated: you should wipe it off, reflux, and try again. For a few pennies more you can buy a solder called *rosin* or *acid core,* in which the flux is built in. Soft solder can be worked with any sort of metal stick and made to fill a gap, but a neater and stronger joint results if the pieces are carefully lined up before soldering begins.

One special use of soft solder deserves mention here, since it relates directly to craftwork. Pewter has a low melting point and cannot be hard-soldered. Lead-tin solders are effective for pewter and, if used sparingly, can make virtually invisible joints. Since the melting points of lead-tin solders (which vary with the exact alloy proportions) are close to that of pewter, some crafters prefer a solder that contains bismuth, a metal with a very low melting point. When added to solder, it lowers the melting point to about 200°F (92°C) lower than that of pewter, allowing a generous margin of safety. Bismuth solder is available from most companies that sell pewter and requires a special flux that can be found at the same supplier. Remember that lead is a health hazard; any vessel that is used to hold food must use a nonlead solder.

Hard Solder

Soft solder may be thought of as metal glue: it binds two units together by forming a bridge of material that is stuck at both ends to the pieces to be joined. This differs entirely from silver and gold solders, which penetrate the metal to be joined and provide a much stronger attachment. To accomplish this, an alloy that melts at almost the same temperature as the pieces to be joined must be used. The resulting bond is for all practical purposes as strong as the metal itself, and it blends in so well that it cannot be seen.

Because of the high temperatures needed for the hard-soldering process, there is a complication. In order to bring the area around the joint to the proper soldering temperature, the entire piece of work must be heated. It is a physical law that heat flows toward a cooler area. If the torch flame is directed at only one end of a piece of metal, the heat will flow along the metal away from the torch and toward the cooler end. Another physical law dictates that at a point away from the flame air will pass over the metal, absorb the heat, and rise. As it rises, it allows more cool air to absorb more heat from the metal in what

could become an endless cycle. You are in fact creating a miniature (and very inefficient) radiator, since this is the principle behind most home heating units. In order to break the cycle, the entire piece of metal must be heated, eliminating the cool end. This stops the flow of heat away from the torch and lets the joint area reach the soldering temperature.

This step is easy enough to accomplish—the problem arises if you are making a piece that requires several solder joints. In order to make the first joint, all the components are heated to the melting point of the solder. If, after filing, bending, or trimming this piece, another section is to be attached, the entire piece must again be heated to the melting point of the solder. Unless care is taken, the first joint will unsolder in the process of making the second. For a piece that involves 10 or 12 soldering operations this can be a real problem. Over the years several solutions have been found, some of which are described here.

Even when a joint remelts, it does not automatically fall apart. In its molten state the solder has a strong surface tension—in many ways it resembles mercury—which tends to keep the pieces together unless some outside force pushes them apart. Outside forces would include gravity, spring tension, thermal expansion, and a bump of the hand. One of the easiest solutions is to complete as many solder joints as possible at the same time. This is a general rule of thumb no matter what other techniques are used. There is a limit to the practicality of this rule, however, and it is unnecessary to devote an hour to balancing a dozen parts in an attempt to line them all up at once.

To raise the melting point of a joint that has already been soldered, the area may be painted with a mixture of water and either yellow ocher, rouge, or whiting. These materials are all available in powder form from jewelry suppliers and are quite cheap. In each case the material is mixed with water to a creamy consistency and painted onto a soldered joint. It is a good idea either to wait until the coating dries or to heat slowly at first in order to dry it carefully before beginning to solder. In painting the mix on the work care must be taken not to drip it onto an area that is about to be soldered, since even a tiny bit will prevent the solder from flowing. This coating does not guarantee that a joint will hold, but it does raise the melting point of the solder enough to stack the deck in your favor.

A more scientific and reliable way of solving the problem involves the use of solders with varying melting points. The first joints are made with a solder that melts at a high temperature, called *hard solder.* The next joints are made with an alloy that melts at a lower point (*medium solder*) and does not interfere with the first, and the last are done at an even lower melting point with *easy solder.* A fourth type, called *Easy-Flo,* which contains cadmium and has a lower melting point than easy solder, has recently become commercially available, but it is not commonly used. For very complicated pieces a fifth step may be added by using a solder called *IT* for first joints. This system can be used along with the painting method to allow even the most intricate pieces to be constructed without incurring unsoldering problems.

A century ago many craftsmen made their own solders—and this can still be done—but nowadays most people buy commercially made solder. It is available from any dealer in precious metals and can be bought by the ounce or by linear measurement. For anyone wishing to make his own solder, the table in this section shows the correct proportions and the melting points that can be obtained.

Solder-composition Table

	% silver	% copper	% zinc	flow point	
fine silver	99.9			1761°F	961°C
sterling	92.5	75		1640	893
IT	80	16	4	1490	809
hard solder	76	22	3	1425	773
medium solder	70	20	10	1390	747
easy solder	60	25	15	1325	711
Easy-Flo solder	50	15.5 (19 cadmium)	15.5	1270	681

Silver solders contain copper and zinc, which are usually added in the form of brass. When making your own solder, melt the ingredients in a hollow carved in a charcoal block, starting with the brass. Stir the mix with a carbon, steel, or hardwood rod to ensure that it is evenly blended. Add a small amount of flux in the form of borax powder (the laundry aid) and remove the torch. As the lump cools, it can be squashed down with a second block of charcoal held in the hand to form a flat blob. This may then be hammered or rolled to a thin sheet, about 26-gauge.

Solder is commercially available in strips about 1″ (25mm) wide and in several gauges of wire. In all cases it is very important that each scrap of solder be well marked, since it is practically impossible to tell one from another once they have been mixed up. It is common practice to scratch an appropriate letter indicating hard, medium, or easy solder into sheet metal. Do this repeatedly over the whole piece so that any scrap that you end up with will be labeled. Lengths of wire solder are sometimes coded by making different-shaped bends in the end; e.g., a round loop for easy, a triangle for medium, and a square for hard.

Silver solder can be used to join gold, copper, or brass but will leave a silver-colored line along the seam. Gold may be soldered by using a lower-karat gold: 15-karat gold is a good solder for a piece made of 18-karat stock. To make gold solder, add about a fifth part by weight of either silver, copper, or a mixture of the two to the gold being used to make the piece. Copper gives the metal a yellower color and reduces the melting point more than would an equal amount of silver. Both are usually used in equal amounts. For example, when using 18K gold, you are working with an alloy that is 18 parts gold and 6 parts other metal, bringing the total to 24 parts, or karats. To a pennyweight (24 grains) of 18K gold add 5 grains of copper-silver mixture. This brings the new alloy to 18 parts gold and 11 parts other metal, or about 15-karat, which would be a proper solder for the piece under construction. By the same method any solder needed may be made. For first joints make the solder as above. For successive joints add some silver and copper to the alloy whenever you need to lower the melting point by a step.

As already mentioned, it is important that the metal to be joined be kept free of oxidation by using a flux. The oldest flux common to jewelry work is *borax,* a salt of boric acid, which is used, among other things, in the production of glass and ceramic glazes. It is available from a local grocery store (look in the laundry-soap section) or may be bought from a jewelry supplier in the form of a solid lump. It is mixed with water to form a milky paste that protects the metal when heated. A product called Handy Flux is basically borax that is premixed into a thick paste. It can be used as is or thinned with water if evaporation dries it out. Either flux works well but has the disadvantage of liquidizing when heated, which can make it difficult to watch the solder flow and form a shiny, glasslike layer on the metal after the work has been cooled. (The removal of this substance is discussed in the section on pickling.) A yellow-green liquid called *battern's flux,* which has a fluoride instead of a borax base, is also popular. It has the advantage of easier application and rarely forms the flux glass, but I've found that it doesn't hold up well under the prolonged heating needed for soldering big pieces of copper or brass.

Borax-based fluxes are usually applied to the metal with a small brush or dabbed on with a short wooden rod. The liquid flux may be applied with a brush, an eye dropper, or a small spray jar (such as a cologne or deodorant container). These spray methods allow the article to be refluxed while hot, which is difficult to do with paste fluxes. Flux can burn away while soldering and might need to be reapplied midway in the process, so this becomes an important factor.

The Soldering Process

With solder and flux in hand, we come to the soldering process itself. *Wire* solder is usually used in whatever length is convenient to manipulate and feed into the joint as it is needed. *Sheet* solder is cut into small squares .04″ or .08″ (1mm or 2mm) on each side and laid into place at the beginning of the soldering process. To cut the little *chips* of solder, cut parallel lines into the sheet the appropriate distance

apart and about 1″ (2cm) deep and then make perpendicular cuts, catching the solder chips on your fingertip to keep them from scattering. Precut solder is available from some dealers, but it seems an unnecessary luxury.

Soft solder, as you remember, can be made to fill a gap. This is not true of silver and gold solders. The proper preparation of a joint—that is, exact cutting and bending so that both pieces fit together well—cannot be too heavily stressed. To check the fit, hold the article up to the light. Any gap wider than the thickness of a sheet of paper must be closed by filing or bending. The metal should be clean of dirt and grease before it is placed on the soldering pad. If it has undergone little handling, it is probably clean enough. If extensive work has been done, a scrub with soap and ammonia might be a good idea.

The pieces should be laid in place exactly as they are to be soldered. This may involve careful bending to make ends or edges line up. It sometimes helps to prop parts: pumice or pennies can be used, as can an iron wire called *binding wire.* It is tied around the work, and the ends are twisted to hold it in place. Final tightening can be accomplished by putting a kink in the wire with the tips of flat-nosed pliers.

When the pieces are arranged, flux is applied. As mentioned previously, it can be painted, dropped, or sprayed on. Some crafters prefer to dip each piece in flux, which is obviously done before assembly. The solder chips are then laid into place, using either the tip of a moist paintbrush (the same one that is used for flux) or sharp tweezers. There is no rule about how much solder to use: too little will make a weak joint, and too much will result in a sloppy overflow that can ruin the lines of a piece. Since the solder flows like water, very little is needed. Pieces 1mm on each side are usually placed about ¼″ (6mm) apart.

It is important that heat be applied slowly, since the first step is to boil the moisture out of the flux. If the flame is applied too quickly, the flux will boil rapidly, causing the solder chips to scatter. I find it a good idea to direct the torch flame vertically down on the metal (which requires the elbow of the arm holding the torch to stick up). This allows a better view of the work and ensures that the heat goes where you direct it. It is absolutely necessary that the pieces to be joined reach the same temperature simultaneously. To regulate the heating, pay close attention to the colors that the metal acquires as it is heated. The proper soldering area is dimly lighted, making the colors more clearly visible. Sterling moves from a brassy color through a pale gray, a brownish gray, a dull black, a dull red, a bright red-orange, and a glowing red-orange to a shiny, mirror-like surface that indicates that the metal is melting. Solders flow between the first red and the bright red: *there is usually no need to heat beyond this temperature.* If the metal has become bright red in color but the solder hasn't flowed, remove the torch. The problem is not a lack of heat but something else. Check to see that all parts are touching, reflux, and try again.

This process is the same for all the nonferrous metals. Gold and fine silver pass through the heat stages a bit faster than sterling, so you really have to be on your toes. Copper and brass have a longer bright-red phase than sterling: when sterling is bright, the melting point is seconds away, so you should back off. Copper and brass become red quickly and stay red for a relatively long time before starting to melt.

Throughout the soldering process the torch should be kept in motion. As explained earlier, it is always necessary to heat the entire piece of metal, even when only one end is being soldered. When you start to solder, hold the torch so that the tip of the flame's inner cone is about 6″ (15cm) above the work and move slowly back and forth along it. As the flux boils and forms a white crust, bring the torch closer to the metal so that the tip of the cone floats just above the surface. Play the torch over the metal with a circular or back-and-forth movement—not quick and jerky but slow enough to distribute the heat evenly. You might think of moving the torch in concentric circles that slowly home in on the joint area. Remember, however, that the entire piece of metal must be heated—say, to the point at which it turns blackish—before beginning to home in on the

joint. When working on delicate items, the torch should always be moving. On large pieces the flame may be held stationary at the joint area for a second or two just as the metal gets red, but it should not rest directly on the solder. This would cause it to oxidize, preventing it from flowing. When the correct heat is reached, assuming that the metal is properly fluxed, the solder will flow like water. It will look like a bright, silvery line spreading along the joint. As soon as the solder has flowed, the torch should be removed.

Specialized Methods

As you become familiar with the soldering process and begin to join increasingly intricate shapes, you will probably want to experiment with other soldering methods. As described above, the simplest and most frequently used technique is to set a chip of solder on the joint between the two pieces. This ensures that the proper amount of solder is being used and lets you begin the operation with everything in place. There are times, however, when it is difficult to get a chip of solder to stay in position, and a good craftsman should be able to devise some alternatives.

Sweat Soldering

One method, called *sweat soldering,* is especially appropriate when a large piece is to be attached to a small one or when it is important for the solder not to flow beyond an edge. Sweat soldering may be thought of as a two-part operation. The pieces to be joined are laid out on the soldering block side by side, not touching, with the top piece upside down. Both pieces are fluxed, and solder is laid onto the piece with greater detail. This section is then heated until the solder melts, forming puddles that harden in place when the torch is taken away. With the solder now held in place, it is possible to line up the pieces. They are laid into position, working quickly to take advantage of the metal's first heat, and the whole unit is heated again until the solder flows.

A particular type of sweat soldering that comes in handy involves coating the tip of a piece of wire with

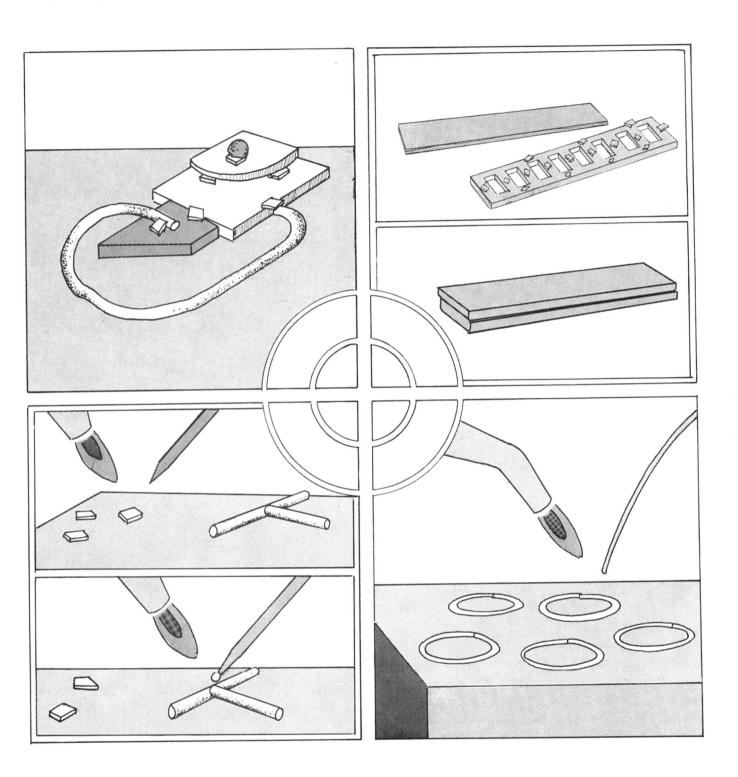

solder before joining it to a larger piece. Imagine, for instance, the problem of soldering a wire post onto the back of an earring. In this case the earring would be laid face down and fluxed. The wire would be held in soldering tweezers, and a piece of solder would be laid out on the pad, safely away from the earring. The wire is held vertically so that its tip touches the solder, and the point of connection is heated. As the solder melts, it will jump onto the wire, forming a tiny blob at its tip. The earring is then heated, with the wire held 1″ or 2″ (2½cm or 5cm) away from the flame. This is close enough to keep it warm without the risk of melting it. When the earring first becomes red, the wire is brought into position, and the torch applied to both pieces. The solder should flow immediately; the torch is then lifted away.

Probe Soldering

Another technique, called *probe soldering,* is useful when making a series of joints, as for a chain, or when working with shapes on which it is difficult to balance a solder chip on the seam. This may also be thought of as a two-step process. A steel *probe* is required; it may be bought (look under "scribes" in your jewelry supplier's catalog) or made from any piece of scrap steel rod, such as welding rod or an old needle file. The item to be soldered is prepared as usual, set on the soldering block, and fluxed. A bit of solder (or several bits if you are working on a series of joints) is laid out on the block several inches away from the work. Heat is directed onto the solder, which will melt and curl up into a tiny ball. The tip of the probe is touched against the ball; and, when the torch is lifted away, the solder is lightly stuck onto the end of the steel. If the probe is too cold, the solder may not adhere; if it's too hot, the solder may coat its tip; a few practice runs will give you the hang of the procedure. With the probe held just beside the work, the torch is directed at the piece itself. When it appears to reach the soldering temperature, as determined by the color of the metal, the probe is swung into position, placing the solder on the joint. When done right, the solder will flow as soon as it touches the work, and the torch

Pendant, sterling, 2″ in diameter. The piece was made with 16-gauge wire. After soldering the lower half on the circle was hammered to form lines of varying widths. The hammering also had the effect of doming the piece, making it appear more reflective.

Pendant, sterling, 3″ high. This piece was constructed from lengths of 16-gauge wire that were soldered together and flattened. To make the piece more interesting, it was slightly curved after polishing.

may immediately be removed. The entire action should be a graceful interplay of the two hands, and with a little practice it is possible to set up a rhythm that is both engaging to watch and handy to use. The only trick to this method lies in reading the temperature of the metal. If the probe is brought into the soldering area too soon, it will draw heat away from the work and run the risk of bumping the pieces askew. If you have trouble with probe soldering, it is a good idea to practice the technique on scrap metal.

An extension of the probe-soldering method utilizes wire solder. In this case the piece is fluxed and heated as before; but, instead of picking up bits of solder on a tool, wire solder is used. The solder can be held directly in the hand, a pin vise, a medical hemostat, or any other holding mechanism that you devise. The hand is usually rested on the workbench beside the soldering pad in such a way that it can be pivoted to bring the solder into the joint. It is very important that the solder not be brought into the torch flame until the work has reached soldering temperature. If it is introduced prematurely, the end of the wire will ball up, forming a glob of solder that is awkward to use and might interfere with details on the finished piece. Once you get the hang of the method, however, it is very efficient and is often preferred by production jewelers. The composition of solder is constant, so there is no difference in melting point, polishing results, or strength between sheet and wire solder.

Mud Soldering

Filigree and similar delicate work can be joined in a process called *mud soldering.* In this method solder filings are mixed with flux to form a paste (mud) that is painted onto the joints. The work is heated slowly with a gentle flame until the solder melts. Filings may be bought from some suppliers or made by rubbing a piece of solder on a coarse file and catching the dust. Jewelry manufacturers use this technique extensively, since it lends itself to automated production.

Pickling

After a soldering operation has been completed—or, for that matter, whenever metal has been heated—it will appear darkened because of oxide formation on its surface. This darkness (brown on gold, gray on sterling, and blue-black on copper) makes it difficult to check the soldered joint, inhibits future soldering, and requires extra polishing. It is common practice to remove the oxide by cleaning the metal in an acid solution called a *pickle.* For copper a standard pickle is a mixture of one part nitric acid and six parts cold water. Silver and gold are pickled in a solution of one part sulfuric acid and ten parts water. In mixing acids be careful to add the acid to the water and not vice versa, since water poured into acid generates chemical heat and might cause the acid to splatter. A commercial product called SPAREX may be used for any nonferrous metal and is often preferred, since it is less corrosive and eliminates the need to keep acid in the shop.

Whichever type of pickle you use, it should be kept in a heavy copper or glass pot with a lid. Most people use a Pyrex saucepan. If copper and sterling are cleaned in the same pickle, there is a tendency for the copper to plate onto the silver. This can become a nuisance if a lot of work is being done in both metals and would justify the use of two pickles, but for occasional use one is sufficient. The pickle turns blue as it absorbs copper and must be replaced when the color becomes clearly apparent. Depending on your work volume, this might be anywhere from a week to a couple of months.

Work may be placed into the pickle cold, but the cleaning action can be speeded up with the addition of heat. The work may be dropped into the pickle immediately after soldering while it is still hot, or the pickle can be heated on a stove or hot plate with the work in it. In practice it is sufficient to quench the piece after soldering while it is under construction, but after all the soldering has been completed, especially if a lot of flux has been used in repeated firings, it is a good idea to heat the piece in the pickle before moving on to the polishing operation. If a heatproof pot is used, it may be set directly on a hot plate or stove. Another solution is to use a crock pot, which can be bought at most discount stores for about the same price as a glass container. Before using the crock pot, the seams must be sealed with heat-resistant caulking, which can be bought in a tube in most hardware stores. Even if the piece is very dirty, allowing it to remain in the pickle for about five minutes is usually enough to remove any stubborn oxides.

It is important that work be held in copper or wooden tongs when it is placed into or removed from the pickle. An electroplating reaction occurs with steel tongs because of the dissimilarity between the ferrous steel and the nonferrous work. It causes copper salts to plate from the pickle solution onto your piece at the point where it is held by the tweezers. This accidental plating is a bother to polish off and should be avoided. For the same reason binding wire (which is also ferrous) should be removed before pickling a piece.

Though the acid solutions used in the jewelry shop are mild enough to handle, they will eat holes in clothing and sting if they get into cuts. It is standard practice to rinse a pickled piece in a dish of water and is even better to hold it under running water. If the piece contains pockets or crannies that might retain the pickle, it is necessary, after all soldering has been completed and the work has been thoroughly pickled, to soak it in a solution of baking soda and water in order to neutralize the acid. If this is not done, the acid will continue to corrode and will form a crystalline deposit around the mouth of the enclosed area.

The primary purpose of pickling is to clean away oxides and flux glass formed in soldering. Another use that deserves mention is to build up fine (pure) silver on the surface of a finished work. Whenever a hot piece of sterling is quenched in strong pickle, the copper oxides that are formed on the surface by heating are dissolved, leaving a thin film of fine silver. The heating and quenching may be repeated to deepen the layer somewhat. Fine silver, you should remember, does not tarnish and is whiter in color than sterling. Because of this some crafters finish a piece with a pickle buildup of fine silver to achieve the desired color. This layer is very thin and would wear off in normal polishing, so care must be taken. A standard approach is to complete the piece (except for setting stones), polish with tripoli and rouge, heat and quench at least five times, and lightly polish either by hand with a rouge cloth or on the buffing machine with a fine scratch brush.

Fire Scale

A very irksome problem that is unique to sterling and 14K gold is the formation of cupric oxides (dirty copper) on and just below the surface of the metal. They appear as a gray stain that seriously detracts from a finished piece and is all the more frustrating since it usually doesn't show up until finishing. It is caused by alloy breakdown during heating, which leaves the copper free to combine with oxygen, creating the blackish copper oxide. This occurs at around 1100°F (587°C) for sterling; since this is below soldering temperatures, the problem is always imminent. In fact, it would be safe to say that on any piece that is soldered or annealed *fire scale* is formed. In some cases in which the heating is gentle and brief, the scale is removed by normal finishing and you may never be aware of it. In heavily textured pieces created by techniques such as fusing the fire scale won't show up and doesn't cause any problem. But it often does show, and you have to do something about it.

With experience you might be able to spot fire scale at the sandpaper stage of the finishing process (see chapter 4), but it sometimes doesn't show up until the tripoli or even the rouge polish. If you're lucky, the scale might be thin enough to be removed by extending the normal procedure only slightly, so the first thing to do is to keep on with the tool at hand (i.e., the sandpaper, tripoli, or rouge) and to see whether it is able to remove the stain. Take note of a particular patch, work on it for a minute, then check to see if it is any smaller. If so, continue until it is removed. If the sanding or polishing seems to have no result, the oxide probably runs deep and you will have to resort to other methods to remove it.

To minimize fire scale in the first place, it's always a good idea to heat as quickly and briefly as possible. This helps reduce the amount and depth of the fire scale. A coating of flux helps protect the surface from alloy breakdown, though it has the disadvantage of promoting the flow of previously soldered joints. A simple method of obtaining a flux coating is to dip the work in flux or to paint or spray flux onto the work at each soldering operation. Since heat causes the flux to puddle up, it might be necessary to repeat the fluxing two or three times to get a good coverage. Another way to obtain the same coating is to use a saturated solution of borax and ethyl alcohol (the type used in alcohol lamps). It is usually kept in a small jar at the soldering bench. Before soldering the work is dipped in this solution, set on the soldering pad, and ignited. The alcohol burns away, leaving a residue of borax over the entire piece. Soldering is then performed as usual, with the layer of borax serving as the flux.

Once fire scale has formed, there are several ways to remove it. None of them is ideal, but each has its own merits. If you have already determined that your scale runs too deep to be removed with light polishing, the most obvious solution is to remove some of the surface, removing the fire scale along with it. This means filing, sanding, and polishing. Besides the extra work this method has the disadvantage of wasting metal (thinning the work) and of damaging details and textures. But it works. If the article has broad, open planes that are easily reached with sandpaper and if the surface treatment will not be affected, this is probably the most efficient solution.

Another way to beat the fire-scale dilemma is to remove the surface and with it the scale by a process called *bright dipping.* Acid is used to eat away the surface of a piece, but, unlike the use of abrasives just mentioned, this method eats everything away equally, leaving the details more or less intact. After the piece has been sanded and polished with tripoli, it is attached to a stainless-steel wire (if unavailable, use copper but replace periodically) and dipped into a solution of equal parts of nitric acid and water. (Remember to add the acid to the water.) The piece

should be submerged only for a few seconds, during which time the unaffected sterling will turn gray and the fire scale will turn black. Rinse the work in water and remove the black film with a fine abrasive such as pumice. Redip, again only for a few seconds, and repeat the cleaning process. Continue until the black areas no longer appear. The acid eats solder faster than sterling, so keep an eye on joints to ensure that they are not scarred.

If electroplating equipment is available, another alternative, called *electrostripping,* is possible. Like bright dipping, this procedure removes the surface layer of the metal, taking off the fire scale in the process. The difference is that electricity, which is slower but safer, is used instead of acid. The article to be stripped is attached to the positive element of a plating unit and suspended in a commercially produced stripping solution. A clean piece of brass is connected to the negative pole and hung in the solution so that it doesn't touch the piece. When the current is turned on, the fire-scale area may become dark, and the whole object will probably take on a dull mat finish. The length of time needed depends on the size of the article, the concentration of the solution, and the depth of the scale, but it might be anywhere from 10 minutes to an hour. When the surface appears to be uniform in color, the piece may be removed, rinsed in water, and buffed.

Another solution that makes use of the plating apparatus is to cover up the fire scale by plating over it. Gold, fine silver, or rhodium may be plated. This is a fairly common practice among jewelry manufacturers, since it is efficient for volume work.

4. Finishing Techniques

It is not an exaggeration to say that the finishing process begins as soon as you touch the metal. The easiest scratches to remove are those that are never made in the first place, and an experienced craftsperson continually checks for trouble spots. As mentioned earlier, hammer heads and anvils should be perfectly smooth. If either has a scar, the time needed to remove it is well justified, since it will save time in polishing. Similarly, pliers should be smooth-jawed and used only where necessary. Of course, these precautions should not interfere with the progress of the work: many marks are unavoidable and must be removed after the forming is completed. The finishing process is a step-by-step progression to increasingly finer abrasives. It is very important that no step be omitted or abbreviated. The first work is done with files.

It is very important that each step in the finishing process be done completely before moving on to the next degree of coarseness. The upper drawing shows a proper progression through the levels of abrasives: deep scratches are changed into medium scratches, which are changed into smaller scratches, and so on. In the lower drawing the first step was cut short, leaving some deep scratches. These persist throughout the finishing. In addition to taking more time skipping steps can result in sloppy work, since the abrasives are pushed beyond their limits.

Filing

Always use as large and coarse a *file* as the piece permits. The use of too small a file tends to waste time, break files, and destroy the crispness of a design. The teeth of a file point away from the *tang,* or handle, so cutting occurs only on the push stroke. Because of this it is a good idea, especially when filing hard metals such as steel, to lift the file on the noncutting stroke, since dragging it curls over the tips of the teeth and shortens the life of the tool.

Because the file is such a simple-looking piece of equipment, many people are fooled into thinking that there is no right way to use it. Wrong. Files can be surprisingly effective when used properly, but practice and attention are needed until you get the

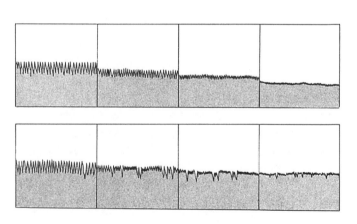

48

hang of it. Hold the work steady by bracing it against a knee or workbench and move only the file. Use the entire length of the cutting edge and pay attention to the angle at which you are holding the file. Filing jewelry is not like filing your fingernails: you should pay close attention to what's happening. Especially when using large files, you might find that the work goes faster and more evenly if you stand up, since the proper file stroke starts at the shoulder, not the wrist. In jewelry work large files are used to remove hammer marks, straighten edges, round off corners, and shape outlines. If you are working with any sort of volume, an attempt should be made to catch the filings, which can be refined and reused.

Large files are followed by *needle* files, which are usually about 6″ (15cm) long and are available in a variety of sizes. They continue the work started by the large files: they shape and smooth areas that are unreachable with the larger tool and can also be used to smooth down the roughness left by the first filing. Another small file that should be mentioned is the *riffle* file, or, as a group, *rifflers*. These delicate files are steel rods with teeth cut in only the last ½″ (12mm) of each end. The tips are made in a wide

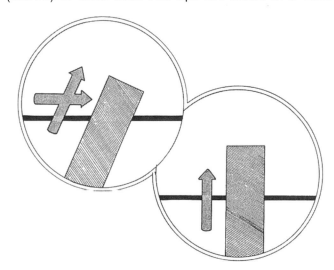

As simple as a file might appear, there is a correct and an incorrect way to use it. Holding the file at a right angle to the metal might create ridges, since each stroke will have a different force and therefore a different cutting power. By sliding the file sideways while pushing it a straighter edge is more likely to result.

range of shapes and can do precise filing that can't be done by any other tool. They have limited use because of their highly specialized nature, however, and are not a must for the beginning jeweler.

When you have finished filing, the surface should have a pattern of scratches that is consistent in depth. It is important that the scratches be made uniform before moving on to the next finer abrasive. To check this, tilt the piece into the light and look at it closely—deeper scratches will show up as darker lines. If possible, it's a good idea to alternate directions as you move from one abrasive to the next—i.e., to run the fine files perpendicular to the preceding coarse files. In addition to preserving the shape this procedure shows deep marks readily, since you know that anything running perpendicular to your current stroke must be removed before continuing.

Sanding

The next step after filing is the use of sandpaper. Unlike files, sandpaper cuts well in all directions. There are several types, and each craftsperson has his favorites. An old standby is *emery paper,* which is deep red in color. A slightly better variety is *emery cloth,* which lasts longer because of its fabric backing. Another choice is *silicon-carbide paper,* which is sold under several trade names and, depending on the company, might be black, dark green, or white. The most commonly used abrasive, silicon carbide is very tough and will last longer than many people suspect. When you feel that your paper is not cutting fast enough, wipe it on a cloth or hold it under running water to empty out the filing dust, and you'll probably find that it will continue to cut for quite a while.

Sandpaper is available in a range of *grits*, or coarsenesses. Most manufacturers rank their paper according to a universal numbering system in which higher numbers indicate finer grits, or smaller particles. For jewelry work a 180 grit may be considered coarse, 240 medium, and 320 fine. Abrasive papers in all grits are made with both *open* and *closed* coats. This terminology refers to the concentration of particles on the backing: a closed coat contains more particles per square inch. Availability and personal taste will help you decide which you want to use. Open-coat papers feel rougher and cut faster than closed-coat papers with the same grit. Most papers are available from a hardware store, and your best bet is to go there and to rub your finger on all their stock before you decide. Buy a sheet of those you like and pay attention as you use them to note differences.

Instead of sandpaper some crafters prefer *scotch stones,* rods of a natural abrasive material that is slightly softer than the abrasives used on paper. The stone is rubbed against the surface, usually while the work is held under running water. This floats away loose grit, preventing it from being pressed into the surface of the metal. (Some people use sandpaper under water for the same reason.) One of the advantages of the scotch stone is that it shapes itself to the contours of the piece being finished, automatically ensuring an even finish.

Most sandpaper is sold in standard-size sheets measuring 9″ × 11″ (22cm × 27cm). For jewelry work they can be cut into smaller squares that are easier to handle or mounted to a sanding stick, which provides greater leverage and control. These sticks can be bought but are just as easily made from any piece of wood about 1′ long, 1″ wide, and ¼″ thick (30 cm long, 3cm wide, and 5mm thick). Lumberyards sell this wood as lattice. A sheet of sandpaper may be attached by laying a piece of masking tape along the two long sides and wrapping it around the stick, pressing the tape in place as you go. Sharper corners are made by running a blunt tool such as a ballpoint pen along the edge of the stick before the fold is made. As a surface wears out, it may be peeled away and torn off, exposing a fresh layer of sandpaper. A similar arrangement may be worked up by using a dowel or several dowels of varying diameters to provide a rounded sanding surface.

Another device that makes sandpaper more effective, called a *slotted head tool,* is made for use on the flexible-shaft machine. It is a steel cylinder about 1½″ long and ¼″ in a diameter (40mm × 6mm) that is attached to a shaft that holds it in the chuck of the machine. The cylinder is split all the way through by a cut running from the top to about two-thirds of its length. A strip of sandpaper (any grit) is inserted into this slot. When the machine is turned on, the paper coils itself around the cylinder and does a very good job of cutting. A strip long enough to go around the cylinder several times is recommended: in this way a worn first surface may be torn off to expose fresh sandpaper underneath.

If a buffing or flex-shaft machine is available, another option to coarse sandpaper is provided by *abrasive wheels.* There are a number on the market, and each has its selling point. They basically consist of silicon-carbide or Carborundum grit mixed with hard rubber or glue and pressed into a specific shape such as a cone, sphere, or wheel. The cheaper wheels tend to wear out quickly and good ones are fairly expensive, but in some cases they can save a lot of time and justify the investment. They cut quickly, so care must be taken to keep the metal moving continually while it is in contact with the wheel, or grooves will almost certainly be cut. Since these wheels are as rough as coarse sandpaper, it's a good idea to stop just before the shape is finished and to allow fine sandpaper to smooth down the marks left by the grinding wheel. These wheels con-

To make sandpaper more effective, many crafters wrap it around a small board such as this one. The edges of the paper are made crisper if the line is creased with a blunt point before folding. If a full sheet of sandpaper is used, the outer layers can be peeled away as they become worn to expose fresh paper beneath.

stantly throw off abrasive grit when in use, so eye protection is a must.

There are some places that are too small for sandpaper and too delicate for grinding wheels: the solution here is *pumice powder*. It may be thought of as sandpaper without the paper: it is bought by the pound as a white powder and is available in three grits (coarse, medium, and fine). It can be rubbed dry onto the metal or mixed with water or any sort of oil to form a paste. The pumice can be rubbed in with the fingers or pressed into a strip of leather that is glued onto a stick in the same manner as for sandpaper. Pumice yields a soft, frosted finish that is sometimes used as the final surface when a bright shine is not desired. Used dry or mixed with water, pumice is also useful as a neutral cleaning material. Before coloring can be applied, the piece must be free of any grease and soap residue, and pumice manages to cut through both well.

At this point the work should be of the correct shape, free of all burs or rough edges, and uniform in color. Especially when dealing with a piece that is going to rest directly against the skin, such as a ring or bracelet, it's smart to close your eyes and turn the piece over in your hands to be sure that no dangerously rough edges have been overlooked. When you are convinced that the entire piece is free of gouges and covered with tiny scratches of uniform depth left by the fine sandpaper, you are ready to begin the buffing operation.

Buffing

Buffing is done in a similar progression from coarse to fine, except that the grits of sandpaper are replaced by buffing compounds. There are many compounds on the market, some made for specific metals and some for commercial operations, but you should feel free to try any of them. The two most commonly used compounds are *tripoli,* which is a form of sandstone and is usually brown; and a ferrous oxide (rust dust) called *rouge,* which is usually red. Tripoli is the coarser of the two and is used to remove the fine scratches left by the sandpaper. Rouge is used for the final polish: rather than remov-

ing material, it pushes the metal crystals around until they make a flat and therefore highly reflective surface. Both tripoli and rouge powders are mixed with grease and pressed into bars to make them easier to handle. The grease makes them somewhat messy and requires some special attention to wash them off.

It is very important that a separate set of buffing tools be maintained for each compound used, since mixing any two of them decreases the effectiveness of both. If even a little of the fine compound gets into the coarse buffs, their cutting power is reduced; if a coarse compound gets into the rouge, it will be impossible to obtain a brilliant luster. Most people use a motorized buffing machine for polishing, but buffing obviously used to be done by hand. This can yield satisfactory results in many instances, and there are cases in which the delicacy or shape of a piece recommends a hand method.

Hand Buffing

Hand buffing is done with flat sticks similar to those used to hold sandpaper but with a strip of leather, preferably chamois, glued to one side. Tripoli is rubbed onto one of the sticks until the leather takes on a dark brown color. This may be done dry, or the tripoli may be dipped in either turpentine or kerosene to dissolve the grease binder. The work is buffed with this stick in a motion similar to that used with the file: the work is held stationary while the leather is pushed over it in a long, smooth movement. When the scratches have been removed, the work is washed in a mixture of water, ammonia, and a liquid soap such as dishwashing detergent. A soft toothbrush is used to scrub the piece, making sure that all the tripoli is removed. Clean your hands as well, since tripoli on your fingers can be transferred to other buffs. Dry the piece with a soft cloth or tissue and repeat the process with the rouge compound. This final shine may also be achieved with a felt-covered stick or a soft cloth into which rouge has been rubbed. The work is then washed again and scrubbed until the suds lose their pinkish color, indicating that all the rouge has been removed. To avoid water spots, the work should be carefully dried. This is done professionally by laying the jewelry in a box filled with warm, fine sawdust. It absorbs the moisture and is blown off when it dries. A soft cloth or tissue paper also works well.

For tiny areas that cannot be reached by buffing sticks string and thin strips of cloth or leather may be used. The strip is secured at one end and pulled taut with your free hand. The compound and the work (in this order) are stropped along the cord to achieve the buffing action. An obvious variation is to secure the work to the bench and to slide the cord back and forth along it. Especially when using string, it is easy to wear grooves, so pay close attention and turn the work around in your hands as it moves back and forth.

Machine Buffing
Safety Procedures

The *buffing machine* is a great asset to the modern jeweler. I don't want to scare you away from using it, but certain precautions should be observed both for your own safety and for the good of the piece you are making. Because the buffs are so soft, it's hard to imagine that they can do any damage. This misconception can lead to problems unless certain proce-

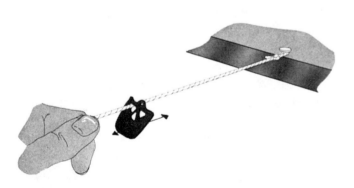

An effective method of finishing hard-to-reach places, called trumming, uses a piece of string that has been rubbed with tripoli or rouge. The piece can be moved as shown, or the work may be held steady while the string is passed back and forth over it. For broader areas a strip of fabric or leather can be used.

dures are followed.

1. Always work on the underside of the wheel so that the part of the buff that touches the metal moves away from you. There is a tendency for the buff to pull the work out of your hands: if you use the above position, the work would be thrown into the hood instead of into your face. The work should be held firmly against the wheel so that a muslin buff flattens out at the edges, but there is no need to press so hard that the motor slows down.

2. Always hold the work in a breakaway grip: never interlock your fingers into the piece. If the machine pulls the work away, it will happen so quickly that you won't be able to let go. Always be on the lookout and hold the work so that it can fly out of your hands cleanly. Never put a ring on your finger to polish it (unless you have an unlimited supply of fingers) or polish a bracelet or necklace by reaching your fingers through the inside.

3. Tie long hair and loose clothing back so that they can't tangle up in the wheel. Again, if anything happens, you simply won't have time to back away or to turn the motor off.

4. Wear goggles. The buffing room is no place for vanity: your eyesight is far more important. At the very least pieces of compound will fly into your face; and, since they are abrasives, they can irritate your eyes. Although less likely, the work itself may be thrown at you and can do harm to unprotected eyes.

5. When polishing frail items, support them on a small piece of wood, hold securely at both ends, and buff only a small portion at a time. Delicate pieces are a great hazard on the wheel, and the best safety precaution is to polish them by hand. Not only is this safer for you, but it is much less risky for the piece, which can be badly disfigured if it catches in the wheel.

6. Never take the wheel for granted. While you are polishing, keep your mind on what you're doing. If you want to have a conversation or figure out what to do next, stop the machine and come back when you can concentrate on polishing.

7. To protect your lungs, always wear a respirator.

Since buffing creates a lot of dust, some arrangement must be devised to contain it. The best system, especially important if a lot of time is to be spent at the wheel, as in a production shop, is a buffing table equipped with an exhaust blower. In this arrangement a separate motor acts as a vacuum cleaner, sucking dust particles down a hole behind the buffing machine to a filter where they are collected. For the small-scale worker this setup is not a necessity, but some sort of hood that can be cleaned out periodically is needed to catch the dust. The simplest type of hood is a cardboard box propped in place behind the machine. A more permanent hood can be made of wood, sheet metal, or both or bought from a supplier. Many hoods are equipped with a light bulb to illuminate the work while it is being polished, and I've always found it a big help.

Buffing Wheels

Buffing *compounds* are used on the machine with *wheels,* which are available in a range of shapes and sizes. They can be divided into two categories: *hard* and *soft.* Most soft wheels are made of fabric, a few stitched together in many layers: the common plies for muslin are 30, 50, and 60. *Leather* buffs are made to work with a pumice compound called *hard white* or *Lea compound* and cut too quickly for many jewelry applications. *Wool* buffs work well with *bobbing compound,* which also contains pumice and is fast-cutting. Most jewelers work with *muslin* buffs, which are appropriate for both tripoli and rouge. They are available as disks about 1″ (2½cm) thick and from 3″ to 12″ (7cm to 30cm) in diameter. Several centers are also available: the plain type is the cheapest, while leather and lead centers cost a bit more. Fabric wheels with no hub can stretch out of shape and it is worthwhile to buy the better quality. With use the outer layer of muslin wears away, leaving the first row of stitches at the surface of the wheel. They may be cut by carefully holding a sharp knife into the wheel as it is turning. After the thread has been cut, stop the motor and trim away any loose fibers with scissors. A softer and more efficient buff will result.

Buffing wheels are sold as plain fabric and must be coated with an abrasive compound in order to cut. Before coating the buff must be prepared, or *dressed.* A new buff should be mounted on the motor and, while it is turning, raked with an old fork or hacksaw blade to pull out loose fibers. They will fall out soon anyway, so you should remove them before applying the compound. When the shower of threads seems to have ceased, stop the wheel and trim all the loose ends with scissors. If they are allowed to remain, they might wear grooves in the piece or snag on delicate work. When the wheel has been properly dressed, it is ready to be *charged,* or impregnated with compound. With the wheel turning on the machine, the compound is held against the buff for slightly less than a minute until it takes on the color of the compound. If too much is applied, it will fly off and make a mess, so it's better to apply sparingly and regularly. With experience you will learn how fast each compound can cut and in this way determine when the rate is too slow, indicating that more abrasive is needed.

Hard buffs are made of felt and come in full inch variety of widths and in a knife-edge shape that is thick at the hub and tapers toward the circumference. *Felt* wheels are made in several hardnesses: the medium grade is preferred for general jewelry work. A handy shape that is a second cousin to the felt wheel is a tapered wooden rod covered with felt, called a *ring buff.* As the term implies, it is used for polishing the inside of rings and any similar small curve. Felt wheels are used when it is important that details and sharp edges are not worn away. They are also handy for directing the buffing operation when scratches have been made in a small area—around a bezel, for instance. Because felt buffs cut straight edges, there is a danger of wearing a sharp-edged canyon in the metal, and it's a good idea to keep the work rotating in your hands continually while it is in contact with the wheel. Felt wheels do not need to be dressed but are charged with compounds in the same way as are fabric buffs. For both types of wheel the compounds may be applied dry but will penetrate the buff faster if the bar is first dipped in kerosene or turpentine.

Polishing

The motor for a buffing setup should be at least ¼ horsepower, larger for production or school work-shops, so that it will not drag (slow down) when in use. Though some craftspeople prefer a motor that makes 3450 revolutions per minute, I've always found the slower (and therefore safer) 1725rpm motor satisfactory. The motor should be securely mounted on a high bench, preferably about 40″ (1m) off the floor. It should be situated so that the shaft spins in a downward direction and positioned so that the shaft is at least 5″ (12cm) above the table. For most efficient use the shaft should be fitted with a threaded, tapered spindle, which allows buffs to be changed easily. Spindles can be bought from jewelry-supply companies. When ordering, specify the diameter of the motor's shaft and the side of the motor to which the spindle will be attached. This last point is important because the threads are cut so that the wheel is tightened as it turns. A right-handed spindle mounted on the left would immediately un-screw the buff when the motor was turned on.

The speed of the motor is not as critical as is the surface speed of the buffing wheel (the distance that a given spot on the circumference of the wheel travels in a minute). A 6″ (15cm) wheel spinning at 1725rpm covers almost 3000′ (915m) per minute, while a 4″ (10cm) buff moving at the same speed travels less than 2000′ (610m) per minute. This means that larger buffs are especially good for fast cutting and final polishing, and smaller buffs for greater deliberation.

A more delicate and controlled polishing may be done with the *flexible-shaft*, or *Dremel, machine*. A glance at a catalog will reveal the scores of minia-ture finishing tools available, from coarse steel files through grinding wheels to small versions of muslin and felt wheels. Small muslin buffs, which must be dressed before charging in the same way as for larger ones, are mounted onto a shaft called a *man-drel* that has a screw threaded into its end. Felt wheels are used on the same sort of mandrel, while felt cones are screwed onto a shaft whose tip is threaded. Mandrels are quite cheap, and it's a good idea to buy enough of them to mount each buff permanently, saving time in tool changing. Re-member that you also need a set of buffs for each compound to be used. It's a good idea to build a collection of mandrels and drills with the same shank diameter to facilitate quick changing. The standard size is 3/32″ (2mm) and offers the greatest selection. For reaching into tight places a Q-Tip makes a handy buff, and it can be coated with pumice, tripoli, or rouge.

Special Buffs

The above information applies to the creation of a bright shine on general jewelry work and is by far the most commonly applied buffing sequence. Spe-cial needs and considerations have led to the de-velopment of special buffs. A *bristle brush* is a wooden disk from whose circumference short bris-tles made of nylon or animal hair project. It can be used with either tripoli or rouge and is handy for reaching into recessed areas. A variation made for the flexible-shaft machine, called an *end brush,* has bristles that stick out in a continuance of the shaft. The polishing method for these tools is the same, except that less pressure is used in holding the work against the wheel. *Scratchbrushes* are wood or metal disks mounted with fine brass, steel, or nickel wires. They are most often used to achieve a frosted or brushed finish on metal after the usual tripoli and rouge polish. They are used at slow speeds and work best when lubricated with water or household oil. It's a good idea to turn the wheel around periodically in order to keep the tips of the wire from bending over, which limits the effectiveness of the tool.

Tumbling

An alternative to buff-type polishing that is espe-cially appropriate for rounded shapes is a process called *tumbling*. In this technique many pieces of jewelry are loaded into a canister with a special soapy lubricant and several pounds of steel shot and sloshed around in a manner that resembles a miniature washing machine. The shot is made just for this purpose and consists of assorted shapes: spheres, rods, tiny Saturns, and eggs. The closed container is laid on rollers, which are turned by a motor. As the work is jostled into contact with the shot, the jewelry is burnished, smoothing out the surface. Variations are possible, depending on the type of work being polished, the ratio of work to shot, and the duration of the tumbling, but this process usually replaces tripoli and sometimes leaves a final polish. Tumblers are designed just for jewelry finishing, but a small lapidary (stone-cutting) tumbler is just as good for small-scale work. The main disadvantage of tumbling is the volume required: to work efficiently, even a small unit needs 50 to 100 pieces of similarly shaped jewelry. But for the production workshop this is not too difficult a stipulation to meet.

It is very important that the steel shot used for tumbling be kept absolutely free of rust. Its action depends on a smooth, shiny surface; and, if it is destroyed, the rather costly shot must be discarded. If it is left overnight, the shot is covered with water to avoid contact with air. If it is left unused for longer periods, it must be dried by spreading it out on a towel and leaving it in a warm place, such as near a heater or under a light bulb.

Coloring

The finishing operations described thus far assume that a piece is polished to a maximum shine all over and are especially appropriate if there are few or no recesses. Many designs, however, benefit from an interplay of raised and sunken areas. In these cases it is common to darken recessed areas, providing greater contrast to the exposed areas, which take and retain a high polish. The process of coloring metal is called *patination*.

Sterling Silver

The most common form of coloring is the darkening of sterling, known as *oxidizing* or *antiquing*. "Oxidizing" is an erroneous term, since the resultant color is due to sulfur, not oxygen. "Antiquing" is probably more appropriate, since the effect is similar to a buildup of tarnish over several years. The implication that you are trying to make something look old, however, is not true. Darkening makes it look better but not necessarily older. The most common coloring agent for sterling is *liver of sulfur*, a form of potassium sulfide. It may be bought from a chemical-supply company or a jewelry supplier and is usually furnished in the form of lumps about the size of an almond. These lumps and the solution made from them deteriorate when exposed to air or light and should be kept tightly sealed in a dark glass bottle. A standard concentration of liver of sulfur is one lump to about a pint of water. Because the solution is constantly weakening, exact measurement is unnecessary. The lump of sulfur will dissolve more rapidly if it is mixed with hot water.

When darkening sterling, the work may be dipped in a cool solution, but the reaction will be faster and more even if heat is applied. The solution itself may be heated in a flameproof dish or some sort of double-boiler arrangement, or the piece may be heated, usually while held in soldering tweezers or attached to a length of wire, and then dipped into the solution while still warm. When using the latter method, it is important that the piece not be too warm, since a thick sulfide scale will be created, which will chip off, leaving an uneven color.

For an even, blue color on sterling place the work in a small steel container and surround it with pieces of pure sulfur (sometimes called *flowers of sulfur*), making sure that the two don't touch. Gently heat the container with a torch until the desired color is achieved. For a greenish tint mix in a Pyrex container 3 parts boiling water and 1 part iodine and add this mixture to 3 parts hydrochloric acid. Pure iodine, not the drugstore tincture, is needed—it can be bought from a chemical supplier. Since it is a reactive material, great care should be taken when using it.

If only the recessed areas are to be colored, the coloring is usually done between the tripoli and rouge stages. It is important in any coloring operation that the piece be thoroughly washed, since any traces of grease left from the buffing compound will make the color spotty. If most of the piece is to be darkened, it is usually immersed in the appropriate solution. If only a small area is to be treated, the solution should be painted on, which saves time in the follow-up buffing process. When the desired color has been reached, flush the work under running water, making sure that no colorant is left behind, including any traces on your hands or on the tools used to hold the work while dipping. After the piece has been dried, it is rubbed with fine pumice powder or buffed on the rouge wheel to remove the coloring from the higher areas. The degree of lightness is determined by the duration of this cleanup process: continue until the piece looks good to you, then stop. Wash with soap and water in the usual way.

The entire work can also be colored, offering an alternative to the conventional bright shine. This process is usually done after the final polish, and it is again critical that the piece be free of grease. One word to the wise before I continue: this overall darkening is not a coverup technique to hide sloppy polishing. On the contrary, any mistakes or shortcuts will probably show up more clearly in a darkened piece than in a bright, shiny one. The process is a very deliberate one, not an afterthought to cover up a mistake. After a careful washing with ammonia and soap rinse the piece well and avoid touching its more exposed surfaces with the fingers. The work is dipped into the chosen solution until the proper color has been achieved. It is then rinsed in water and burnished by hand with a scratchbrush, usually applied in a random or circular motion. This removes some of the color, blends the various hues together, and bonds the sulfide layer more permanently to the surface of the metal. The work may be redipped and burnished several times, each time yielding a mellower color. A scratch buff, normally used on the buffing machine, works well for this treatment; a suède brush, sold at shoe and department stores for the care of leather, may also be used.

A range of sterling colors can be made with either of the following solutions: 1 gram of barium sulfide to 7 ounces of cold water or 1 gram of ammonium sulfide to 7 ounces of hot water. When clean sterling is quickly dipped in either mixture, it takes on a golden color. If it is allowed to remain in the solution a little longer, the work will assume a crimson color. If the work or solution is heated, the reaction will cause the sterling to turn brown. This color is mellow at first but will flatten if too much heat is applied.

Gold

Achieving a deep black color on gold can be difficult, since one of the advantages of gold is its resistance to chemical corrosion. The same liver-of-sulfur solution used on sterling may be used on gold, but in this case both the metal and the solution should be warm, and several dippings are needed. Another blackening agent is pure iodine; but, because of its volatile nature, it is not a good item to stock on a permanent basis. Good results can be obtained with a commercial preparation called Silvox, which must be used with steel to get a deep black color. This is done by applying it with the tip of a nail or swabbing it with a piece of steel wool held in tweezers. The same preparation can be used to darken sterling, but the color is comparable to that of liver of sulfur, which is cheaper. Retail jewelry stores sometimes use a special black paint to darken recesses, but I feel that the chemical treatments are better. The paint does not create a pleasant shading transition from dark to light and tends to chip off easily with wear.

Copper and Brass

Both copper and brass offer a wide range of color possibilities. The same mixture can be used for either metal; brass requires a longer immersion or a stronger mix. A great deal of variety can be obtained just from the strength of the solution, the temperature at which it is applied, and the duration and number of applications. Experimentation is the best way to get a feel for these colorants.

Liver of sulfur in water works nicely, especially on copper. It should be mixed to about one-third the strength of the sterling solution. Also try 1 part copper sulfate mixed with 2 parts hot water or 1 part ammonium sulfate mixed with 2 parts hot water. Quick dips, especially when followed by rubbing with a scratchbrush, yield a rich brown. After coloring with any of these solutions wash with soap and water and dry as usual.

In any coloring operation it's a good idea to proceed slowly, darkening the metal in careful stages until the best hue is obtained. Patinas can always be made darker by redipping, but they cannot be easily lightened. If the work becomes too dark, it must be pickled to remove all oxides, rinsed, and recolored all over again.

C-1

Peter Moss Handler. Ring, sterling, 14K yellow and rose gold, deer antler. The antler is held in place not only by the pivot pin that runs through the top section, allowing it to move, but also by pins soldered onto the backs of the stars and "nailed" in place.

C-2

Denise Levar. Hairpiece, bronze, brass, sterling, copper, 4" in diameter. Pieces of four metals were inlaid by careful sawing, domed, and pierced. The contrasting colors were emphasized by oxidizing the hairpiece in liver of sulfur. in liver of sulfur.

C-3

Chuck Evans. Bracelet, sterling, gold plate. This hollow bracelet was made by repousséing four panels of 20-gauge sterling. The panels were then soldered together with a lining and made into two halves that are connected by a hinge. After plating the work was buffed to allow the silver to show through at the raised areas while keeping the recesses gold-colored.

C-4

Rick Guido. *Mountain Climber* (badge), plastic, brass, gold charm, 3" high. Rivets are used to hold the metal sections onto the plastic. Plastic can be cut and shaped with conventional jewelry tools but should be polished with a special compound.

C-5

Curtis K. LaFollette #1 (pendant), sterling, mokumé, 1½" wide. The sterling section was carved in hard wax with a drill bit and large files. After casting this element was soldered onto a slightly domed section of mokumé.

C-6

Gail M. Markiewicz. Ring, 14K gold, pearl. The model for the ring was formed from soft wax that was molded with a warm needle. A perfect fit for the uneven pearl was guaranteed by shaping the wax around it while it was in place. Photo by John Heller.

C-7

Patricia J. Daunis-Dunning. Bracelet, sterling, copper, 2" wide. The copper and sterling sections of this piece were soldered together as a flat band, which was then cut, repositioned, and resoldered before shaping. To increase its reflectivity, the band was curved by shaping it on a stake. The colors were produced with a strong oxidizing solution.

C-8

Chuck Evans. Pin, bronze, sterling, pearls, 2" in diameter. The almost regular pattern of silver squares across the face of the piece is a solder inlay. After preparing it the disk was cut and decorated with piercing. The sterling side pieces were forged and soldered into place.

C-9

John Heller. Pin, sterling, 14K gold, rose quartz, 4" in diameter. The wax pattern for the sterling section was made by pressing the desired shape and texture into clay. Hot wax was then brushed into this recess, creating the pattern. The gold section was shaped from soft-wax sheet, cast separately, and soldered to the sterling half. Photo courtesy of the artist.

C-10

Ring, sterling, 14K gold, ivory. The pattern for the sterling element was carved from hard wax, cast, and finished. Soft wax was then formed in place, and the gold was cast directly onto the sterling half. Rivet wires were soldered in place after the ivory was cut to the correct shape.

C-11

Curtis K. LaFollette. Flask, sterling, 8" high. The body of this piece was formed in a Masonite die. Notice that the flange was allowed to remain and in fact complements the design of the piece.

5. Surface Techniques

If you knew nothing at all about metalwork when you started this book, you should now be able to make a finished piece of jewelry. The steps discussed so far—tools, soldering, bending, and finishing—are basics and will be repeated in almost every piece that you make. Jewelry made with these basic techniques, however, is limited by the stock shapes of the metal: the sheet and wire as they come from the supplier. By looking at the finished piece the starting materials and the processes used become obvious.

Line, shape, and texture are three basic components of any design, but the techniques discussed so far deal only with the first two. The sleek shine of polished metal is a beautiful hypnotic; but, as rich as it is, there are many surface treatments that can rival it in beauty. Some of the techniques discussed in this chapter are worked on the metal before assembly; others are appropriate only after the piece has been fabricated. Some are best used alone, but most can be used in combination with others and in a thousand variations to produce an incredible stockpile of surfaces.

Texturing

The only final state of metal mentioned so far is a smooth surface, either buffed to a high polish, frosted, or colored. Another possibility is to *texture*

the metal before any work is done. There are many ways to do this, among them the following.

1. Using a ball-peen hammer, strike the surface in a random pattern, covering the metal with concave facets. This is a handy way to camouflage fingerprints on a piece that will be handled.

This test piece of copper shows three ball-peened surfaces. The largest facets were made with the domed face of a planishing hammer; the middle section was made with a machinist's ball-peen hammer; and the smallest marks are the result of the ball peen of a chasing hammer. Smaller-scale work generally requires smaller facets to achieve a proportioned look.

C-2.

C-1.

[Note: The illustrations on this page and the three following pages appear in color on the book covers.]

C-3.

C-4.

C-6.

C-7.

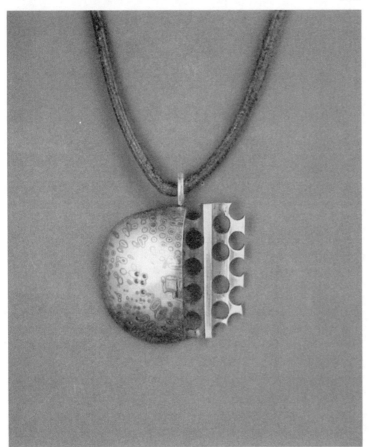

C-5.

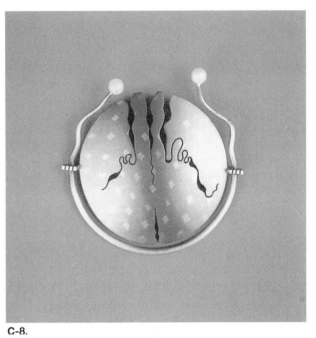

C-8.

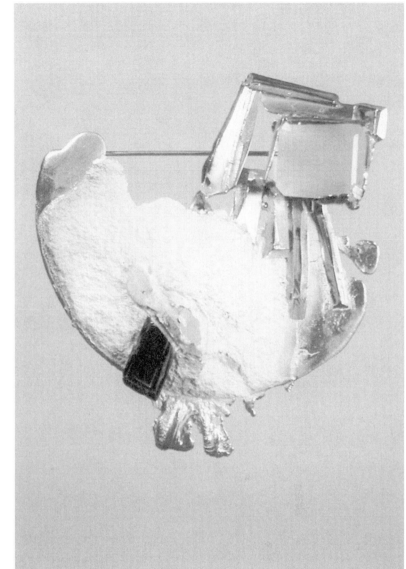

C-9.

C-10.

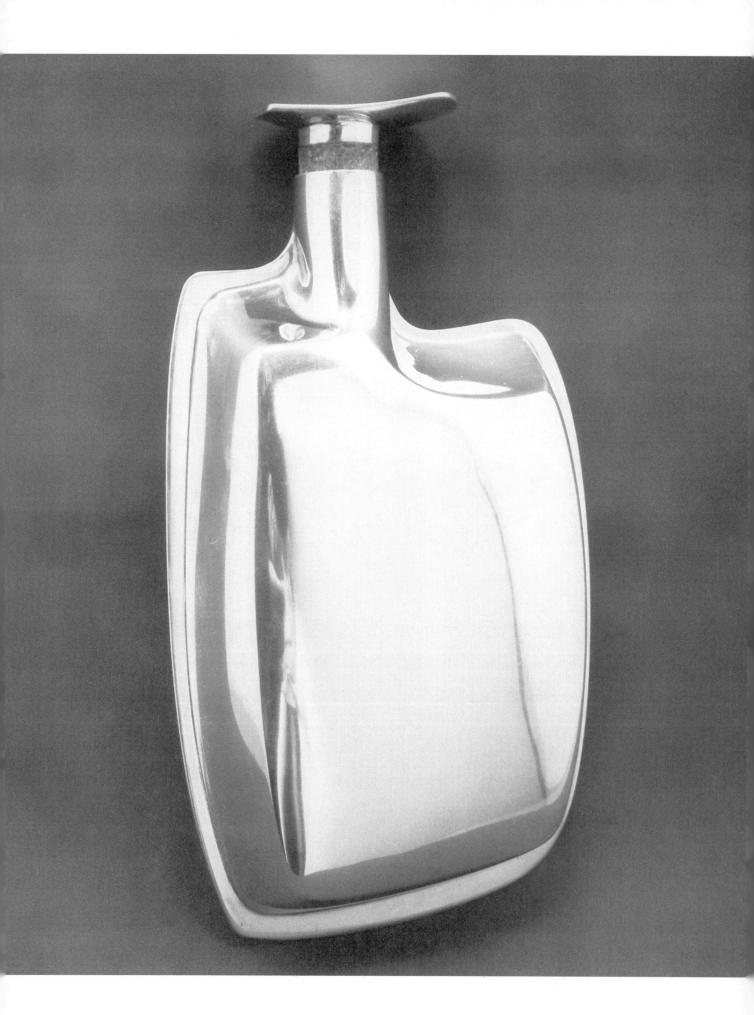

2. Using the ball-peen hammer, make a row or circular pattern. Try using several different-size balls: large balls are found on machinist's hammers, small ones on chasing hammers. Even smaller dents can be made with a dapping punch. It can be held in the hand and struck with a hammer, but a faster method is to clamp the tool in a hand vise or vise-grip pliers at right angles to the handle so that it becomes a hammerlike apparatus.

3. The wedge of a riveting hammer makes a rich linear pattern and can also be handled in a random or an organized way. A planishing hammer, when held at a steep angle, makes arc-shaped marks.

4. Nonferrous metals are soft enough to pick up many textures when they are hammered into the surface. A pitted anvil, concrete, cast iron, or any other hard, rough surface can be used as a support against which metal is pounded to texture it.

5. An old hammer face can be scarred with files or punches to create a rough surface that can be transmitted to metal flattened with the hammer.

6. A coarse, grainy texture can be created by punching a series of dots into the metal with a scribe or centerpunch. A bolder texture can be made by deliberately poking through the metal with a sharp scribe. Work on a piece of softwood that will not dull the point when it pushes through.

Texturing Tools

There is a type of punch made just for texturing, called a *matting tool.* It resembles a repoussé punch, except that its surface is incised with a texture. It is available commercially in specific patterns, such as a honeycomb or grid, or with a random roughness. The tool is used simply by pounding overlapping blows into the metal while it is supported on steel. Use a heavy hammer and anneal the piece before starting.

A shallower texture can be made by using the flexible-shaft machine and a small steel bur. Almost any bur shape or coarse grinding stone can cut a texture; ball-shaped burs are slightly easier to control. The piece may be covered with the scratchy lines made by this tool, or they may be scribbled

or looped regularly. Unlike most other surface techniques, this method is localized and can be used like an eraser to camouflage mistakes that have been made in assembly.

Roll Printing

Rich textures can be pressed into sheet metal with the use of a *rolling mill.* A sandwich unit of the raw sheet, the texture material, and a piece of brass is put together and passed through the mill. Brass, which is the hardest of the common nonferrous metals, is used to protect the rollers and to concentrate all the pressure on the softer metal. Some possibilities for texturing materials are sandpaper, fab-

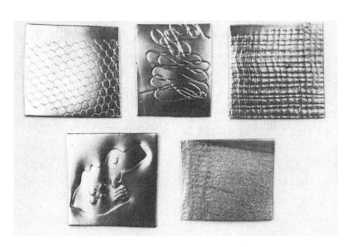

Samples of roll-printed textures. These patterns were made with lace, binding wire, burlap, a shape cut from copper sheet, and sandpaper.

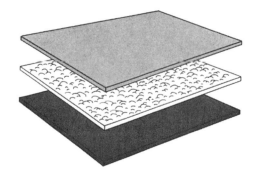

To protect the rolling mill and get a deep impression, brass, the hardest of the common nonferrous metals, is used as shown for roll printing.

ric, lace, window screening, and shapes cut from copper and brass.

Before trying to run a pizza through the mill, stop to think through the possible effects, both good and bad, of what you're doing. This technique offers exciting possibilities, but, like any other, it has its limitations. Some materials are inappropriate and will just waste your time. Others will damage the rollers and leave a very expensive piece of equipment out of commission. Anything made of steel (saw blades, paper clips, pins) must be annealed before being passed through the mill. Heat it to bright red and allow to cool slowly in air. Even when annealed, steel materials should be used only with metal that is thick enough to cushion their shapes. A little common sense should tell you which materials are simply too frail to press into the metal (grass, for instance) and which are too hard or large to pass through the rollers safely. Set the distance between the rollers as closely as possible by eye before trying to pass the unit through and give up immediately if it takes all your strength to turn them.

Stamping

A huge variety of textures and patterns can be transferred to both sheet and wire by the simple technique of *stamping*. It is similar to leather tooling and involves the use of hardened steel tools to press

These punches were made in the shop as a specific design need arose. The punch on the right, called a matting tool, is made by hammering the steel onto an old file. The tool on the far left is a Philips screwdriver with the tip ground off.

designs forcibly into the metal. Stamping tools look like chasing and repoussé tools: in fact, there is little difference between the processes of stamping and chasing. *Chasing* refers to work that is done in a continuous motion, usually on curved metal. In stamping the tool is lifted and repositioned for each blow, and the metal is usually flat. It is important that the metal to be stamped be annealed and thick enough to absorb the force of the blow without creating a weak spot.

Stamping tools can be improvised from household materials. Heavy, flat nails such as those used in masonry can be shaped on the tip and used for stamping. Screwdrivers and chisels can be ground down to form stamping tools, but they have their limitations. Not only are the shapes restricted, but the tips wear down quickly and need to be refiled. Commercial stamping tools are available; but, since they often come in trite shapes (such as supposed Indian motifs) and are mechanically perfect, they frequently fail to harmonize with handcrafted work. Punches and stamping tools are not difficult to make, and it is worth your while to take time out from jewelry production to learn how to do it. Not only do these tools cost about one-fourth of their commercial counterparts, but they are unique and appropriate to the need at hand.

To make stamping tools, special steel called *drill rod* or *tool stock* is required. The three types available are *air-hardening, oil-hardening,* and *water-hardening,* which refers to the liquid that produces the crystalline change needed to harden the steel. Air-hardening steel requires exacting temperatures and is not suited to handcrafting. I prefer water-hardening to oil-hardening steel, since the latter requires you to keep a gallon of oil in the studio. Aside from this inconvenience there is no difference in the way in which the two steels are worked.

Tool steel is available from local dealers in most cities and even in small towns—look in the Yellow Pages under Tools or Steel. It is usually supplied in 12' (3½m) round or square rods that measure 3/16" (5mm) or more in diameter. For jewelry tools ¼" (6mm) or smaller diameters are usually preferred.

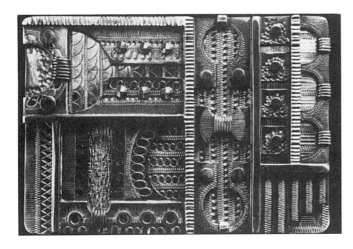

Nancy Moore and Tom Streb. Belt buckle, sterling, copper, and brass, 2″ × 3″. The richness of this form was achieved by stamping, engraving, and wrapping elements that were then riveted together. Photo courtesy of the artists.

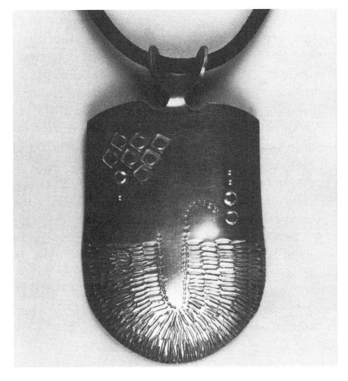

Pendant, copper, 3″ high. Rich surface patterns can be devised with even the simplest punches.

Though you might want to try other lengths, 4½″ (11cm) is standard for hand punches. It can be cut to length with a hacksaw or a jeweler's saw. Most tool stock is furnished in the annealed state; but, if it must be softened—if you are using old tools to make new ones, for example—heat the steel to a bright red color and allow it to cool slowly, preferably by burying it in sand.

In some cases the punch shape is filed directly into the end of the rod. Broader shapes for chisels and some repoussé tools require the tip to be flared out to make a wider blank before shaping. Some flattening can be done on the cold metal; but, if radical changes are to be made, the metal must be hot-forged. Holding the steel in tongs or vise-grip pliers, heat it to a red-hot color with a torch but don't let it get so hot that it starts to throw off sparks. Quickly hammer the metal on the anvil, stopping as soon as the red color disappears. Reheat and strike again if necessary until the proper shape is achieved. Anneal by bringing the metal to a red heat and slowly cooling. Once formed, the blank can be shaped on a grinding wheel, with the saw, or with files. When using a power machine, be careful not to heat the steel so much that it turns color: this will harden it prematurely.

Fine detail may be worked into a stamp by using flexible-shaft burs, drills, or needle files. Take time in shaping the tip, since the tool will be a permanent acquisition. The design may be checked midway by pressing the stamp into clay. The outside edge of the stamp should be beveled to allow clearance for the metal to bulge as it is compressed by the stamp. The top edge should also be lightly beveled to prevent chipping from the force of the hammer. When the shaping is complete, the tool should be sanded to remove any file marks.

If the tool were used in this state, it would soon lose its crispness and wear out. To avoid this, the blank must be hardened. The last 1″ (2½cm) of the shaped tip is heated to a bright red color. Some experience is needed to judge the proper temperature accurately: insufficient heat will not harden the steel, and too much can melt it, destroying the design. The best description of the desired color is a bright orange-red but not one that gives off sparks. When the tool reaches this temperature, it is quickly submerged in a large container of oil or water, depending on the type of steel. This step is easier if the tool is held over the liquid with tongs while heating so that it can be immediately thrust into the water. Since the liquid around the tool is instantly heated, it's a good idea to swirl the tool around as it is dunked to bring it into contact with cool liquid.

The tool is next tested to ensure that the steel is hardened. If the procedure was properly followed, the same file that was used to shape the tip will now slide along the tool without scratching it. If this is not the case—if the file easily cuts into the steel—it is probable that a high enough temperature was not reached. Go back and try again. When the steel is properly hardened, it is brittle. If struck with a hammer, it would probably shatter like glass. To relieve this brittleness, the tool is again heat-treated in a process called *tempering.*

Drawing a temper is a procedure that requires a careful reading of temperature changes as they are indicated by variances in color. In order to see the color of the steel clearly as heat is applied, it is necessary to clean the tool with sandpaper, since the hardening leaves it with a gray scale. The tool is again held in tongs, and the flame of the torch is held stationary about 1½" (4cm) from the carved tip. Bands of color will start to move out from the flame in both directions, but you should be concerned only with those that are moving toward the shaped tip. The first color to appear is a dark blue; as the blue patch moves down the shank, a brown or brownish yellow band appears just ahead of it. The next band toward the tip is straw yellow in color: this color indicates the proper temper. When the straw-yellow band reaches the tip, plunge the tool into the cooling liquid, again moving it around slightly as you do so.

The tool can now be sanded to brighten its appearance, and it should be tested by stamping a piece of scrap metal. If properly hardened, it should stand up to many years of use on soft metal without showing any wear. The other end, by the way, is left untempered to absorb hammer blows. The process might sound a bit involved on paper, but after only a few tries you'll memorize the steps and find it as easy as it is helpful.

Engraving

Engraving is an ancient and versatile method of decorating in which small, sharp tools are used to shave away little bits of metal. The form of engraving with which you are probably most familiar is the cutting of monograms and inscriptions on charms, watchcases, and trophies. This is usually done on a machine in which a diamond-tipped bur spinning at high speeds is used to cut into the metal. This requires much less skill than does real engraving and leaves a shallower mark that has none of the richness of a hand-engraved line. The cutting of initials is a valid use of engraving, but it is unfortunate that the scope of the art has been so limited. Pictures, symbols, and textures can be engraved, and they offer a vast potential to the craftsperson who is willing to invest the time needed to become proficient in this art form.

The tools used for engraving are called *burins* or *gravers;* they are made of high-quality steel and are about 4" (10cm) long. They are held in a small wooden handle that is gripped tightly in the heel of the hand. For proper cutting it is critical that the tools be accurately shaped and periodically resharpened. This work is done on abrasive stones saturated with oil. Proper shaping requires both a coarse and a fine stone, which are often sold glued back-to-back, and a fine grit of sandpaper for the final polishing. The angles at the tip of the tool are exacting and can be best cut with the aid of a holding device.

Gravers are made in several stock shapes, and each must be prepared and honed before the work can begin. The drawing shows some common graver shapes, the proper angles of their faces, and the lines that they cut. The first shape, called a *square graver,* is the most commonly used and probably the easiest to control. It cuts a fine line

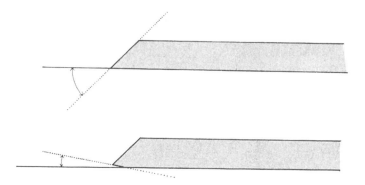

Meticulous honing is very important in engraving and can best be done with a holding device. Whether cut by hand or with such a device, the angles of the gravers are the same. They vary, depending on the type of metal being cut, the length of the tool, and the size of the hand that is holding it, but this drawing shows a universal starting point. The face angle should be 45°. The underside, or belly angle, which controls the angle at which the tool is held and the depth of the cut that it will make, should be around 12°.

when held straight into the metal and can be rolled over to widen the cut. This action is used to create a line that gracefully moves from thin to wide and back to thin again. This graver can also be used to score a groove for a sharp bend or for any sort of cut-in design. The second tool, a *flat graver,* is harder to control, since it removes more metal than the others. It is used for carving and in the finishing process for cutting away scratches and solder traces that are impossible to reach with files or sandpaper. The next two tools, the *round* and *knife-edge gravers,* respectively, are used for cutting slightly deeper lines than those possible with the square graver. While these lines can be decoration in themselves, they can also serve several other purposes, including inlay, as described later in this chapter. The last graver, called a *liner,* cuts a series of parallel lines in a single stroke. It can be used to create a frosted surface by cutting a single pattern of lines or by crossing a first cut with a second one at an angle.

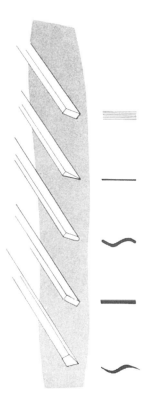

In the hands of a professional engraver each tool has specific uses, and a large collection is not uncommon. For general use the shapes shown above will answer most needs. From the left they are square, flat, round, and knife-edge gravers and a special tool called a liner.

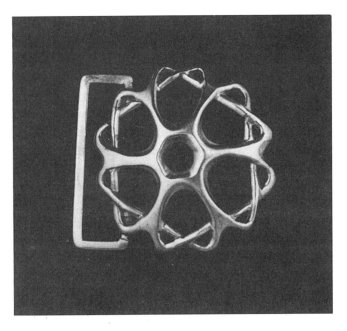

Belt buckle, sterling, 2″ in diameter. This buckle was made with a technique called carving. The design is started by piercing from a thick sheet. The interwoven effect is achieved by removing metal from the appropriate areas. This can be done with a flat graver, a small chisel, a file, or a combination of the three.

This cross-hatching makes a rich pattern that will last a long time, since it is cut deeply into the metal. In addition to the obvious use of this texture as a design element lining comes in handy for decorating an otherwise plain pin or pendant back and goes a long way toward hiding errors.

Heat Texturing
Scarring

Metals may be joined without the use of solder by melting them together in a process called *fusing.* In *scarring,* an extension of this process, a sheet of metal is textured with the torch as a method of preparing stock that is then cut up and used for jewelry pieces. A relatively thin-gauge sheet of metal—say, 20-gauge or less—is fluxed and heated just until it turns shiny, indicating that the surface is starting to melt. The torch may then be quickly withdrawn to leave the sheet slightly bubbled and coarse on the surface. Repeated applications of the torch increase the coarseness. For more obvious textures filings may be dropped onto the metal just as it reaches the molten state. If filings of the same metal are used, they will appear as small bumps; filings of a different metal will start to alloy with the surface, sometimes producing subtle color variations. The torch must be withdrawn as soon as the filings are dropped, since a delay of a few seconds will cause the metal to fuse completely into the surface, smoothing it out. While the metal is molten, it may be poked, jabbed, or torn with a soldering probe. With a little experimentation this technique can be used to create rich surfaces that offer great contrast to the smooth shine usually expected on precious metals. As mentioned previously, the usual practice is to scar a larger sheet than needed and to use only the best parts, since the effects are random and there will probably be some uninspiring areas.

Reticulation

A more sophisticated form of heat texturing, called *reticulation,* can be used to create a controlled pattern that is recognizable by its finer lines and more consistent roughness. It may be worked on sterling, but for best results a special alloy is used. To make reticulation silver, copper is added to sterling: a good mix is 17% copper to 83% fine silver. It may be mixed from scratch or made by adding slightly more than 10% copper to a given weight of sterling. This mix is melted in a crucible, fluxed, stirred with a carbon rod or hardwood dowel, and poured into a preheated ingot mold. The resulting ingot is rolled out to about 18-gauge. This alloy may also be purchased in sheet stock from Hauser and Miller Refiners (4011 Forest Park Blvd., St. Louis, MO 63108).

Reticulation samples: at the upper left is a piece of Nu-Gold, untreated but taken to a high temperature. Beside it is a piece of sterling that was painted with yellow ocher and heated. On the lower left is a section of sterling that was heated and quenched in pickle ten times before being textured with the torch. The last sample shows reticulation alloy (830 parts silver, 170 parts copper) that was heated and quenched in pickle ten times before its final heating. This is the most dramatic and best controlled form of reticulation.

Whether you are using reticulation alloy or sterling, it is necessary to build up a skin of fine silver on the surface of the sheet. This is done by heating the metal at about 1100°F (590°C) and quickly dropping it into a pickle. The heating produces silver and copper oxides that are dissolved by the pickle, leaving fine silver on the surface. The process is most effective if the pickle is clean and potent: in fact, some people prefer a pickle of 1 part sulfuric acid to 10 parts water to the usual commercial product. The heating and quenching process must be repeated a minimum of five times for the reticulation alloy and at least twenty times for sterling. Care should be taken throughout to handle the surface as little as possible, since it is easy to scratch through the fine-silver layer.

The sandwich that is created in the quenching operation contains an interior of a low-melting copper-silver alloy and thin outside layers of higher-melting fine silver. To create the rich texture associated with reticulation, the unit is carefully heated to the point at which the interior becomes molten while the skin remains solid. The torch is then removed, and the cooling interior contracts, buckling the surface skin into ridges and craters. In practice the sheet is set on a preheated soldering pad or firebrick and heated locally with a standard flame. The flame is gently moved in a circle, allowing the small area to be heated and cooled. When the surface starts to wrinkle, the flame is moved slowly along the surface, drawing the texture with it. Care must be taken not to overheat the metal, since this would realloy the fine-silver layer with the rest of the sheet. If the surface becomes shiny, overheating is indicated. In this case it is necessary to repeat the quenching process in order to reestablish the skin. With experience you can control the texture formation by tilting the torch or by changing the gas-air mixture. When finished, the reticulated piece can be cut up and used for any type of fabrication. It solders and polishes like sterling.

Nu-Gold and nickel silver tend to break out of alloy at high temperatures, making them natural for a reticulationlike effect. It is not necessary in either case to build up a skin by quenching in pickle. A high-temperature torch is needed, however, and best results will be achieved if the underlying soldering pad is preheated.

Harold O'Connor. Brooch, silver, gold, 2″ wide. Sheets of metal were prepared by reticulating; the best-textured sections were then sawn out and fabricated into the pin unit. Photo courtesy of the artist.

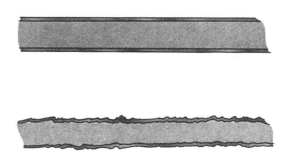

Reticulation makes use of the principle that metal contracts as it cools. A layered metal with a low-melting interior is made by repeatedly dissolving copper out of its alloy in pickle. The metal is then carefully heated until the inside layer becomes molten. The flame is removed and the interior contracts, causing the outside surface to buckle and creating a rich landscapelike texture

Etching

Etching is an ancient technique in which acid instead of mechanical force is used to create a recessed area in metal. It is a simple matter of exposing certain areas to acid so that they are eaten away while protecting other areas that in contrast appear raised. The acids used in etching are called *mordants;* the corrosive action is called the *bite;* and the acidproof material used to protect selected areas is called the *resist.*

As a rule the work is assembled prior to etching. An exception would be small pieces such as pin backs, which might be hard to cover with resist. Such articles should be soldered on later. The piece should be properly shaped, but it is not necessary to give it a final polish, and no stones should be set. The metal is cleaned by pickling and by rinsing well in water; it is then dried, taking care to minimize handling.

Wax, nail polish, and spray paint can be used as resists, but the most common material is a thick, dark brown paint called *asphaltum.* It is available from jewelry suppliers and art-supply stores. Asphaltum dries slowly and has a tendency to chip

Nancy W. Barrett. Sterling bracelets, 1″ and 1½″ wide. The patterns of these bracelets were made by carefully painting the resist. An 18-gauge sheet was used, and the sterling was oxidized to provide greater contrast between the raised and the recessed areas.

Rings, sterling. The linear pattern of these rings was achieved by scratching through a resist and etching the metal. In both cases the band was soldered, then painted with asphaltum. A needle was used to scratch through the paint, exposing a thin line of metal that was eaten away in an acid bath. The controlled scene on the left shows the results of a "proper" etch. For a more dramatic effect the other ring was set in an acid bath that was heated on a hot plate. This speeds up the biting action of the acid, producing more energetic and less predictable results.

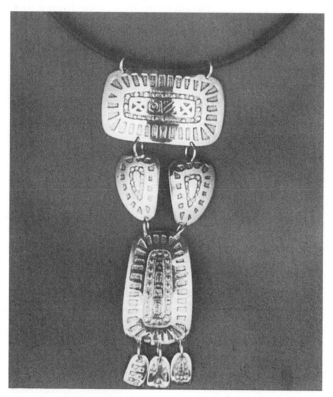

Nancy W. Barrett. Sterling pendant, 4″ high. The lines on the piece were painted with asphaltum resist, and the metal was placed in acid, eating away the exposed areas. Each panel was etched separately, polished, and assembled.

when it is thick, so care should be taken to paint it onto the surface as thinly as possible. The drying process may be hastened by setting the work in a breeze or a warm spot.

If relatively broad areas of the design are to be either left raised or eaten away, the resist can be painted on with a brush. Remember that all painted areas will be left at their original height, while all exposed areas will be recessed. Acid, unfortunately, has no sense of design and will eat any exposed surface. Be sure to cover the back, edges, and any accidental chip in the resist. The entire piece can also be coated with resist. It is usually painted on,

taking care to apply it as thinly as possible. When the resist has dried, the design can be scratched through with any point, such as a needle or scribe point. The line thus exposed can then be eaten away by submerging the piece in acid.

Some of the common mordants used in jewelry etching are listed below. Acids are sold in at least three grades: *chemically pure* (CP), which is 100% acid; *technical,* which is about 75% pure; and *commercial,* which is usually between 40% and 50% pure. The grade that you use obviously affects the mordant proportions. All the mixtures in the chart refer to pure acid, the strongest form available. If you are using commercial nitric acid to etch sterling, for instance, you would have to revise the proportions: since you are starting with a mixture that is already half water, you should add an equal part of water to the acid being used to obtain the right strength. Always add acid to water. To mix in reverse generates heat that might cause the acid to splash dangerously. Stir the mixture thoroughly with a wood, plastic, or glass rod. Always work in a well-ventilated area. The fumes produced as the acid bites into the metal are dangerous. Work near a sink: whenever you remove the work from the acid bath to check its progress, rinse it thoroughly under running water. If acid should splatter on you, rinse all affected areas quickly.

Tea strainer, sterling, 3½" high. After the body of the piece had been fabricated from 20-gauge sheet, the word "TEA" was painted in asphaltum using a sharpened dowel. The metal was immersed in acid for about a half hour to reach the proper depth.

alloyed gold:	hydrochloric acid	8 parts
	nitric acid	4 parts
	iron perchloride	1 part
	water	40-50 parts
fine or sterling silver:	nitric acid	1 part
	water	3 parts
copper or brass:	nitric acid	1 part
	water	1 part
steel or iron:	hydrochloric acid	2 parts
	water	1 part
	or	
	nitric acid	1 part
	water	10 parts

As the metal is being etched, tiny bubbles are formed. They stick to the surface of the sheet, preventing the acid from making proper contact. This can slow or even stop the cutting action. To remove the bubbles, the work should be brushed with a feather or a piece of string or at least agitated in the dish regularly. Be careful to use a soft touch, since it is easy to chip the asphaltum off.

As the bite progresses, lift the work out of the acid regularly with wooden tongs to check its depth. Rinse the work under running water and, in an inconspicuous corner, slide a needle across the surface, allowing it to catch in an etched line. If it snags easily and holds tight, the line is deeply etched. If the needle passes right over the line, it is still shallow and needs further etching. When the etching is complete, the piece is rinsed in water. The resist is then dissolved in turpentine by dunking or rubbing with a cloth. Soap must then be used to remove all traces of turpentine before proceeding with further soldering, coloring, and buffing.

The acid sometimes gets under the resist and lifts it up, exposing more of the metal than the design calls for. You should watch for this so that you can catch it right away. Lift the piece out of the acid, rinse in water, and pat dry. Touch up the exposed area with any sort of resist, allow it to dry, and return it to the acid.

For best control acids should be allowed to work slowly. The mixtures shown here require about half an hour. It is sometimes necessary to prime the reaction to get it started, however, which is done by adding heat. A glass container of acid may be set into a dish of hot tap water in a double-boiler arrangement to speed the reaction up. A less controlled but sometimes desirable effect can be obtained by heating the acid on a hot plate. This creates a great fizzing and a rapid bite that might cause some of the resist to flake off, resulting in a coarse texture.

The range of acid strengths available, the effects of evaporation, and the fact that metal nitrates and sulfates are being absorbed into the acid all combine to change the strength of the mordant. Some time-consuming testing may be required to determine the strength of the acid at hand before engaging in the actual etching. One method of checking

the solution is to use an auto-battery-testing device. It looks like a large eye dropper and can be bought at auto-supply stores for under $1. Models vary, but most utilize a number of balls that float or sink, depending on the strength of the acid. It's a good idea to establish the strength desired through etching tests and then to measure it with your gauge. You can then simply mix the acid until the gauge indicates the proper reading. Battery testers read in several ways: the one that I use shows the proper mix for sterling mordant at the level at which a car battery would be at half charge.

After etching acids can be stored in small-necked glass or plastic bottles with stoppers made of either of these materials. Do not use metal lids, since they corrode in only a day or two. Be careful to mark each container completely, showing the concentration, date, and type of acid. Solutions may be safely stored for about a month; if no etching is planned within that time, you should probably discard the acid and make up a new batch when it is needed. Unless you enjoy having the plumbing replaced, don't pour the acid down the sink. I usually empty it in a little-used corner of the yard.

Inlay

All the surface techniques discussed so far in this chapter are direct: marks are made on the metal by mechanical or chemical action for the purpose of decoration. *Inlay* differs in that it consists of two steps: the metal is prepared, often using the methods just discussed, before the inlay work is done. For all the inlay techniques described below except the marriage of metals a recess can be formed by sawing, stamping, engraving, or etching. In most work the cavity does not need to be deep. It is more important that the upper edge or outline be neat. Inlaid areas may be broad patches or fine lines and may be worked in any jewelry metal.

Solder Inlay

Solder inlay is an appealing technique because of its range of application and relative ease of construction. A specific unit may be decorated with solder inlay, or a sheet may be prepared to serve as a blank from which pieces can be cut as they are needed. If sections are to be assembled after the inlay is made, hard solder should be used for the inlay. If the inlay is to be done last, easy solder is a better choice.

A recess is prepared in copper or brass by stamping, etching, or engraving, and the metal is thoroughly fluxed and heated to a dull red. Silver solder is then melted into the cavity. This is easiest to do with wire solder, which can be fed into place as needed, but strip solder can be made to work without too much trouble. The area around the recess will probably be covered with a layer of solder in the process, but an attempt should be made to keep it as thin as possible. When the recess is filled, the work is cooled and the excess solder is filed away to reveal a silver-colored line flush with the surface. Though it is not crucial, the surface will be easier to clean up if the piece is slightly convex. Since the reflectivity of copper, brass, and silver is similar, the inlay does not show well if it is brightly polished. It looks better if the piece is buffed and then dipped into a dilute liver-of-sulfur solution. Some people prefer to dip before washing, since the grease in the rouge coating slows down the darkening reaction, lessening the risk of overblackening the piece and having to reshine it.

Wire Inlay

In *wire inlay* wires of one metal may be forced into grooves in a sheet of metal in a contrasting color for a variety of results. The grooves may be prepared in a number of ways, but engraving is especially suitable. The line should be cut with a knife-edge graver, making two separate cuts at the angles shown. For the wire to be permanently locked into place it is important that the groove have undercut sides. Etch-

Buttons, copper with solder inlay, ⅝" in diameter. The pattern for these buttons was stamped into a sheet of copper that was then cut with a disk-cutting die. After doming in the dapping block each dome was flooded with solder. The excess was filed flush with the surface, revealing the patterned inlay. After polishing the buttons were oxidized in dilute liver of sulfur to show the two-tone effect most clearly.

ing usually makes grooves with a slight undercut, and, though not as smooth-edged as an engraved line, they are well suited to this kind of inlay. The bottom of the groove should be roughened with the same pointed graver. The tool is pushed into the bottom of the groove at a sharp angle, abruptly stopped, and jerked upwards, leaving a bur that will stand up and catch onto the inlay metal to hold it in place. When the groove has been prepared, the inlay metal is drawn to a round wire just as large as the groove is wide and thoroughly annealed. This is an important step that should not be overlooked. The softened wire is then held over the groove at one end of the design and pounded into place with a small planishing hammer or the ball peen of a chasing hammer. The wire is usually held coiled in the hand and fed into place as the work progresses. The hammer forces the wire into the groove and pushes it out into the undercut area, hardening it in the process and locking it tightly in place. At sharp corners or at the end of the design the wire may be cut with snips or a small, sharp chisel. When completed, the inlay is planished a last time to even the surface and may then be sanded and polished as usual. When done on steel, this process is called *damascene,* since it is historically identified with the city of Damascus, where it was a specialty.

Colored Inlay

Chips of gemstones may be inlaid easily in the *colored-inlay* technique. While it is not as strong as the methods just described, it can hold up for years if not abused. Though tiny inlays are possible, the results are more attractive if the recess to be filled is at least 2mm wide and 1mm deep. A good way to form such a recess is to use the overlay technique discussed in chapter 3. After the work has been sanded but before the tripoli stage, the stones are laid into place with epoxy. Any stone may be crushed, but only opaque, bright-colored stones will create a colorful inlay. Turquoise, malachite, chrysocolla, coral, and jet are recommended. Ivory, bone, and exotic woods may also be used. Stones can be cut to the right shape with a grinding wheel, and soft material such as wood can be cut with the jeweler's saw. The stones are frequently crushed by wrapping them in leather or heavy plastic and breaking them with a hammer.

I prefer to work with fast-drying epoxy, though any kind may be used on flat work. Pieces with a sharp curve, such as a ring, definitely require the fast-drying variety. The epoxy may be left clear or colored as described below. A cyanoacrylate-base glue (Eastman 910, Super Glue, Krazy Glue) should not be used, since it won't fill gaps. The epoxy is laid into the

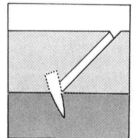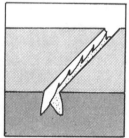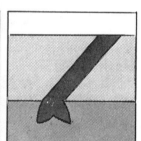

The groove for a wire inlay may be prepared by stamping, etching, or engraving, as shown here. It is important in all cases that the groove have an undercut, since this is what holds the wire in place. The wire is tapped into the groove with a planishing hammer, pushing it out into the undercut and simultaneously hardening it.

70

recess, and the larger chunks of stone are pressed into it. The medium-sized pieces are arranged around the larger with tweezers. The remaining stone dust is mixed with a bit of epoxy to make a thick paste, which is pressed over the entire area to fill all the spaces between the stones. At this point the chips extend beyond the metal, but remember that the stone layer at the metal's surface is critical, since all the excess is removed. Be sure to press down hard enough to force the small particles into the recesses where they are needed. Allow the epoxy to set completely. The excess stone material is removed with a grinder, band sander, or sandpaper. Excess ivory, bone, or wood can be filed away. The inlay is sanded down until the clear edge of the metal is reached. It is then polished as usual with tripoli and rouge. Stone inlays may be further polished with a lapidary compound such as tin oxide to heighten the shine, but this is not essential.

Few colorants can be used with epoxy, since their chemistry changes the action of the glue, making it unable to bond well. An exception is Chinese paste, a powdered glaze material available from greenware ceramic suppliers. It is available in many colors, though it may be hard to find, since it is rarely used nowadays. The paste is mixed with clear epoxy and laid into place with a small tool such as a needle. Care must be taken to remove any air bubbles. The inlay is piled up slightly higher than the metal surface and allowed to dry. It is then filed, sanded flush, and polished with tripoli and rouge if desired. It will not take the shine of the inlay materials mentioned above but is quick, bright, and durable. Similar bright-colored inlays can be made using polyester-resin materials, which are sold at hobby shops. They are available in a wide range of colors. Be careful to pop all air bubbles and finish with files, sandpaper, and buffing.

Marriage of Metals

Though the term "marriage of metals" is somewhat general and can logically refer to any technique in which more than one metal is used, it is at least more correct than to call this technique an inlay process. A simple form of the *marriage of metals* may be made by soldering wires of different metals side by side. The effect is usually heightened if the resulting strip is flattened, which can be done with a hammer or in the rolling mill. A more sophisticated use of the technique is to cut shapes that fit together like puzzle pieces from two or more metals. The shapes are soldered to yield a sheet of metal that can be worked like any other. In order to make a smooth joint at the point at which the metals touch, the contact must be very good, so controlled sawing is the name of the game.

There are two ways to approach the sawing of marriage-of-metal pieces, and only by trying each can you decide which is better suited to your talents. In one method a hole is drilled in one metal, a saw blade inserted, and a line cut to what will be the outside of the hole. A sheet of contrasting metal is then clamped or glued on top of the first, and the design is cut through the two pieces at the same time. Since the saw kerf leaves a space between the two pieces, it is important to use a small blade—something in the neighborhood of 4/0. This method is slightly cumbersome in the early stages but ensures a good fit, since any error made in one piece is repeated in the other.

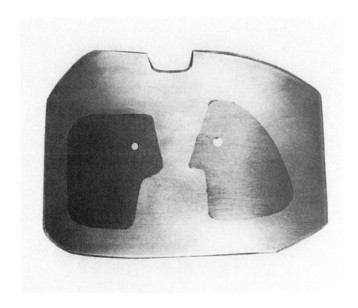

Belt buckle, brass, copper, sterling, 3" across.

The other method can be worked with any saw-blade size, since the kerf does not enter into the final assembly. The design, either the shape or the hole into which a shape will be set, is drawn onto one of the metals and cut out. It is then traced onto the other metal, using a sharp scribe or a fine-line pen. The second section is next cut out, taking great care to saw accurately on the outside of the drawn line. Since some gapping is almost inevitable, it is wise to start with sheet stock that is slightly thicker than the desired result. After the two pieces have been fit together (some filing may be necessary), they are flattened with a planishing hammer to press the metal out and close the gap. The work is now fluxed, and small pieces of solder are placed at about every ½″ (10mm to 15mm) along the seam. The piece is then heated, checked for gaps, resoldered where necessary, and sanded. Here again, the effect may be lost if the work is taken to a high polish. The buckle shown was polished with tripoli to remove scratches, lightly rubbed with coarse pumice, and dipped in a dilute liver-of-sulfur solution.

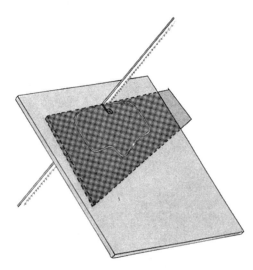

One method of making sawn inlay is to glue the two pieces of metal together and to saw through both at the same time. This can pose a problem where the shape is to be pieced—i.e., cut out from inside a sheet. The solution, shown here, is to drill a hole in the waste section, insert a saw blade, and cut to the outside of the proposed shape. The second piece of metal can then be set into place by sliding it against the blade. Cutting can then be done through both pieces simultaneously.

A simple and effective variation on this technique uses round wire to make inlaid dots. A hole is drilled to match the diameter of a piece of wire; a short section of the wire is inserted into the hole; and a bit of solder is laid at the base of the wire. After soldering the wire is snipped off and filed flush to reveal a circle of contrasting color. For larger circles a disk cutter can be used to cut holes and matching plugs.

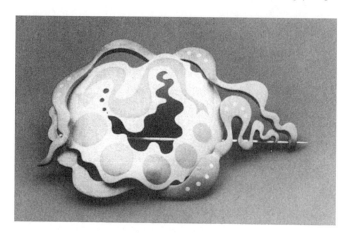

Pat Feinberg. Pin, inlaid copper and sterling, 3″ across. Shapes were carefully sawn from two metals to fit together without any gaps. The round insets were formed with a disk-cutting die, which was used to make a hole in one metal and a plug of the other. The smaller dots were made by matching a round wire with a drilled hole. After soldering it in place the excess wire is filed away.

Lamination Inlay

Lamination inlay, a variation on the side-by-side technique, consists of layered metal sheets. A rolling mill presses two pieces of metal so tightly together that they appear to be made of one sheet. In some cases the bottom sheet is pressed up through holes in the top until the two sheets reach the same level; in others the top piece is made, soldered onto the larger bottom section, and pressed down into it. Intuition and experience can help you decide which solution is appropriate to your needs—usually either one will work, so the point is not critical. In either case the top piece is made of very thin stock (22- or 24-gauge), while the lower one must be thicker than the intended result. The pieces are soldered together in a very good joint, since even the smallest area left unsoldered will spoil the effect. When this is done, the metal must be thoroughly pickled and dried. It is then passed repeatedly through the rolling mill until the surfaces blend together. This naturally distorts the design; and, while it can have amusing results, the technique is not appropriate for exact shapes.

Mokumé

Mokumé is another technique that is not a proper inlay but fits most naturally under this heading, since it involves the use of several metals. Some people describe this process as *Japanese wood-grain,* and in some cases the results can take the wavy line pattern associated with wood. It is an ancient oriental technique and only one of a great number of similar procedures that use mixed metals to form subtle color variations.

Many alternatives are possible, but a standard mokumé method is as follows. Cut equal-size squares of several nonferrous metals of about 20- or 22-gauge: copper, brass, fine silver, and sterling, for instance. They are then soldered together in a sandwich. The solder must flow completely, making

a bond that is absolutely free of gaps, so this process is easier said than done. I flux all the squares, lay the first one down, and flow solder over its entire surface. Wire solder works well, since it can be fed onto

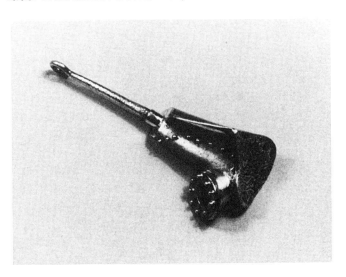

Harold O'Connor. Pendant, sterling with a mokumé panel, 2″ high. As small as it is, this piece manages to combine several techniques harmoniously. The body of the piece was fabricated from several pieces, decorated with shot, and highlighted with a piece of mokumé. The bale or cord attachment was forged to a taper, formed into a loop, and soldered into place. Photo courtesy of the artist.

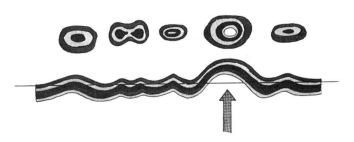

In making a lamination inlay the smaller inlay material may be soldered on top of the parent metal, as shown in the upper drawing, or the inlay may be soldered behind a pieced area, as was done with this heart. In either case the soldering must be complete, and the effect will be distorted as the laminate is passed through the rolling mill.

The wood-grain effect of mokumé is achieved by first pounding bumps in the back of a multilayered sheet. These bumps are then filed off to reveal the layers of different metals. This drawing shows how various effects can be made by using different bulges. A gradual bump, as shown on each end, will make a long oval that will show a lot of each layer. Two small bumps that are close together will create a figure-eight pattern. Sharp, angular bulges will create small ovals with thin lines, and a bulge that goes deeper than the thickness of the sheet, as shown at the arrow, will leave a hole in the mokumé when it is filed flush.

the sheet until the whole surface is coated. I then pick up the next sheet with tweezers and preheat it, keeping the solder molten. I lay the second sheet into place and heat the two until the solder shows around the edges. The top of the unit is again coated with solder, and a third layer is soldered on. Three or four layers should be built up in this way.

When the soldering is complete, the piece is dried and flattened to about 20-gauge. This can be done with a planishing hammer, but a rolling mill produces more even results. The sandwiched sheet, which has doubled in size due to flattening, is then cut in half. The two halves are soldered on top of each other to double the number of layers. Again, care must be taken that the solder completely covers the sheets that are to be joined. The resulting sheet is again flattened to around 20-gauge and may be cut and redoubled again. As the number of layers increases, the resulting pattern becomes more subtle and intricate. A minimum of 6 layers, a maximum of 48, can be used.

When the last layering is done, the sheet is again flattened, this time to about 18-gauge. It is then worked from the back (the rougher side can become the back) with rounded tools such as repoussé or dapping punches, pressing out bulges that should reach about two-thirds of the way through the thickness of the sheet. The location of these bumps and the consistency of depth determine the pattern created on the other side.

After the bumps have been made, the front surface is filed to remove all the raised areas. As each knob is leveled, layers of the metals underneath are revealed in a pattern similar to that of a contour map. The surface is worked with files, sandpaper, and buffing compounds in the usual way. When the mokumé is shiny, the color contrast is difficult to see: it is common practice to follow the rouge stage with a quick dip in a dilute solution of liver of sulfur and water, which instantly brings out colors and patterns that were invisible in the shiny piece. This surface should be rinsed in water and burnished with a soft brass brush.

Any pits that you discover while filing a mokumé sheet indicate places at which the solder failed to make a complete join. If there are only a few in the middle of an otherwise gorgeous section, they can be filled in with easy solder. This is a risky operation: if the solder between the sheets flows, the entire effect will be ruined. It is not uncommon to leave an occasional pit on the panel or to work around it in some way. Because of such problems it is standard procedure to make up a sheet of mokumé from which the best sections are cut out and used. When attaching mokumé to other sections of a jewelry piece, use as little solder as possible and paint the mokumé with yellow ocher to safeguard it.

Mokumé is only one of many similar techniques. By flooding solder onto chains, twists, folds, and spirals and flattening them out many mixed-color patterns can be devised. Your willingness to experiment is your only limitation.

6. Moving the Metal

To beginning students and the uninitiated metal is a hard material, but the experienced metalworker realizes that, even though the result may be firm and permanent, through careful working metal may be made to stretch and to compact. All the techniques presented in this chapter are based on this fact.

Annealing

This topic was mentioned in chapter 1 but bears elaboration here. When viewed microscopically, metals form a more or less orderly arrangement of crystals that might be pictured as a pile of balloons. If a weight is set on top of the balloons and stress is applied, they will slide along one another to make room for the weight. When they can slide no further, they begin to stretch out, flattening under the weight. This process, of course, has its limits. The weight will eventually break the balloons; the metal will tear or crack. In the case of balloons there is no recourse, but a process called *recrystallization* can prepare a metal to handle more stress. As the metal is heated, the material from one crystal (balloon) is redistributed, and a new "generation" of crystals is formed. The idea here is not that each balloon is reinflated and returned to its own shape but that, by reorganizing the crystals, the original structure is remade. This structure has all the malleability of the original. The process of *annealing,* or recrystalliza-tion, may be repeated indefinitely, making possible complex forms that utilize metal's ability to stretch and compact.

Industrial annealing is done in electric furnaces that use exacting temperature gauges. In the work-

The photo on the left shows annealed brass magnified 250 times. The picture on the right shows the same piece after it had been work-hardened. Brass is used only because it displays the crystalline structure clearly: any of the nonferrous metals will produce similar changes. The lines between the crystals (the different-colored areas) allow metal to slide or distort without breaking. In the work-hardened piece these slide planes have been "used up"; the metal will break if it is worked further. Photo by John G. Cowie, Worcester Polytechnic Institute.

shop annealing is done with the torch, usually the same one that is used for soldering, though larger workshops may have a giant-sized model for annealing large pieces. Temperature changes are read by careful observation of the colors through which the metal passes as it is heated. Because these are most clearly seen in a darkened area, large workshops often set aside an enclosure for annealing that shields out bright studio lights. If such an arrangement is unfeasible for the home workshop, it is necessary to experiment in order to determine the color that each metal turns in your particular lighting when it is in the softened state.

Annealing is a cumulative and a reversible process. Heating the metal will soften it, and holding it at the proper temperature will soften it further. The process is reversible for alloyed metals (such as sterling) due to a hardening reaction that takes place along the bond between the two metals at high temperatures. The metal softens as it is heated up to a certain point, at which the process reverses itself, and heat tends to harden the structure. It is thus possible to under- or overheat the metal and to miss the annealing effect.

Each metal has its own temperature range for annealing, and it is important to learn it if proper softening is to be achieved. It's often a good idea, when working with a metal for the first time, to make several attempts at annealing. Heat the metal to a certain color, cool it, and bend it in the fingers in order to determine the success of the procedure. A list of commonly used metals and their annealing temperatures is given below. All color references refer to a dimly lit area: make allowances if you are working in bright light.

1. *Sterling* should be heated to about 1100°F (590°C), which is the first dull red. It is then quenched in pickle or water.

2. *Yellow* and *green golds* are similar to sterling: they may be heated to around 1200°F (650°C) and either quenched or cooled in air.

3. *Rose gold* is heated to the same temperature but must be quenched quickly to achieve softening.

4. *White gold* is heated to cherry-red, or 1400°F (760°C), and may be quenched or air-cooled.

5. *Copper* and *bronze* are heated to a bright red—about 1400°F(760°C)—and quenched immediately.

6. *Brass,* including *Nu-Gold*, is taken to the same temperature and bright red color as copper but must not be quenched, as this tends to harden it.

7. *Pewter* does not appreciably work-harden and therefore does not need annealing.

When annealing wire, it should be wound in a coil and held closed by wrapping the ends around or by tying it with copper or iron binding wire. Be careful to use a broad flame and to heat evenly, since it is easy to melt sections of a thin wire if you're not on your toes.

It should be noted that *work hardening* is not always an undesirable state. In fact, it is not unusual to follow the heating sequence, which softens the metal, with a hardening operation. Examples of cases in which strength is needed in the final product would include pin stems, flatware, tie and money clips, bracelets, and necklaces.

Milling
The Rolling Mill

Stock shapes of sheet may be thinned in a *rolling mill*, a type of heavy-duty wringer similar to that used in an old-fashioned washing machine. A pair of hardened steel rollers is mounted into a steel frame that is in turn bolted to a stand or workbench. A geared wheel at the top of the mill controls the distance between the rollers, and a handle (sometimes two) on the side turns the rollers, which pull the metal through. Though the mill has several other functions, its most common use is to make sheet metal thinner. Because of the cost of precious metals it is difficult for the craftsman to keep every thickness of sheet on hand in quantity. When a rolling mill is available, a thick gauge may be bought and rolled thinner as the need arises. No, you cannot make metal thicker by putting it through the mill backwards!

The use of the rolling mill is simple: the metal should first be annealed, and the rollers adjusted so that the piece just slips between them. The top adjustment is then moved about half a turn, bringing the rollers closer together. The sheet is fed through the rollers by turning the crank. The adjustment knob is then reset, bringing the rollers closer again, and the process is repeated.

It is important that the thickness not be reduced too much at any one pass. Turning the handle might require a slight effort but not two hands and a lot of groaning. Thinning the sheet in small steps is better for the machine and avoids the chance of pressing the metal too thin. As the metal is thinned, it also becomes longer. This lengthening occurs in only one direction as the piece is passed between the rollers. Depending on your needs, the piece may be stretched in one direction or rotated with each successive pass through the mill, stretching it equally in all directions.

A rolling mill is a surprisingly expensive piece of equipment, and certain precautions must be followed to keep it in top shape. The rollers are made of polished, hardened steel and must remain clean and in perfect alignment in order to do a good job. Since they are made of steel, they will rust if they get wet, which would ruin them. For this reason any metal passing through the mill must be thoroughly dried. The rollers are made to be used on soft metals such as gold, sterling, copper, and brass. No other materials should be stretched in the mill, since they would scar the rollers. In order to keep them smooth, the rollers should be periodically wiped clean and coated with a thin layer of Vaseline or oil to prevent rust if they are not to be used for some time.

The rolling mill can be used to flatten wire as well as sheet metal. When passing a wire through the mill, it's very important that it enter and leave the mill perpendicular to the rollers. A diagonal pass will form a curve in the metal that is almost impossible to straighten. To keep the wire at right angles to the rollers, it should be pulled taut as it enters the mill and exits on the other side. Two people might be necessary for this job, with one person turning the crank while the other guides the wire.

Special rollers are available that have a series of grooves cut into the surface. Depending on the shape of the grooves, these rollers can be used to narrow, taper, or add a fancy design to wire. Beaded wire, which looks like a line of connected balls, and fancy bezel, which has a raised pattern along its length, are made in this way. To taper wire on the mill, the section to be reduced is rolled several times, bringing the rollers together a bit more after each pass. It's possible to taper with flat rollers, but the grooved style does the job more neatly and quickly.

The Drawplate

Loosely speaking, the *drawplate* does for wire what the mill does for sheet: it makes wire smaller in diameter and longer. The drawplate has no moving parts: it is simply a thick steel plate about as long as a hand, which is pierced with a series of holes of decreasing size. Each hole is tapered so that it is larger at the back of the plate and narrower as it passes through. Holes with different cross sections are available: round, triangular, square, and half-round are the most common. As the wire is pulled through the plate, it can be made smaller, changed in shape, straightened, and polished due to the burnishing action of the steel. Like the mill, the drawplate is an expensive piece of equipment and should be handled carefully. It must be kept free of rust and should be coated with Vaseline or oil for long-term storage. For everyday safekeeping it can be wrapped in a piece of plastic or a cloth lightly soaked in oil.

The wire is pulled through the plate with the aid of heavy-duty pliers called *drawtongs*. They are equipped with a curved handle for a better grip and with rough jaws that tightly clamp onto the metal. To start a wire through the plate, the tip must be brought to a tapering point. Small stock—under 16-gauge—can be filed; for economical reasons larger wires should be forged with a hammer. The taper should be gradual and at least 1″ (2cm) long, not just a point filed onto the tip. The drawplate is then clamped into a vise so that the series of holes to be used is exposed; the smaller end of the holes should be facing you. The tip of the wire is pushed through various holes from the back until the hole that just fits it is found. The point is then fed through the next smaller hole and grabbed tightly with the tongs. The wire should be pulled through with an even, continuous motion, backing up as necessary. Though possible, it is better to avoid regripping the wire midway along its length, since this will scar it and might cause it to break. The wire is then pulled through successively smaller holes until the desired diameter is achieved. It is necessary to anneal the wire about every five holes; the rule is that the metal should be softened whenever it becomes springy and hard to pull. The wider side of the large holes may be rubbed with beeswax, which melts as the wire is pulled through and helps to lubricate the action. I don't use it when drawing fine wires, since it tends to clog the smallest holes.

Though it is rarely used in small workshops, a handy tool to know about is a *drawbench*. It is a

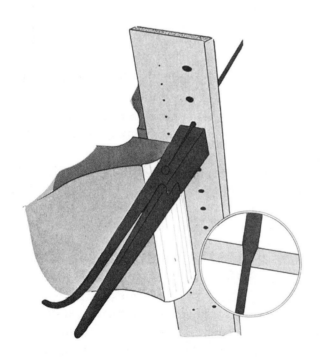

The drawplate is used to make wire thinner, to change its cross section, and to construct tubes. To be most effective, it should be gripped in a heavy vise as shown, but another holding apparatus uses a strong board laid across the opening of a door jamb. The round inset shows how the wire is compressed as it passes through each hole.

tablelike arrangement that increases leverage and allows wire to be drawn more easily. At one end of the bench is an apparatus for holding the drawplate, a vise or two solid pegs behind which the plate can stand. The other end is equipped with a wheel and, running from its axle, a cord or chain that is used to grab onto the wire. Special tongs with two curved ends are needed. The wire is tapered and pulled in the usual way—the only difference is that the pulling is accomplished by turning the wheel instead of walking backwards.

In addition to the obvious use of the drawplate to make wire thinner, it is handy for several other tricks. Kinked wire may be straightened out by pulling it through the drawplate a few times. If a wire is going to be used unsoldered and should be especially firm, as in the case of some jump rings, it may be made springy with the plate. In this case wire larger than desired is drawn down and left unannealed, which leaves it harder than usual for its size. The drawplate is also used to make handmade chain links more consistent in size. Tongs are not usually needed, since a great deal of stress is not involved. Drawplates are also used for tube making, which is discussed in chapter 9.

Repoussé

Repoussé is an ancient technique that involves raising and recessing areas of a metal sheet for decorative interest. The term means "pushed out" in French, which is appropriate, since most of the forming is done from the back and raised, or pushed out. Repoussé can be worked on any metal item from a large tray to delicate earrings. The materials needed are a surface against which the metal is to be shaped, tools to do the pushing, and a hammer with which to deliver sufficient force.

The surface most frequently used for repoussé is *pitch*, a tarlike material that is gooey when heated and firm but yielding at room temperature. Repoussé pitch is a mixture of straight pitch (a distillate of coal or petroleum or a tree resin), plaster of paris or brick dust, and tallow or linseed oil. The proper mixture of these ingredients creates a pitch that is soft enough to yield under the punches but firm enough to support the metal adjacent to the blow, leaving a clear mark. It should also be adhesive enough to grip the work and hold it while hammering but not so sticky that it is difficult to remove. Jewelry-supply houses sell ready-to-use pitch, which is usually adequate and easier than making your own. The pitch is supplied in hunks about the size of a fist. They are melted in an old saucepan over a low heat until liquid enough to be poured into a suitable container.

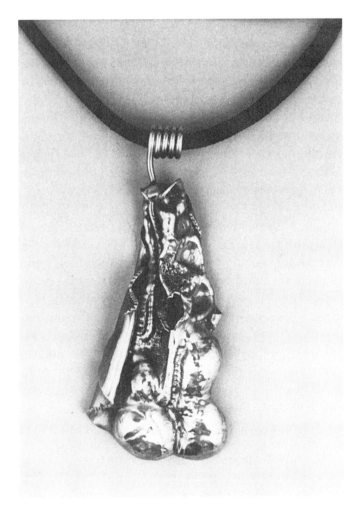

Pendant, sterling, 3″ high. Except for the wire bale, which was soldered in place midway in the process, this piece was made entirely with repoussé techniques. Tool marks, a natural part of the process, are allowed to remain and are in fact used as a design element.

An alternate working surface is *microcrystalline wax*, also known as *foundry wax*. It is a petroleum by-product that has the look and consistency (but not the taste) of caramel. It is sold in slabs about 2″ (5cm) thick that can be used as is, eliminating the need of a container. Because of its low melting point the wax should not be heated with a torch. In fair weather the work will sink into the wax with the first few hammer blows. In the winter it might be necessary to hold the wax under warm tap water to soften it. Similarly, if the weather is very warm, cold water might be needed periodically to keep the wax firm. Work proceeds quickly on this surface, since no heating and cooling time is involved, but it is a bit less exact, since the metal moves slightly with each blow.

When working on large pieces such as trays, the pitch is poured onto a board onto which sides about 1″ (2cm) deep have been made by nailing wooden strips along the edges. A more useful vessel for jewelry work is a *pitch bowl*, a hemisphere of cast iron that is heavy enough so that it won't slide around the bench while in use. The bowl sits in a doughnut-shaped ring made of rubber or leather and can be tilted at any angle to accommodate the direction of the tool. This is a great advantage, since it means that the tool can always be vertical, allowing a heavier blow than is possible when it is slanted. Pitch can also be used in a shallow metal dish such as a cake pan or a cast-iron frying pan; but, since they must always remain flat, these vessels have their limitations.

Any light hammer can be used for repoussé, but a *chasing hammer* makes the work most comfortable. It has a broad face, so it is more likely to hit the tool than the hand holding it, and a thin, springy handle that lets it spank the tool sharply, giving it an extra push. It is relatively light and equipped with a bulbous handle, making it possible to use it for hours at a time without tiring.

Repoussé tools (or *punches*) are lengths of steel about 4½″ (12 cm) long that are filed to blunt shapes on one end. They may be bought in standard shapes, but many craftspeople prefer to make their own to meet specific needs (see chapter 7). These tools are generally rounded, since sharp edges might break through the metal. A beginning student might use only five or six tools, but an experienced craftsperson who does a lot of work in this technique would probably have a collection of forty or fifty. After pushing out (also called *bossing up*) from the back greater detail is worked from the front in a process called *chasing*. The tools used for this technique resemble repoussé punches in length and diameter but are slightly sharper and often have clear shapes such as a chisel, a V, or a crescent on their tips. Again, they are commercially available; but, since standard shapes are not always suitable to the job at hand, many crafters make their own.

To begin repoussé, a piece of metal slightly larger than needed is cut out with the shears, leaving the corners, which help to hold the work in the pitch. A typical thickness for jewelry pieces is 20-gauge; but, since the proper thickness is dependent on the size, the height of the relief, and the type of piece, no

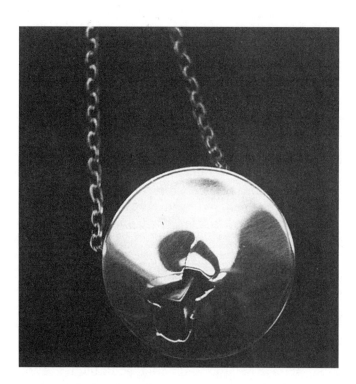

John Fix. Pendant, sterling with copper breaking through, 2″ in diameter. Photo courtesy of the artist.

precise rules are possible. A high relief requires a thicker starting piece, since the metal is thinned as it is stretched. A delicate item that will not get much wear, such as an earring, can be made of thinner stock.

The metal should be annealed and dried, and the design should be drawn on what will be the front side of the sheet. The pitch is then gently heated until it becomes soft, at which point the metal is laid on it. An alternative procedure is to heat the metal and set it in place, allowing it to heat the pitch. With either method the metal should sink down into the pitch. It might need to be forced down with a bit of pressure: it should sink enough to form a small ridge of pitch that curls up over the edge of the metal and holds it in place. When heating the pitch, it should not be allowed to catch fire and burn, since the oil or wax in the mixture will evaporate and leave it brittle. When the pitch is firm enough to support the work—that is, to keep it from sliding when struck—the tooling can begin.

The first step is to create a permanent outline of the design that is visible on the back. (This step can be omitted for any free-form areas.) With the front side up, a line is chased over a pen or pencil drawing of the proposed design. A chisellike tool called a *liner* is guided along the line as it is hit with the hammer just hard enough to make an outline on the back of the sheet. If the tool is held at a slight angle, it will advance itself as it is struck, making a smooth line. When the outline is complete, the metal is removed from the pitch by lightly heating it and pulling it free with tweezers. It's a good idea at this point to bend over the corners of the sheet, providing a tab that slides into the pitch and anchors it in place. The pitch is softened and the metal is again set in place, this time with the back facing up.

As a rule the bossing up moves from the outside of the design inward, using rounded punches. At this stage a good deal of metal is probably being moved, so hefty hammer blows are in order. By holding the tool at a slight angle the hammering can continue in a fast rhythm. After some work it is not unusual for the metal to curl upward and to break out of the pitch. This is often an indication that it is becoming stiff and needs to be annealed. If pitch is stuck to the sheet, this excess may be melted and dripped back into the pot if care is taken that it doesn't catch fire. Alternatives are to wipe off the excess with a cloth soaked in benzene or to ignite the piece while holding it in tweezers and to let the flaming pitch drop off onto a scrap board. The metal is then annealed and dried; the pitch is reheated; and the piece is put back into place. If the backside bossing up was interrupted when the sheet broke loose, it should again face up. If the back was completed, the metal is laid into the pitch with the front facing up and chasing is begun with the sharper tools.

At this stage the vague bumps left from the first step are refined, creating outlines and details. After working the entire surface you will probably find some areas that require greater height, indicating that more work must be done from the back. If the metal has not pulled itself out of the pitch by the time you have finished working on one side, the piece may be removed by quickly playing the torch directly on the metal and pulling it up with tweezers. The piece should again be annealed, and the process repeated from back to front.

The metal is inverted as tooling is done alternatively on the back and the front. Most jewelry pieces require three or four workings on each side, but it's not impossible for a piece to be reversed as many as twenty times if high, detailed relief is involved.

When the shaping is finished, the work is removed and pickled. The extra metal around the form is then cut away with a saw. The rough edges left by this operation may be "tucked under" by working them lightly from the back one more time, forcing them to curl under and out of the way. An option is to create a flat edge by rubbing the piece face up on sandpaper and then to solder the repoussé section onto a flat sheet, forming a hollow piece with a flat back. When doing this, remember that any enclosed area must provide some way for trapped air to escape, usually a small hole drilled in an inconspicuous place in the back.

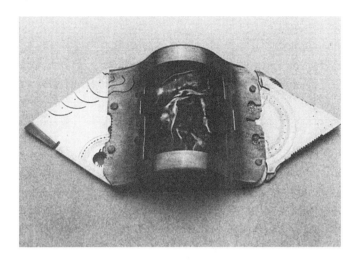

David LaPlantz. *It's Coming Out Both Sides* (pin), copper, brass, nickel silver, 3″ across. A variety of techniques—sawing, stamping, repoussé, filing, and riveting—combine to make the most of every bit of the surface. Photo courtesy of the artist.

Shallow Forming

Many small forms that are to be only slightly convex can be made with a simpler process called *shallow forming.* Small ornaments such as leaves, hearts, and flowers can be pushed out from the back, using repoussé tools and a block of lead 2″ (5cm) across and at least ½″ (1cm) deep. Lead serves the same purpose as pitch: it is hard enough to provide some resistance but soft enough to allow the metal to take the shape of the punches. Wax is slightly softer than lead but can be substituted in this process.

Broad, shallow, raised areas that are not to have a specific outline—swells, curves, and such—may be formed on a sandbag, using a hammer with the appropriately shaped peen. The bag should be made of rugged fabric and filled with playground sand: a good one can be made by sewing up both ends of a piece of blue-jeans leg.

The difference between repoussé and shallow forming is that in the latter the metal is cut to shape before tooling and a depression of approximately the right shape is made in the support block. The hammering is done as in repoussé, bossing up the general shape from the back before turning the work over to refine the contours with sharper chasing tools. Because lead burns pits in gold and silver

81

when heated above 600°F (315°C), care must be taken that no traces are left on these metals after forming. Lead is also a health hazard, and you should get into the habit of washing your hands after using it.

Small domes can be made with either the repoussé or the shallow-forming method, but the work is much faster and neater when made in a *dapping block*, a steel cube several inches on a side that is incised with hemispheres of varying sizes. Each depression has a corresponding punch, a piece of steel rod about 3″ (8cm) long with a steel ball on the end. A circle is cut and laid into a depression about twice as big as the disk. It is struck down with a ɔunch, using a heavy hammer and two or three blows. The disk can then be moved to a smaller depression and struck down with a matching punch to deepen the dome. This procedure can be re-

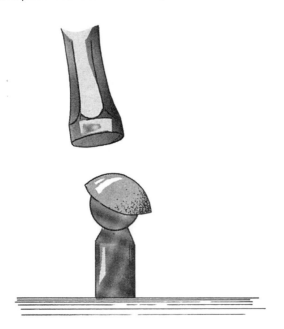

Most dapping blocks create domes that are less than a full hemisphere. To deepen a dome started in the block, grip a punch in the vise and pound the edges down over the ball shape as shown. The hard part here is not the striking but holding the dome in such a way that only a small section overhangs the punch, which is out of sight beneath. If too much is allowed to overhang, the hammer blow will be deflected; if not enough overhangs, the dome will not be affected.

peated several times, but the dapping block will not make a perfect hemisphere. If this is desired, a punch slightly smaller than the dome is clamped

Die Forming

A *die* is any device made of a hard material that Is used to form a softer material. The drawplate and dapping punch are both forms of dies. A fairly recent development in metalsmithing is the use of inexpensive *silhouette dies* to create hollow forms. Most dies are made in halves: the material being formed is compressed between the halves and forced to take the shape of the die. A common example would be a bottle cap, which is made by pinching a disk of thin metal between dies that shape it into a cup with crimped sides. The dies used by metalsmiths differ in that they provide only an outline, or silhouette, of the desired shape. The height and shape of the vertically in a vise and the edges of the dome are pushed over the ball with a planishing hammer. Dapping can be worked on other than solid disks: a circular design of soldered wire could be domed in the dapping block, for instance, or a section of a circle given height in this way. To make domes larger than are possible with the dapping block, follow the steps shown for die forming, stretching, or sinking.

Peter Moss Handler. *Donald's Teaball,* sterling, 14K gold, fossilized walrus tooth, 2″ in diameter. The two halves of this container were formed in the same Masonite die, guaranteeing their fit. Notice how the flange is used to provide a rim and a straight edge for the hinge.

pieces made in the dies can be determined by hand methods and may be altered from piece to piece.

One of the advantages of *die forming* is its speed. It's probably the fastest way to give a piece of flat metal a prescribed hollow shape other than a dome. It is also handy in that the starting point is a given outline, which makes it useful when a hollow form of specific outline is needed. This matching is convenient in another case: when two parts are to be assembled and require a good fit, the die is highly recommended. When making a container such as a perfume bottle or a hollow shape such as a spout, the silhouette of the desired form is made into a die, and two halves are punched out and then soldered together. Because both pieces were made from the same outline, they will achieve a tight fit easily. When making top and bottom halves of a container, such as the tea ball shown, die forming provides the answer to the ticklish problem of making the lid fit the bottom.

There are many die-forming methods and many variations on them just waiting to be tried. Only a few basic approaches are discussed here; the rest of the field is left open to experimentation.

Masonite Dies

One type of *Masonite die* has a three-layered arrangement. The top two layers are of ¼" (6mm) tempered Masonite, which provides a sharp, durable edge. The lowest layer, made of plywood at least ½" (12mm) thick, is included for strength. Matching pieces of these woods are cut out to make the die; a square or rectangle at least 1" (2.5cm) larger than the proposed metal shape is recommended.

The silhouette of the shape is drawn on a piece of Masonite and cut through all three layers. It is critical that the hole be identical in each piece. To align the pieces properly, they are bolted together dy drilling holes in the corners. Large bolts, about 3" (8cm) long, are passed through the holes and fastened into place with wing nuts. Any nuts would hold, of course, but wing nuts speed up the process, since they can be removed by hand. With the die pieces clamped together in this way, the proper shape is cut

out with a coping or jeweler's saw. Remember that either a side- or a top-view silhouette is possible. The sawing might be slow, since the die is so thick, but haste will only break blades and increase your frustration. When making sections that are to be fit together, it is very important that the inside wall of the

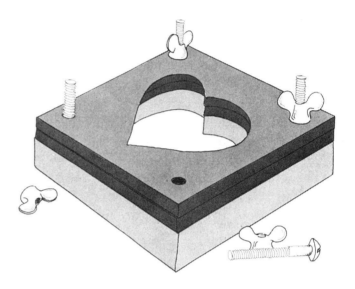

In this die the metal being formed is held in place by sandwiching it between two matched pieces of Masonite. Wing nuts allow faster tightening and opening of the die.

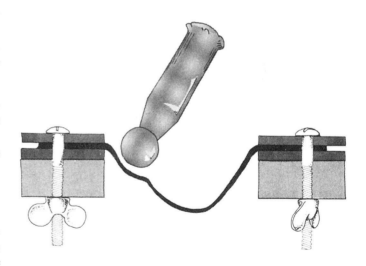

83

die be absolutely vertical. The sections are pounded in from reverse sides of the mold and must be mirror images of each other; if they were both made from the same side of the mold, they would be identical, rather like having two right-handed gloves. If the saw is allowed to tilt while cutting, the underside of the die will be larger or smaller than the top hole, resulting in a less than accurate fit.

An alternative to hand sawing is to use a band saw to cut out the die hole. Because the band is a continuous loop, it cannot be undone and inserted into a hole drilled into the inside of the die area. For small dies that are made to be used on soft metals such as sterling and copper, the plywood seems to supply sufficient rigidity even when the saw has cut its way in from an outside edge. When using this method, it's a good idea to allow slightly more wood than usual around the die hole. In addition to its speed the band saw has the advantage of making absolutely vertical sides.

When the die form has been cut out and checked for evenness, a piece of metal is prepared. This is usually 14- to 20-gauge in thickness, depending on the intended depth of the project. It is cut to a size that allows about ½″ (12mm) around the die hole. After annealing, the metal is clamped between the pieces of Masonite, using finger pressure on the wing nuts.

When raising relatively shallow forms, the plywood provides the height necessary to keep the work from hitting the table. For deeper work the bolts should be inserted with the heads facing up, raising the die above the table by the length of the bolts, which now act as legs. To keep the die from sliding around the table while hammering, it can be set on a sandbag or pillow.

To shape the work, the metal exposed in the die hole is pushed down by striking dapping punches with a medium-weight hammer. When working on thin metal, punches made of hardwood doweling may be substituted. On large shapes it is possible to strike the metal directly with the hammer, but marksmanship and the force of the blow must be carefully controlled. The tool is moved around the outside or top edge of the form, using overlapping blows. If the tool is held at a slight angle, it will move itself along more or less automatically. After moving around the entire edge a second pass is made just inside the first. The procedure is repeated in concentric circles until the center of the form is reached. The idea is to squeeze the metal from the outside toward the middle, where it is needed for greater height. No metal is supplied from outside the die form, so there is a limited mass to be worked. By carefully pushing metal from the outside inward deep forms may be made without dangerously thinning the sheet.

After the entire surface has been struck once with the tool, the metal will probably be stiff enough to require annealing. Since die forming depends on the ability of metal to stretch, it is important not to overlook this step. As a matter of fact, you may find that half the time needed for die forming is taken up by annealing. The wing nuts are loosened; the die layers are spread apart; and the metal is removed. If long bolts are used, the nuts can stay in place, speeding up reassembly. The sheet is then annealed, pickled, and dried in the usual way and reinserted into the die exactly as before. It is again hammered in concentric circles from the outside inward until annealing is required. This process is continued until the desired depth is achieved.

When the metal has reached the proper depth, there will probably be some irregular bumps and bulges due to uneven striking. They can be smoothed out by working from the inside with the largest possible dapping punch. Light surface treatments such as texturing and making ridges and valleys can be worked while the metal is still in the die. After a final annealing the form is reinserted in the die and tightened into position, and the entire unit is inverted. Tooling done from the outside in this way requires a soft touch, since at this point the metal is thin and, of course, unsupported within the hollow. If deep surface treatments are desired, the form is laid in pitch (or filled with pitch and laid onto the pitch bowl) and worked with standard repoussé methods. When doing this, it is a good idea to keep the flange around the metal intact, since it helps to keep the shape rigid. After working in the details the piece can be reinserted in the die to check and true its shape.

When the forming is completed, the excess around the shape can be trimmed with a jeweler's saw. In some cases the flange is partially or entirely retained and incorporated into the design. In the tea ball shown earlier, for example, a section of flange was left to provide a straight edge along which the hinge could be soldered. When the flange is meant to blend into the body of a piece, the transition from flat to raised areas can be either gentle or sharp, depending on how near the top edge the tools were worked in forming.

The decanter shown here was made in another type of Masonite die. In this case the silhouette is drawn on several sheets of Masonite and sawn out, with care taken only on the piece that is to be on top. The pieces are then assembled, mounted onto a plywood base with glue and countersunk bolts, and allowed to dry overnight. A piece of 14- to 20-gauge metal is prepared as described above, allowing a flange of about 1″ (2.5cm). Holes are drilled about 1½″ (4cm) around its perimeter. Corresponding but smaller holes are then drilled into the Masonite form, and the metal is screwed onto the die with sheet-metal screws (#10 preferred). They thread themselves into the wood and hold the metal firmly in place.

To "find" the outline of the piece, a wood or rawhide mallet is lightly tapped over the surface until the die edge appears. From this point the forming process continues as with the first die. As annealing becomes necessary, the screws are removed completely and the metal is lifted off. One of the advantages of this method is that the assembly allows easier access to the metal being formed, since there is no top layer of Masonite.

When matching asymmetrical shapes are needed, this type of die requires that two separate dies must be prepared, since it cannot be inverted and worked from both sides. The easiest way to ensure a perfect match is to saw out the top Masonite piece for one

die, flip it over, and trace it onto another section of Masonite. The two dies are then assembled as described above.

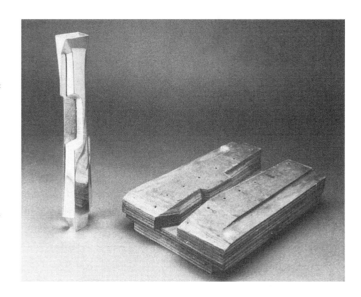

Curtis K. LaFollette. Sterling decanter, 14″ tall. This piece was made in the Masonite die shown beside it. The flange was designed to be folded over after forming was complete in order to make up one of the facets of the shape. The handle area was textured with a chasing tool; this provides the practical benefit of hiding fingerprints while adding richness and variety to the work.

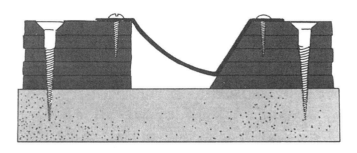

This cutaway view shows one of the possible layering sequences for a Masonite die. The wood parts are held together with glue and countersunk screws or bolts, and the metal is held in place with small screws. Note how the angle on the right was formed by pressing the metal down against a side of the die. In this way angular sides can be made to match on all pieces formed in the die. In such a case it is best to glue the Masonite together and to file it to shape before attaching it to the plywood base.

Steel Dies

An alternative to the Masonite dies is a ⅛″ (3mm) *mild-steel die*. The steel for this can be bought from any steel supplier; and, because it is awkward to cut, you might want to obtain a size that is ready to use. The forming methods and the results obtained are no different for steel than for Masonite dies. As does the second Masonite method, steel dies allow access to the rim of the form. Since the die is so much thinner, the possibility of tilting the saw while cutting out the die hole becomes less critical, and matching forms are easier to achieve. To make matching halves, the die is simply inverted and worked from the other side.

As shown in the diagram, the layering of a steel die is quite simple. The metal to be formed is screwed directly onto the steel itself. It is possible to use bolts and wing nuts, but a faster method is to thread holes of the correct size into the steel sheet itself. Before doing this the die hole is drawn on the metal and cut out with a jeweler's saw. A size 0 or larger saw blade is recommended. When the die hole has been made, four additional holes about ⅜″ (1cm) away are lo-

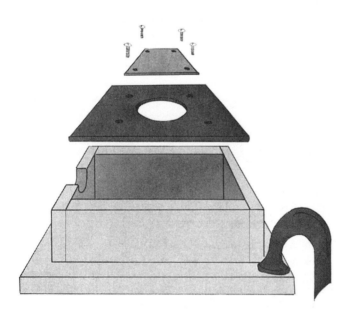

This drawing shows the layering of a steel die. The wooden box is not essential to the technique but makes a handy base that keeps the screws from being damaged by heavy blows. It is easiest to use if it is clamped onto the workbench.

cated roughly at corner positions. These holes are drilled and then threaded with a tool called a *tap*, which is a screwlike gadget used to cut threads inside a hole. It can be bought at a hardware store and won't cost much more than $1. Taps are available in many sizes and are measured both by diameter and by the number of threads per inch. The size is not crucial, but it is important that you get the right-size drill bit for the tap that you are using. It might be a good idea to get the bit, tap, and screws at the same time to ensure a matched set. Use round-head screws about 1″ (2.5cm) long. While you're at the hardware store, you might also want to pick up a handle for the tap: it makes the tool much easier to use. When drilling or tapping steel, the area to be cut should be lubricated with a light household-type oil. Once the die has been made, it will last indefinitely, so it's worthwhile to take enough time to make it correctly.

Cut out a piece of metal to cover the four screw holes. They are marked on the sheet and drilled larger than the screws that will go through them. When the metal is first screwed onto the die, the hole is covered up. A series of light taps with the hammer will reveal the outline of the die, but a faster method is to hold the metal in place beneath the die and to trace a pencil line around the hole. The metal can then be screwed into position on top of the die, with the pencil mark showing the location of the hole beneath. The die can be worked while sitting on its screws, as mentioned before, but there is some danger of damaging the threads of the bolts. An open box such as the one shown in the diagram can be used to support the die while forming and is easily put together from any type of wood.

Silversmithing

The next set of techniques fall under the heading of *silversmithing*, which refers most accurately to methods used to form flat sheets into hollow shapes such as vessels with the use of hammers and steel forms called *stakes*. Silversmithing is a field of study in itself: it would be impossible to describe it fully in these few pages. The procedures and results are so versatile, however, that it would be unfortunate to skip them altogether. A brief introduction is offered here. Those who become interested in this field can find more information in more specific sources.

The first step in all the silversmithing techniques mentioned is to make a *template*, or silhouette guide, of the proposed shape. It should be cut out of cardboard; both the positive and the negative halves are needed. The first use of this pattern is to determine the size of the disk needed to start a given shape. It also serves as a reference during the work and a reminder to keep on file.

Sinking

Sinking, perhaps the most common silversmithing process, can be thought of as dapping on a large scale. Like dapping, it slightly stretches the metal and is worked from the inside to push a flat sheet into a bowl shape. Unlike dapping, which depends on concave and convex shapes of exactly the right size, sinking (also called *beating down*) uses a single round-faced hammer and a contoured woodblock to create a range of shapes.

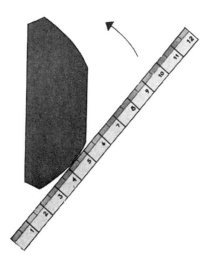

To roughly determine the disk size needed to start a sinking operation, a ruler can be slid around a template as shown. For a stretched form the starting and finished diameter will be the same, since any depth is achieved by thinning the metal. In a raising process the diameter of the starting disk can be found by adding the width and height, as determined from the template.

A template is made of the desired shape and measured with a ruler as shown in the drawing to determine the size of the starting disk, which is cut out of the metal sheet with shears. For bowls up to 10″ (25cm) in diameter, 16- or 18-gauge stock is usually sufficient, since this technique stretches the metal only about two gauge sizes. After cutting the edge of the disk should be filed and sanded to remove any sharp burs, which might cut the hand while forming or start a tear as the metal is stretched. The disk is then annealed and dried.

A forming block is usually made in the end of a log or hefty piece of wood. It can be cut with wood chisels and should be sanded smooth until a symmetrical depression at least 3″ wide × 1″ deep (8cm × 3cm) is formed. To prevent moisture from penetrating the block and causing it to split, the wood should be oiled or sealed with several coats of shellac or varnish. Any round-faced hammer can be used for sinking, but a blunt or broad curve does a neater job than does a machinist's ball-peen hammer. Whatever you use, the face should be cleaned of any nicks.

The disk is held at a slight angle with its edge across the center of the forming block. The hammer is struck about ½″ (1cm) in from the edge where the metal is pushed down into the depression. The disk is rotated slightly, and another blow overlapping the first is struck. After the entire circumference of the disk has been struck, it is moved forward and another course of blows is struck about 1″ (2cm) in from the first. The work continues in this way into the center of the disk.

At this point the metal has been formed into a lumpy, shallow dish. If a check against the template indicates that more depth is needed, the process is repeated, again starting from the outside and working toward the center in concentric circles. Before hammering again, however, it will probably be necessary to anneal. If this step is overlooked, the bowl will be stiff and hard to form, which wastes time and risks a lopsided result. When annealing, turn the bowl upside down so that the heat can be evenly distributed. If the torch is aimed into the bowl, the heat will concentrate at the bottom of the curve and the rim will not be properly softened.

When the desired depth has been reached, the lumpiness of the surface can be smoothed out by a process called *bouging*, which utilizes a mallet made of wood or leather and a rounded stake that copies the shape of the bowl as nearly as possible. Like the hammer used in the initial stages of this technique, the stake should have a perfectly smooth, shiny surface, since any marks will be stamped into the bowl and will be difficult to remove. The stake is held in a stake holder or vise, and the bowl is moved over it while the mallet is struck in a quick, tapping motion to knock down the lumps and true the shape.

The result at this point resembles a dapped hemisphere, except that it is larger. The form can be used in a variety of ways, from containers to jewelry pieces to hollowware. If the object being made is a dish, attention must be given to the bottom, since the shape at this point will rock back and forth. One solution is to make a collar of sheet metal, solder it into a loop, and attach it to the underside of the dish. Remember to do any filing, shaping, or ornamenting before the base is soldered on, since the bowl is most easily accessible at this stage.

If the dish is to have a flat bottom, the next step calls for a *bottoming stake*. It is a steel cylinder; a sawn-off section of a baseball bat can also be used. The stake is secured with the flat surface up, and the dish is centered by eye over it. The bottom is then tapped down onto the stake with a mallet. With the mallet directed straight down, the transition from bottom to sides will be slightly rounded. To make a sharp line, direct the mallet at an angle to hit the edge of the bottoming stake. If each step is done correctly, the resulting bowl will be symmetrical and true; if this is not the case, it can be filed into shape. The usual finishing procedures are applicable.

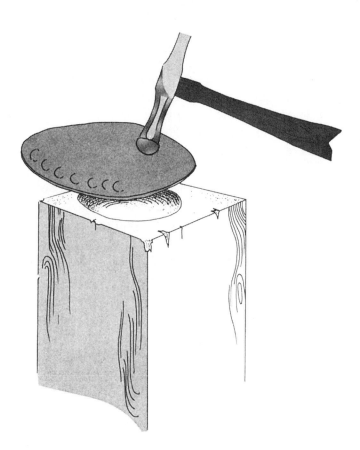

Sinking is perhaps the most common of all the silversmithing techniques. It can be used by itself to create shallow dishes and is the first step in raising. It can be worked over any rounded depression: a bowl shape cut into the end grain of a log is a common form. Any round-faced hammer can be used, but one that closely resembles the curve of the desired piece will leave the fewest marks.

Merle E. Wegner. *Pump Cup*, copper, 4½" in diameter. The body of the cup was raised; the handle was forged; and the detailed crumpling on the underside of the cup was done with repoussé punches. Photo courtesy of the artist.

Stretching

Instead of working into a depression, as just described, the *stretching* method is worked on a flat steel surface such as an anvil. It utilizes a round-faced hammer, as above, and requires a thick starting disk, since any height must be allowed for by a decrease in the thickness of the sheet. A disk the same size as the desired finished diameter is cut out of 14-gauge or heavier stock and annealed.

The hammer is struck directly down on the metal, starting in the center and moving outward in concentric circles almost to the edge. The metal will lie flat on the anvil as the work begins but will start to turn up at the edge after the first few series of blows. The disk is supported just enough to allow the force of the hammer to pinch the metal down against the anvil—that is, the disk is allowed to find its own angle and is supported there without any attempt to flatten it or tilt it upward.

After the edge has been reached, the metal should be annealed, after which the process can be repeated as often as desired as long as the hammer can reach into the cup being formed and the metal is thick enough. The thickness can be checked with a degree gauge or the fingers. If the stretching has been done carefully, the result will be smooth, evenly round, and perfectly flat at the edge. If a course of blows has been skipped or some blows have been struck harder than have others, the shape may need to be refined with a file. One advantage of the stretching process is that it leaves a thick edge, which is not only pleasing to the eye but also makes the rim thicker and therefore stronger than is possible with any other forming method.

Raising

Both the methods just discussed are most appropriate to round symmetrical forms. Since all the work is done from the inside, the possible shapes are limited to those that allow a hammer to enter the form. When a design calls for irregular shapes, especially when they are to be deep, hollow forms, a process called *raising* becomes necessary. This technique is perhaps more complex than the first

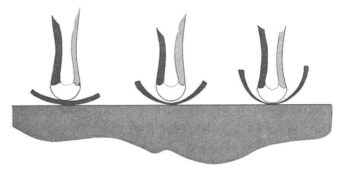

These three drawings show the sequence of a stretching operation. This technique has the advantage of leaving a thick edge but is limited in that the hammer must be able to reach into the shape.

John Fix. Wine goblets, sterling, 7″ tall. The cup section was raised; the bases were sunk; and the stems were forged. The insides of the cups were plated with gold to provide a color contrast. Photo courtesy of the artist.

two—more practice may be needed to get the hang of it—but the range of forms that it allows certainly justifies your time.

Stretching and sinking both thin the metal to some degree, but raising is a compressing operation that actually makes the metal thicker toward the upper half of the shape. The work is done with a cross-peen raising hammer; an 8- or 12-ounce head is common. Complex shapes require a variety of hammers to reach into tight places, but they can be accumulated as familiarity with the technique and personal style develop.

During raising the metal is held against a polished-steel form called a *stake*. The most common shape for forming is called a *T-stake*: some shapes used in the final stages are appropriately called *mushroom stakes.* The stakes are held in a vise, anvil, or stake holder and should be mounted at a height that allows the worker to deal a blow without having to rock backwards or bend over. Some people can hammer while sitting, but I find it more comfortable to stand.

The first step, as before, is to make a cardboard template. The maximum height and width are added together to determine the diameter of the required disk. Since raising is a compressing operation, 18- or 20-gauge metal is sufficient for most projects. A center point is found and marked with a center-punch, and the disk is cut out with shears. Again, the edge should be filed smooth to remove any burs that might cut the hand or become potential stress cracks.

An experienced silversmith can make any curvilinear form to precise specifications, but the beginner is advised to remain flexible enough to respond to the accidents that are bound to happen. To get started, the disk is domed out in a sinking operation as just described. Be sure to keep the center-punched dot on the outside of the bowl. Any lumps made by the hammer are smoothed out with a mallet, working over a mushroom stake. The diameter of the base is then measured on the template, and this distance is marked on the outside of the bowl, using a divider and the centerpunched mark. This is the

only line that is scratched into the metal; and, since it is located at the point at which the sides start to bend up from the base, it is easy to remove later. This base line determines the place at which the raising is to begin and also provides a reference for the concentric hammer blows that will come next.

As shown in the diagram, work begins with the base circle held against the T-stake. To determine the location of the stake, which is out of sight beneath the disk, the metal is *sounded* or tapped lightly with the hammer to discover the point at which the metal is touching the stake. A solid ring indicates the point of contact, while a thud shows that the metal is unsupported at that point. With the disk held in place, the cross-peen of the raising hammer is struck just above the line, pushing the metal down against the stake. The disk is then rotated slightly, and another blow is struck just beside the first. This continues until the disk has made one complete turn. Holding it in the same position, a similar circle of blows is struck just above the first. The disk is then slid back so that the area being struck is always kept within about 1″ (2.5cm) of the end of the stake, and a third circle is struck. Note that the work is done with the holding and not the hammering hand. Once the metal is properly located on the stake, it is fed into position by rotating the disk, and the hammer is directed at the same spot in a mechanical motion.

At this point the area just hammered should begin to take on a conical appearance. If this is not the case, check the angle at which the metal is being held and the location of the hammer blows on the stake. They should always be close to the end of the stake, indicating that the form is constantly sliding toward the worker with each new circle of blows. If everything seems to be in order, raising is continued in concentric circles until you are within about ½″ (1cm) from the top. At this point a planishing hammer should be substituted for the cross-peen. It will do less damage to the stake if a blow accidentally lands too high. After making one complete series of circles to the top (which is called a *course*), the metal is annealed, pickled, and dried, and the process is

A complex process is made to look easy here. The raising is started in the first step by sinking into a wooden form. After checking the template a line is scribed to mark the point where the base will meet the sides of the vessel. With the shallow dish held at a 35° angle, a cross-peen raising or forming hammer is used in the actual raising process. A series of blows is struck around the bowl just above the scribed line. A second series is struck just above the first. The bowl is then slid backward slightly, and a third round of hammer blows is struck. This continues up the side of the form until the top is reached. A similar course of blows is struck after annealing the vessel and so on, until the desired shape is achieved. By checking the template the starting point for each new course can be determined. When the shape has been achieved, the metal is smoothed and the shape refined over a stake (or stakes) with the appropriate curve in a process called planishing.

Curtis K. LaFollette. Raised sterling bowl, 9″ in diameter.

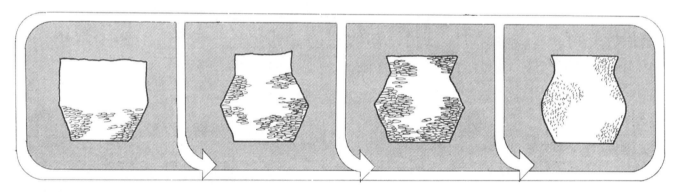

When raising a vessel with several curves, the shape is first
roughed out as an angular blank as shown. The location of
the angles is determined by checking the metal against the
template. After the vessel has been brought to its full height, it
is rounded over curved stakes, usually using light hammers.

repeated. By periodically referring to the template you can see where each new circle of blows should begin. Each time the top is reached, the work is annealed and the process is repeated.

It is important that raising proceed at its own pace. It is a big mistake to attempt a shortcut by omitting or abbreviating a step. This will almost certainly waste more time than it saves and end up in a misshapen result. Once you develop a smooth rhythm, however, you'll probably be surprised to see how quickly you can shape the metal and how easily it flows under the hammer.

John Fix. Sterling teapot with rosewood, 7½" tall. The top and body of the piece were raised; the spout and finial were formed in a Masonite die. The wooden handles are riveted on. In addition to adding color and richness wood is used to insulate against the heat of a liquid put into the pot. Photo courtesy of the artist.

Planishing

When the template shape has been achieved in the metal, the next step, *planishing*, begins. This is the process of smoothing out the hundreds of bumps left by the raising hammer. It is done with a planishing hammer with an 8- to 12-ounce head and polished stakes that copy as exactly as possible the curves of the piece being made. Depending on the complexity of the shape, several stakes might be needed in the course of the planishing process.

If you look carefully, you'll see that the planishing hammer has both a flat and a domed face. The flat face is used on curved areas, where it makes the most of each blow. The convex surface is needed to planish flat surfaces, since the flat face would leave marks as its edge struck the metal.

While raising depends on hitting the metal just above the point where it touches the stake, planishing requires that the metal be pinched between the hammer and the stake. If this is done, the metal will thin slightly at that point, smoothing the ridges down into the low areas to make an even surface. If direct contact is not made, the hammer will fold the metal down, distorting the shape. Again, the important work is done by the holding hand, with the hammering hand used only to deliver a pattern of

The snarling iron is used to hammer outward from within a closed shape. A blow struck on one end recoils through the rod and makes the other end spring up. For large work it might be necessary to have a helper to do the striking, since both hands might be needed to hold the vessel in place.

93

consistent blows. Once the point of contact is found by sounding, the work is slowly rotated and the hammer remains stationary, usually hitting the same spot on the stake. The planishing is generally worked from the bottom of the vessel up in the same direction as raising.

The purpose of planishing is to replace the coarse cross-peen marks with small, facetlike dents. They can be reduced to increasingly tinier marks by repeated planishing: five to ten courses of planishing may be needed to smooth the surface adequately. The small remaining marks can then be buffed away if desired. Some craftsmen prefer to leave them, since they scatter the light in an attractive way and attest to the handmade character of the work. As a rule, the piece is not annealed after planishing, since it is usually desirable to leave it as rigid as possible.

Seaming

While it is true that almost any shape can be made from flat sheet with a raising operation, some are easier to form from a cylinder. The steps for cylinder raising, which is called *seaming*, are pictured in the diagram and represent a commonsense extension of the techniques used in angle raising. In addition to a cylinder the starting shape can be a cone, a truncated cone, or any other tubelike form. The work begins with a template from which the starting form is calculated. Sheet metal is cut out and bent around a form. It is soldered with hard solder. Since this join must bear a lot of stress, an overlapping connection is preferable to the usual butt joint. It is made by filing matching angles on the two pieces that are to be joined. This has the effect of doubling the surface area that is to be soldered, increasing the strength of the joint. The cylinder is laid over a stake and hammered with a cross-peen to compress it as needed. When working on a tall form, the shape may appear to tilt to one side. This may be avoided by alternating the direction of turning when moving from one course of blows to the next. If the first series of blows was struck as the piece was turned clockwise, for the next series turn counterclockwise.

Raised shapes are treated in the same way as any other fabricated unit in terms of soldering, decorating, and other finishing processes. You will find, however, that, when a large, hollow form is heated for soldering, it tends to warp and might pull away from a piece that is being attached. Because of this tendency heavy iron binding wire is used to tie pieces together before soldering. When soldering the base into the form after the shape has been otherwise completed, a bottom that fits tightly into the container should be constructed. It might be necessary to prop it in place with pumice or charcoal, since it is difficult to tie in place with binding wire.

Forging

Forging is the process of shaping rods and wires with a hammer. It is a versatile technique that can be used to make both large pieces that require heavy hammers and bulging muscles and delicate jewelry items that are worked with a rhythm that would please an elf. Forging can be either *hot* or *cold*: steel and iron are almost always worked hot, since they are otherwise too tough to shape; but copper, sterling, and brass are often worked cold—i.e., at room temperature. The nonferrous metals can be worked hot and move more readily when warm; but, since this technique requires that the work be held in tongs instead of in the hand, it's difficult to get good detail. When working hot, the nonferrous metals must be allowed to lose their redness before hammering begins.

As with raising, one of the appealing elements of forging is the involvement and physical exertion that it requires. A great variety of effects are possible, from coarse surfaces that show the technique to highly refined and graceful tapers. Each craftsperson approaches forging in a unique way: for some it is a great release for frustrations, while for others it causes more than it releases. With experience you will find that the smallest detail may be controlled with the hammer; but, when starting out, it's a good idea to be flexible and to let the metal have some say in how it wants to move.

In theory any vessel can be raised from a flat piece of metal. Some shapes, however, can be made more quickly by starting from a cylinder or cone in a process called seaming. The correct-size blank is determined from the template, marked out, and cut. It is then soldered closed with a lapped joint, which is needed to stand up to the pressure of hammering.

The forming is done over stakes in a progression similar to the final steps of raising. As a last step the bottom is soldered in place. For beginning exercises a piece of copper pipe from a plumbing supplier can be used as a ready-made starting blank.

The tools needed are a hammer or two and an anvil or surface plate. The best anvil is a good-sized steel unit (say, a minimum of 75 pounds) that has a mirrorlike face and a smooth, symmetrical horn. Anvils are sold by the pound from tool companies, and new ones are not cheap. They can occasionally be bought secondhand from farm auctions or junk shops, and a machine shop can usually regrind the surface for $20 or $30. A section of railroad track can be used in a pinch. A real forging hammer—one that is used with a forge in blacksmithing—is quite heavy, has a short handle, and is flat on one end and wedge-shaped on the other. A lighter variation that works well for precious-metal forging is called a *tinsmith's hammer*. Raising and forming hammers are also good for this process. A planishing hammer like the one described for raising is also needed.

Forging is not a complex process, and a bit of common sense is all that is needed to grasp the principles involved. When metal is hit with a flat-faced hammer, it is pushed out in all directions. The flat face squashes the metal and allows only a limited degree of control. When a wedge shape is used, the metal is pushed in only two directions, as shown in the diagram. Because of this it is possible to control the flow of the metal. If a rod needs to be elongated, all the stretch can be worked along the length. If it is to be flared, all the metal can be spread to the sides without "wasting" any by pushing it along the length. This control is the essence of forging. Of course, a few tricks are helpful along the way.

It is very important that the hammer strike the metal evenly. If it is tilted to either side, up, or down, the metal will start to curve away from the direction of the blow. The handle of the hammer can serve as a guide to the angle of the hammerhead. Of course, you can't stop yourself in mid-swing to see how you're doing; but, if you carefully watch the results and the position of the handle after the blow has landed, you can note any problem areas. As a rule, keep the work pointing in the same direction as or at right angles to the hammer handle. This makes striking more direct and easier to control.

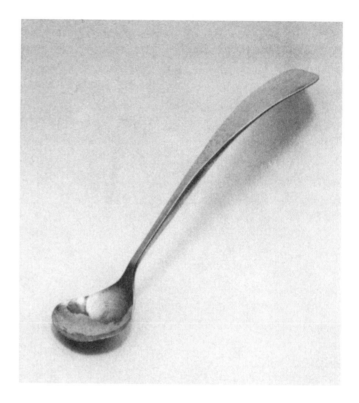

Thomas J. Keaney. Copper spoon, 8″. This spoon was started from a ¼″-square rod and shaped almost entirely with hammers.

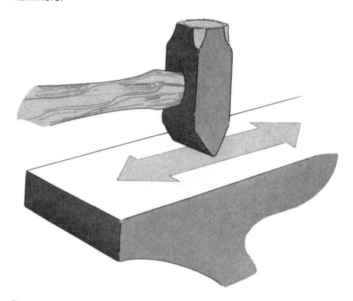

Because of its wedge shape the cross peen pushes the metal in only two directions, as shown by the arrow. This allows it to control the flow of material with much greater accuracy than can a flat-faced hammer. Cross peens are found on forging, raising, forming, and riveting hammers.

Although some people can forge sitting down, it is more common (and relaxing) to work standing up. The anvil or surface plate should be mounted on a sturdy stand so that its striking surface is about a hand's length below waist height. The use of a higher surface will decrease the force of the hammer blow, and a lower surface will give you a backache from stooping down. There is a tendency to bend close to the work in order to see what is happening. This is an uncomfortable habit to fall into, so be on the watch for it from the start. Do your hammering from a standing position, with your head directly above the metal.

An equal emphasis should be placed on force and control. Force alone is good only for smashing the metal from one shape into another. Control is of no use if the hammer is only lightly brushed against the metal. It is not a matter of mastering one and then picking up the other: both force and control should be learned from the outset, and both will increase with experience.

As the metal is shaped with the cross-peen of the forming hammer, it will be scarred by deep gouges. They should be smoothed out periodically with any flat-faced hammer. If this is not done, the peaks can be pushed over, forming an enclosed pit that is impossible to detect. In the subsequent filing stage it is possible to remove the metal covering the hole and find yourself with a nasty pit in the middle of an otherwise smooth surface.

The cross-peen hammer is so responsive that with only a little experience you can feel the metal stiffen and become ready for annealing through the hammer. Don't fool yourself into thinking that you can beat the system by putting off an annealing step. Since the metal is hard, those few extra blows have only a slight effect, and you run the risk of tearing the metal by stressing it beyond its limits. If pushed too far, the metal will tear at the edge. If this happens, the tear should be cut off immediately. Like a run in a nylon stocking or a crack in plate glass, the tear will grow if it is allowed to remain.

The forging sequence is difficult to describe, since it is unique to each piece. The drawing may serve as an example. As much forging as possible should be done while the metal is straight and therefore most accessible. After an area has been flattened, however, it is almost impossible to bend, so any curve that is to be flattened must be rounded before it is forged out. Any shape of rod can be forged, but a square is easiest to control. When starting with a round section, it is not uncommon to square it off first. This can be done with a planishing hammer or in the rolling mill. When the piece has

John Fix. Bracelet, sterling with moonstone. The element that holds the stone was fabricated from sheet and then attached to the rest of the bracelet, which was forged from heavy rod. Photo courtesy of the artist.

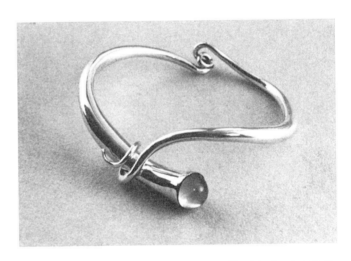

The sequence of construction is more critical in forging than in most other techniques. As much work as possible should be done while the piece is straight, since it is then easiest to handle; but curves that are to be flattened, such as the sides of this bracelet, must be accurately shaped before hammering, since they are almost impossible to bend once they are flattened.

been forged to the proper shape, it is planished just like raised work, taking care that the planishing blows are not so heavy that they overstretch the metal. Planishing may be followed by filing, but a good forger tries to shape the metal almost entirely with a hammer. Sandpapering and buffing can follow if desired.

One of the most common forged forms is a taper. As shown in the diagram, there is a specific procedure for tapering. The rod should be squared if it is not already in this form. The cross-peen of the hammer is struck across the rod, pushing the metal along its length. This is done on one surface, starting at the top of the taper and moving down to the end. The ridges made by the wedge-shaped peen are smoothed out with a flat-faced hammer, and the rod is straightened. The opposite side of the rod is treated in a similar fashion, again moving from the thick end of the taper to the narrow. The other two sides of the square are then hammered in the same way. The procedure is followed a second time, starting slightly lower along the taper. Again, the second side to be hit should be opposite the first. After two passes check to see whether the metal should be annealed by trying to bend it. If you have been compressing the metal a lot (i.e., hitting hard), it might be required. When softened, the process is repeated again, starting slightly closer to the tip than the last time. This procedure is continued along the length until a taper is formed. It is simple enough to understand: the area at the top of the taper is hit only once, on the first pass. The tip is hit on each pass; because it is hit more often it is smaller. The result of this

process is a square taper. To round it off, the square is held on an edge and struck with the hammer. If it is struck along the entire length, an octagonal taper will result, which can then be rounded off by rolling the rod in the hand as it is lightly planished. These instructions refer to tapering a hefty rod: when work-

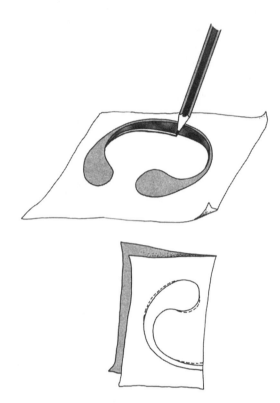

Here is a little trick used to check symmetry: it can be used in many ways but is especially handy for forged work. After refining the shape draw around it on thin paper. By folding the paper and holding it up to the light you can see where the two lines separate, indicating an uneven shape.

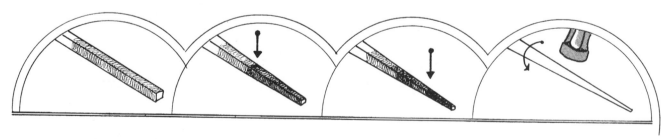

A cross peen is used in the specific sequence shown to forge a taper. The arrow in the second drawing indicates the point at which the second pass of hammer blows should start. Note

that the starting point is closer to the end for the third drawing. Three passes might be sufficient for a small gauge of wire, but quite a few more would be needed on a larger rod.

ing on something small, such as wire under 10-gauge B & S, there is a possibility of hitting the metal too hard with the cross-peen and making it too flat to be struck properly from the adjacent side. In such cases do not strike the opposite side but otherwise forge in the same way.

The biggest problem in tapering is the accidental formation of a rhombus, which, as we all remember from high-school geometry, is an equilateral parallelogram or a lopsided square. The problem with this shape is that a hammer blow directed against its side is automatically deflected, throwing the square even further out of whack. The advantage of a square is that each blow compresses the metal straight down, which means that it can be controlled and shaped. When a rhombus is accidentally formed, which is easily done by tilting the hammer as it hits the metal, each blow squashes the shape further off to the side. It's a good idea to check for this shape periodically by carefully examining the rod during forging. If a rhombus is discovered, anneal and correct it right away. If it's discovered soon enough, it is sometimes possible to knock the metal back into a square shape by holding the rod on an edge against the anvil and hitting it with a flat hammer. If the problem is out of control by the time that it is discovered, you'll have to file off the corners, as shown in the diagram. Forging can then continue as usual.

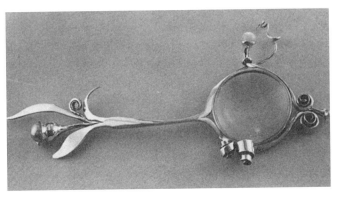

John Fix. Magnifying glass, sterling with moonstone and pearls, 8″ long. The eight units that make up this piece were forged or fabricated individually and then soldered together. The conical shapes that hold the stone and pearls were bent from flat sheet; the magnifying lens is held in a bezel. Photo courtesy of the artist.

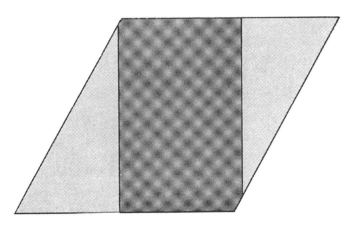

Candleholder, copper, 12″ wide. A ½″ rod was hot-forged to make the two shapes that were soldered together to make this piece. The flat tips were made in a process called upsetting, which involves pounding the metal from the end straight back on itself. The candles are held on tapered spikes.

7. Nonmetallic Elements

With the many varieties of metals and alloys, the surface treatments that can be worked upon them, and the coloring that can be incorporated, a jeweler could work for many years using nothing but metals. There inevitably comes a time, however, when the need arises for an accent that can be better provided by a nonmetallic material. A study of this aspect of jewelry making is a study of attachments, since the problem is not so much one of finding or shaping the material as it is of devising a strong and pleasing way to fasten it to the jewelry piece.

There are an unlimited number of nonmetallic elements available to the jeweler, and more are being invented each year. A partial list of appealing materials would include gemstones, beach stones, pebbles, plastic, bone, ivory, ceramic items, wood, feathers, electronic parts, fabrics, rubber, glass, fossils, mineral crystals, and shells. In all these cases the heat needed for soldering prohibits the non-metal from being built into place. Some method must instead be devised of completing the heating stages before the more fragile material is attached. There are only two ways to set a nonmetal element: the way that will hold and the way that won't. Within the first category there are many possibilities. Some are standard operations, and each has its own variations. It is also not unusual for a specific design or material to suggest a unique solution. One of the tantalizing opportunities of jewelry making is the chance of coming up with a new answer to the ancient problem of attachment.

Gemstones

The most common nonmetallic element is the polished stone, which offers a huge range of size, color, value, and challenge. Stones were originally used because they were believed to contain inherent magical or medicinal powers. As they came into use as money, they were used in jewelry as a symbol of wealth, a form of investment. This is still common today. A large diamond engagement ring might mean love, but it certainly means money. And, of course, stones can be used as elements of a design, as ways to add color or a focal point to a piece of jewelry.

Shapes

The process of gem cutting, called *lapidary,* is an art in itself, and space does not permit a description here. Some jewelers cut their own stones or work closely with a lapidary, but beginning students can choose from quite a range of commercially cut stones. Stones are available from local craft stores, through the mail (see appendix 4), sometimes from silver and tool suppliers, or at regional rock shows held by local lapidary clubs.

Polished stones are available in three categories. *Tumbled stones* are free-form pebbles that have been polished by abrasion in a rotating drum. Because they have no flat sides, they are usually difficult to set well and offer limited potential. *Cabochons* (often called "cabs") are stones that are polished with a smooth, curved surface. The reverse side may be curved but is usually flat, forming the underside of the stone. Cabs may be round, oval, square, or any other shape and are available in several thicknesses or heights. They are attractive, easily obtainable, cheap, and easy to set, making them the type most frequently used by jewelry students. *Faceted stones* are generally transparent or translucent gems whose surfaces have been cut and polished in small planes called *facets*. A standard arrangement of facets for a round stone contains 56 individual planes and is called a *brilliant cut*. Faceted stones are available in many shapes, and each shape has several possible facet arrangements. As a rule, faceted stones are slightly more expensive and more difficult to set than are cabs but are certainly not out of reach even for beginning students.

Setting

Capping

As mentioned above, tumbled stones do not lend themselves easily to fine-jewelry pieces, since their round edges make a firm grip difficult. One solution (of dubious merit) is to use a *bell cap*, which is a snowflake-shaped piece of thin metal that is pushed over the pointed end of a stone and glued in place. The top of the bell is usually equipped with a small ring that can then be used to hang the piece from a necklace or whatever. Commercial bell caps are unreasonably thin and look like the stamped-out bits of mass-produced mountings that they are. When no other solution is feasible, the crafter can make a cap that coordinates with the design at hand, which will look far better than the store-bought variety.

Wrapping

Medium- or large-size tumbled stones can also be *wrapped* in much the same way as a package is tied with string for mailing. The wire used should be thin and soft enough to be tightly shaped around all the contours of the stone, and the beginning end should be located at the top. The wrapping is finished by twisting the two ends together at the top of the stone, forming a loop with the last ½" (1cm) of wire.

A variation of wrapping that allows more of the stone to show and generally makes a neater job requires the use of a *separating disk*, a wafer-thin disk of silicon carbide that is used with a Dremel tool

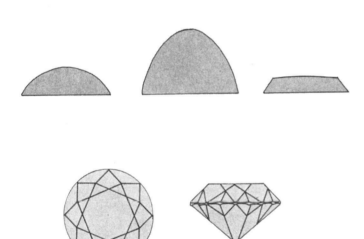

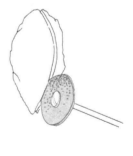

It is difficult to find a good way to hold a tumbled stone. This method uses a separating disk to cut a groove along the circumference of the stone. A soldered and polished loop is then laid into the groove and tightened by twisting. The nail shown in the drawing serves as a handle during twisting and also leaves a finished loop that can be used to hang the stone.

or flexible-shaft machine. With this wheel a groove is cut around the circumference of a flat tumbled stone. A loop larger than the stone's circumference is made, soldered together, laid into the groove, and twisted at one end until it is tight. A rod is used to help with the twisting and at the same time to form a loop through which a cord or chain can pass.

Bezeling

Cabochons are usually set in a *bezel*, which is a metal collar that surrounds a stone and is pushed down on it to hold it in place. The setting shown in the photo, called a *box bezel*, is a basic attachment upon which many variations are possible. The wire used to form the collar may be made of sterling, gold, or copper and may be formed by cutting a strip out of thin sheet or by flattening a wire with a hammer or in the rolling mill. A convenient approach is to use a fine-silver bezel wire prepared commercially just for this purpose. This wire is 26-gauge and is made in ⅛″ and ¼″ (3mm and 6mm) widths. Its fine-silver content gives it the advantages of a higher melting point (meaning that it's less likely to melt as you are soldering it) and of greater malleability, making it easier to push down over the stone. The principle is simple enough; the collar is made to the correct size and soldered in place with the sides standing straight up. After soldering and polishing are completed, the stone is laid into place and the bezel pushed down to meet the angle of the stone, thus holding it securely in place. The steps in the construction of a box bezel are shown in the diagram.

1. The wire is shaped around the stone, marked, and cut with scissors or snips. The cut edges are filed square. Shaping on small stones is made easier by forming a loop of wire of the approximate size by eye and testing it against the stone. When it fits well, the bezel is soldered closed with a small piece of hard solder. Check the fit. If too large, a section must be removed and the loop resoldered. If too small, it can be stretched a little by forcing it along a bezel mandrel. When the fit is correct, the top and bottom are trued by rubbing the bezel on sandpaper held on a flat surface.

2. With the stone removed, the bezel wall is filed to a knife edge at the top. The bezel should be left at its full thickness at the bottom but should become thinner toward the top edge. This makes the setting easier and allows a neater result. Since filing may distort the shape of the bezel, true it up afterward by forcing it over the stone.

3. The bezel is then soldered onto a flat sheet, using medium solder. This sheet forms the back of the bezel, which keeps the stone from pushing out the bottom. It's better to solder the bezel onto a sheet that is larger than necessary, since the bezel loop might slide around slightly during soldering and the larger sheet allows for this. If you were to start with a circle or oval exactly the size of the stone, marksmanship in soldering would become critical. The thickness of this back sheet depends on the size of the stone and the wear that the piece must withstand. For a large stone in a stress position, as on a bracelet, 20-gauge would be recommended. In other cases 24- or even 26-gauge sterling can be used. In addition to the obvious advantages of economy and weight reduction it makes sense to use a thin gauge, since it makes the process of soldering the bezel onto the sheet a bit easier. The difficult part of this operation lies in soldering a small unit (the bezel) onto a larger one. The job can sometimes be made easier by propping the sheet up, allowing the heat to reach it more evenly. This can be done with a penny or a pumice pebble.

Neal Rosenblum. Pendant, sterling with agate, 3″ across. A well-made bezel has a beauty all its own. When the design of the piece and the coloring of the stone are intricate, the simple framing of the bezel can visually tie the piece together.

102

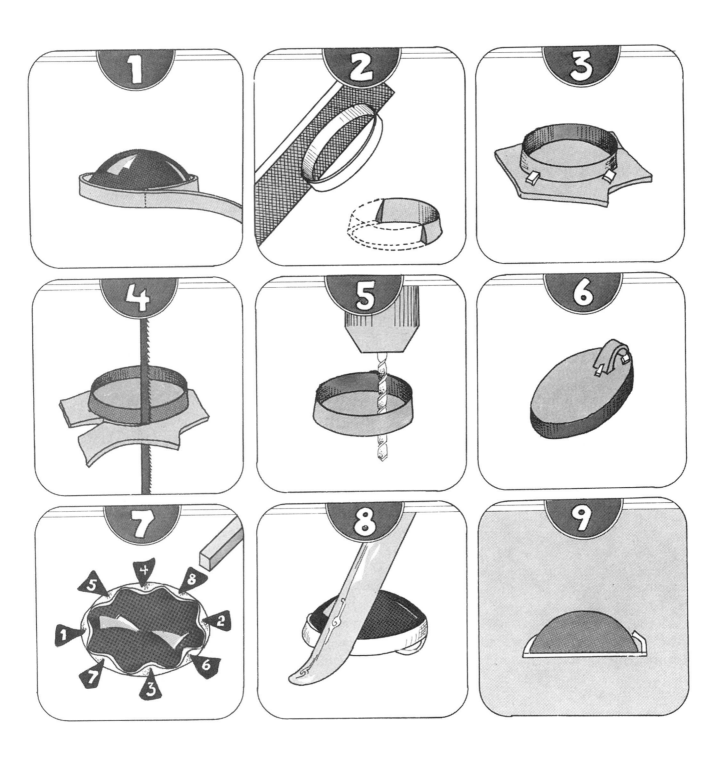

4. After soldering and checking to see that the join is complete all the way around the loop, the excess sheet is trimmed away with a saw or scissors, and the remaining edge is filed smooth until it disappears. This forms the tiny box from which the bezel takes its name.

5. Where possible, it's a good idea to drill a hole in the back plate so that, if the stone gets stuck when it is being tried in place, it can be poked out from behind. This is not possible in many cases, such as when a stone is clear or translucent and a hole would look like a flaw. When a hole is made, it can be a single round hole, a decorative series, or an ornamental design made by inserting the saw blade and piercing. The stone is then set into the bezel to determine the necessary height. Thick stones with near right-angled sides require a higher bezel than do thinner stones. There are no rules for determining the amount of metal needed to fold over the stone; intuition and experience must be trusted. Insufficient bezel will fail to hold the stone securely; an excess will make the setting process more difficult and cover up part of the stone. With the stone set in place, the edge of the bezel that sticks up beside it is observed. If it appears to be too high, the bezel wall may be lowered by filing or sanding. An option is to raise the stone to bring it to the proper height for the bezel. This can be done with cardboard, but it is better craftsmanship to use metal for the riser. A sheet of metal (usually copper or brass for reasons of economy) is cut to the exact size of the stone with the jeweler's saw, or a loop of wire of the appropriate size is formed to lie under the stone. The wire loop may be left unsoldered but must fit tightly inside the bezel.

6. The bezel is cleaned up with sandpaper or a Scotch stone and water until it is symmetrical and free of file and saw marks. It is then soldered onto the necessary attachment: a ring shank, a bale (loop) for pendant use, or whatever. This should be done with easy solder so that the previous joints won't be jeopardized. The work is then sanded again (if needed), buffed, and washed.

7. The stone is laid into place. It's possible that the sanding and buffing may have curled the bezel inward so that the stone no longer fits. It may be bent out with a blunt tool such as a file tang or a repoussé punch. To make setting easier, small work is often held in a ring clamp. Flat work is set on a soft surface such as a towel laid on the bench. The bezel is then pushed into place with a tool that is surprisingly enough called a *bezel pusher*. It is a short length of square steel rod fitted into a bulbous handle. It is held firmly in the cup of the hand and used in an upward rocking motion to lay the bezel against the stone. For the metal to be compressed equally around the bezel it is important that the crimping sequence shown in the diagram be followed. If the pushing were to start at one point and move from there around the stone, the last push might create a pucker that would be difficult to remove. After the eight points shown have been pushed in, the tool is used in the same rocking motion to push in each of the remaining bumps, again moving across the stone each time. This is done until all the bumps have been smoothed out.

8. The small scratches made by the last operation may be removed by careful filing and polishing or with a burnisher, as shown. When the bezel is smooth and shows no bumps or gaps around the stone, a high luster may be obtained by using a rouge cloth or a rouge wheel on the buffing machine.

9. The cutaway drawing shows a proper and an improper bezel. On the left notice that the bezel lies against the stone for its full height and that the top of the bezel makes a smooth transition into the stone. This explains why the bezel was filed to a knife edge in step (2). On the right notice that the bezel fits sloppily around the stone, that the top of the bezel forms a trap for dirt, and that only a tiny corner of the bezel is doing any holding.

These steps outline a logical and time-tested progression for making a box bezel. Each craftsperson and each situation will develop variations. There are a thousand tricks and shortcuts, many of them legitimate and helpful, waiting to be discovered.

Each of the steps just shown has a reason for being included, though, so I would recommend discretion in cutting corners.

Note that the box bezel is used when the stone is unsupported from the back by the piece itself. When backing is provided for the stone, as when a stone is being set on a sheet of metal that is larger than the stone and cut in a pendant shape, the backing plate (and steps 3 and 4) can be omitted. When doing this, it is advisable to put the solder on the inside of the bezel when joining the bezel to the piece, since excess solder can make an unsightly blob. In this way any scar would be covered up by the stone. In

either case this join should be made with a minimum of solder, since too much may disturb the fit of the stone.

A variation on the box bezel uses *gallery* or *step bezel*, a commercially available fine-silver strip that is made with a ledge or step at midheight on the inside. In forming the loop around the stone the bezel is fitted so that the edge of the stone rests on this ledge, eliminating the need for a bottom plate. Careful sizing is a must, since the ledge is small and there is little room for error. A well-cut stone that has a sharp angle at the base is also needed to make this type of bezel work well. The forming, filing, and setting procedure for this type of open-back bezel is the same as given above. Open-back bezels have many uses and are a legitimate shortcut but should probably not be used unsupported in something that needs to be strong, such as a bracelet or belt buckle, since they don't have the structural strength of a box unit. Step bezel is available in both plain and decorated styles.

Bezels usually lie flat and are easy to solder in place, but a special step is called for when a bezel is to be soldered onto a curved surface, as in the case of a stone mounted onto a band ring. If the bezel were soldered to a flat strip that was then curved around to make a ring, the bezel would be com-

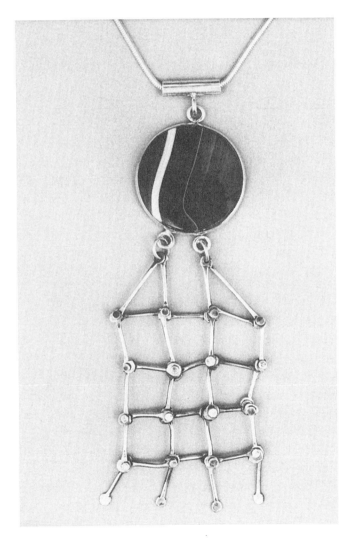

Pendant, sterling and banded agate, 5″ high.

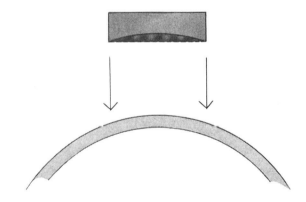

In order to solder a bezel onto a curved piece of metal, the underside of the bezel must be filed to match the shape of the curve. If the bezel is soldered onto a flat sheet that is then bent, it will be distorted when curved. To cut away the underside of the bezel, use a half-round file or sandpaper wrapped around a mandrel or dowel.

pletely distorted and would no longer fit the stone. The bezel should instead be cut to size, soldered closed, and filed to a knife edge around the top. The underside of the bezel is then cut to a curve that matches the arc of the ring. This can be done with a file or by wrapping sandpaper around the ring mandrel and rubbing the bezel along its length. When it has the proper curve, the bezel is soldered onto the otherwise completed ring shank. Most bracelets can be designed so that the stone can lie flat, with the curve beginning at either side of the bezel, so this is not usually a problem. Bezels for large stones might require some curve fitting, however, and this is worked in the same way.

A delicate setting can be made by shaping the top edge of a bezel with a saw, a file, or both. This is usually done after the bezel has been completely made and is equally appropriate for plain or step bezel. The first ring shown in the photo has a bezel ornamented by sawing, while the ring next to it uses a bezel cut with a round needle file. A standard file-edge-bezel shape is the *sawtooth*. It can be purchased ready-made or cut with a triangular file. An advantage of this type of bezel is that it can be easily pushed over a stone and is therefore especially handy for soft materials.

Another variation on the plain bezel, shown on the third ring in the photo, is called a *tooled-edge bezel*. To make this, a collar of metal thicker than for the usual bezel (in this case 18-gauge) is shaped to contain the stone and soldered closed. After it is sol-

dered to a base plate and trimmed, the rim of the collar is filed flat across the top, and the bezel is soldered to a shank and polished. The stone is laid into place, and the bezel is bent slightly inward so that it begins to hold the stone. A chasing tool in the shape of a dull chisel is used on the top edge and is struck lightly with a hammer to set the stone. The tool is held vertically and pushes a tiny flare of metal outward (for decoration) and inward (to hold the stone). The stamping must be done slowly and with enough precision to ensure that little pressure is put on the stone. Firm holding of the ring is important and can be supplemented with the help of a friend or by using a ring clamp fastened in a vise. Sharp edges are then polished off as a final step.

A similar attachment shown in the last ring in the photo, called a *collar bezel*, also starts with a loop that is made of heavier-than-usual stock. It should be 18-gauge for a small stone and 14-gauge for a large one. The bezel is constructed as described for a box bezel, except that the rim is left thick all along its height. When the assembly is complete and the work has been polished, the ring is gripped securely and the bezel is pushed over with a blunt repoussé tool. The action is identical to the setting process of a standard box bezel, except that the thickness of the rim necessitates the use of a hammer to push the metal against the stone. As the tool is repeatedly moved around the stone, its angle is elevated so that, while the first pass is made with the tool almost horizontal, by the last pass it is vertical. When the metal has been pushed so close to the stone that no gaps are showing, it can be shaped to a flat or rounded contour with files. The rim is then polished with a leather-coated polishing stick or a piece of cardboard whose edge is rubbed with compound. It goes without saying that either of these last two techniques is not suited to fragile stones.

Prongs

There are many ways to make *prongs* and no single basic structure that would be comparable to a box bezel. There are, however, certain principles of construction and setting that are relevant to all the

Rings, sterling with assorted stones. These rings show four of the most popular variations of the standard bezel. From left to right they are called the sawn bezel, the filed bezel, the tooled-edge bezel, and the collar bezel.

methods discussed in this section. Prongs are tiny metal fingers that are bent over a stone to hold it in place. They must be large enough in height and thickness to secure the stone but not so large that they can't be pushed into position. In almost all cases the prong should be rounded on the tip so that it won't catch in fabric, which would lift it up and loosen the stone. Whenever the material being set is symmetrical, as in the case of a round or oval stone, it is important for both aesthetic reasons and for proper grip that the prongs also be symmetrically arranged. On square or rectangular stones the prongs should be at the corners to protect them against chipping. As a rule, prongs are pushed into position alternately, always working opposite the last prong pushed, and are lowered in sequence: that is, all the prongs are pushed halfway into place before the final locating is attempted.

Prong settings for cabochons are usually easier to make than those for faceted stones. The drawing shows four fabricated prong settings: the first three are suitable only for cabs, while the fourth can be used with either type of stone. The first two settings are easy to make, since they require only a saw and careful measurement. The outline of the stone is traced onto the metal, and the prongs are marked out. Material from inside the outline is used to form the prongs and is bent up after sawing to allow the stone to be put into place. The second style has an inner core that is sawn out and removed completely, with saw lines cut to the circumference mark of the stone. Half the prongs thus formed would be on top of the stone, while the other half would secure it from the back. In this case the stone could be slipped into position and the prongs pushed down from either side. Be careful, however, to think ahead and to mark out an even number of prongs.

The third example in the drawing shows prongs made by soldering short lengths of wire directly to the jewelry piece. Because it is difficult to locate the wires accurately by simply holding them in place while soldering, it is a good idea to drill holes into which the wire fits snugly. The location of the holes can be carefully planned and marked to guarantee a

proper fit. Wires are then fed through the holes and soldered; any excess protruding through the back can be snipped and filed away.

The fourth setting in the drawing requires a band of 18- or 20-gauge metal whose outside diameter is exactly the same as that of the stone. Note that this band does not go around the stone but rather forms a sort of pedestal upon which the stone rests. The height of the band varies for cabs, depending on taste, but must at least equal the height of a faceted stone. For a cab the top edge is filed and sanded smooth; for a faceted stone a bevel is filed on the inside edge to accommodate the stone's underside. Short wires (square and half-round types are preferred, since their flat sides provide maximum grip) are soldered into a symmetrical arrangment around this collar. The soldering can be tricky, since the wires must stay in position around the loop and must not lean away from the vertical. To keep the prong wires in place, I file a point on each section and push it into a charcoal block around the collar. When the soldering is completed, the wire projecting on the bottom can be trimmed off and the tips of the prongs cut to the proper length.

Two tools, both sold in sets of assorted sizes, are important in setting faceted stones. *Setting burs* are small rotary files that are used in a flexible-shaft

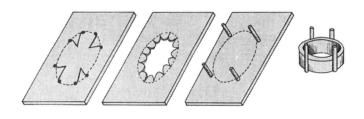

Though the bezel is the most common method of setting a cabochon, it is not the only one. The first two methods shown here use a saw. The prongs are bent up out of the sheet itself and pushed down against the stone for final setting. In the third example prongs were located by drilling holes in the sheet. Wires were then soldered into the holes, and the excess was filed away. The last example uses a band of metal to support the stone, while prongs hold it around the side. This setting may be used to hold a faceted stone by beveling the inside edge around the top of the collar.

machine or any sort of drill. They are made to conform to the underside of round faceted stones and automatically cut a proper bearing when the prongs are arranged symmetrically. A standard set consists of burs ranging in size from 0.3 to 10mm. *Beading tools* are thin steel rods about 2″ (5cm) long that have a hemispherical depression cut into one end. They are supplied in a range of sizes and come with a squat handle. After a prong has been pushed into place with a bezel pusher, the beading tool is used to push the prong further against the stone and at the same time to round it off in order to protect it from snagging. The advantage of this tool is that no metal is removed, as would be the case if the prong were rounded with a file. Beading tools make attractive circular marks when used as a stamping punch and are also used to form rivets, which are discussed below.

Casting Prong Settings

Casting is discussed in detail in chapter 8, but mention should be made here of the particular type of setting that is used with this process. It is common to build the prongs in wax and to cast them along with the piece. Each stone and design has its own considerations, but some basic principles are worth discussing. It is usually better both structurally and aesthetically for the prongs to blend into the jewelry piece to which they are attached and to appear to grow out of the surface. While this also applies to the fabricated methods just mentioned, the effect is easier and more dramatic with casting techniques. The drawing shows the building process for a single prong in soft wax. In this case round wax wire is used and is attached and shaped with a biology needle.

The location of each prong is predetermined to ensure a symmetrical arrangement. The prongs are then attached with a hot needle and positioned so that they lean back slightly from the center of the setting. Wax is then added or pulled down from the top of the prong to spread out to each side, blending into the adjacent prongs. This sets up a triangular stress pattern that any bridge builder would quickly recognize. If the prong were simply stuck on without

any relationship to the other prongs, the setting process would result in a tug of war, as a push against one prong would move the opposite one backwards. The tips of the prongs are usually left longer than is necessary, allowing more precise trimming to be done in the metal.

After the piece has been cast, it is cleaned as usual. During cleaning and buffing the prongs can be bent, so they should be checked to see that they are in position and straightened with pliers if necessary. A bearing or ledge is then cut into each prong with a graver or setting bur. It must be deep enough to allow the stone to rest securely but not so deep as to weaken the tip. The stone is then laid into place, and the prongs are cut to the proper length with snips. The prong should be cut level with the *table*, or top, of the stone. It is then filed at the tip, leaving a tapered point. Prongs made of sterling are usually pushed over by hand, using a bezel pusher. For gold prongs it is sometimes necessary to use a blunt chasing tool and a light hammer to tap them into place. It should be obvious that care is needed with each blow to prevent the tool from slipping and hitting the stone. A *loupe*, or strong magnifying

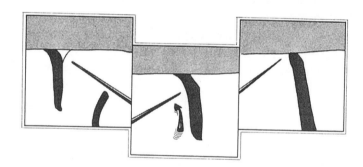

How to make a prong in wax: in the first step a wax wire is held in place and connected to the wax model with a hot needle. It is cut off with the same needle but left about twice as long as is required to hold the stone. Wax from the top of the prong is then pulled down the shaft to strengthen the base of the prong. In the third step additional wax is supplied to strengthen the base of the prong. Care should be taken that this buildup is not too large, since an excess will make it difficult to set the prong. Wax is supplied by touching a wire to the heated needle: it will run down and fall off the needle at the right spot.

glass, should be used to check the fit of the prong on the stone; when it is in firm contact, the tip of the prong is smoothed with the beading tool and/or a burnisher. Final polishing may be done with a rouge hand buff.

As mentioned earlier, there is no limit to the number of ways to set stones. The drawing shows some other settings; perhaps they may point in a direction that you want to pursue.

There is no end to the ways in which stones can be set: these are just a few suggestions. The setting at the upper left can be made for a cab or a faceted stone. The tips are curled to the side to allow the stone to be set in place, then straightened with pliers. At the lower left rivets are used to secure a plate that has been sawn and filed to match the shape of the stone. At the upper right a dark shape indicates how a stone would sit on these simple prong arrangements. At lower right a ring is built around a stone cut in a square-rod shape. The band was pierced and a plate with tabs cut to fit the hole. With the stone in place, the tabs were bent over to hold the unit together.

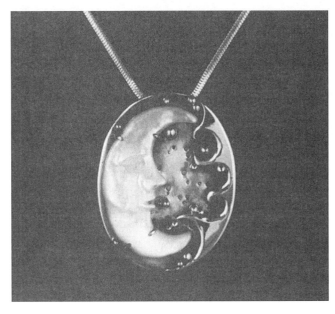

Lilly Fitzgerald. Pendant, sterling and 14K yellow gold with carved mother of pearl, 2″ high. The moon face was carved with files and a flexible-shaft tool, refined with sandpaper, and polished with conventional buffing compounds. Bone, ivory, antler, coconut shell, plastic, and some soft stones can be carved in this way to give character and individuality to a jewelry piece.

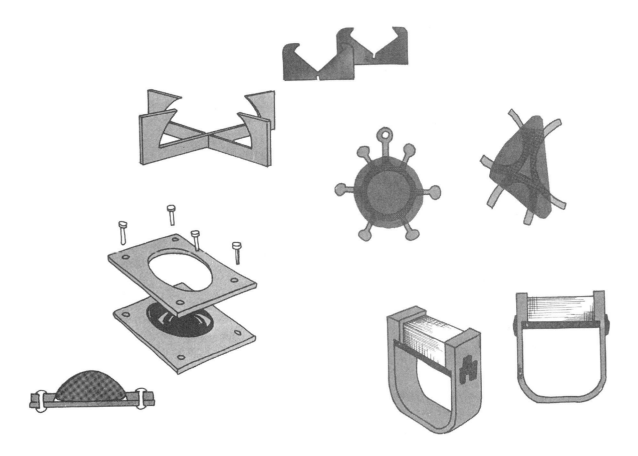

Riveting

Another clever device used to hold a nonmetal element to a jewelry piece is a *rivet*. It is a short length of wire or tubing that penetrates the pieces to be joined and flares out at either end, locking the pieces together. In planning the location of rivets remember that a single rivet allows the piece to rotate unless some method is used to hold it steady. One solution is a rim that lies along at least one side of the nonmetal element; another, of course, is to use more than one rivet. For this technique a hole must be drilled in the pieces to be joined. It's sometimes handy, though not a necessity, to glue the pieces together in order to hold them in alignment while drilling.

A wire must be chosen that fits snugly in the hole. You can drill a hole to match a special wire or draw the wire to match a given hole, depending on the equipment at hand. At any rate, it cannot be too heavily stressed that the fit *must* be snug. To check it, drill a hole the proposed size in a piece of scrap wood and fit the wire in it. When you're sure that you've got a match, drill the holes and anneal the wire.

Both ends of the wire may be flared with the wire in position, but a slightly more controlled result can be made by forming the first rivet head separately. The end of the wire is filed square across the end, and the piece is gripped in a pair of strong pliers or a vise, leaving a tiny tip of the metal projecting from the jaws. If pliers are used, they should be supported against the workbench. The tip of the wire is then tapped lightly with a *rivet hammer*. This small hammer has a flat face on one end and a thin wedge on the other. The wedge, or *cross-peen,* is used to start the metal flaring, and the flat face is used to flatten and smooth it. The wedge end is first tapped across the rivet a couple of times and then at right angles to the first blows, forming an X in the end of the wire. When the wire seems to broaden, the hammer is turned around and the flat face is used to direct the flaring evenly. Blows struck with this side of the hammer are directed straight down and angled at the circumference of the wire. In the process of

forming this first rivet head (remember that two heads are needed for each rivet) the wire may slip down in the pliers or vise a couple of times and need to be pulled up so that it can be properly struck.

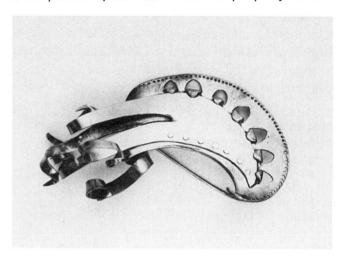

Diane Jaffe. Pin, bronze and nickel silver, 4″ across. This piece uses tabs and rivets to hold it together, achieving a range of shapes in the process.

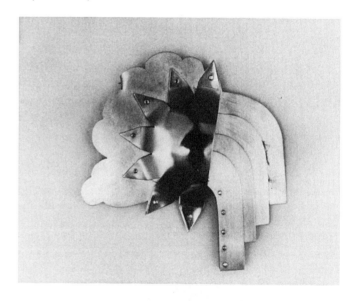

Laurie Luxenberg. *Rainbow Pin,* copper and brass, 3″ high. This piece was made without solder: rivets hold the pieces, including the pin stem, together and at the same time provide interesting accents. One of the advantages of cold attachments such as this is the clean finish that can be given to the metal: it would be darkened in any heating operation.

When the rivet head is formed, the wire is fed through the pieces to be joined and cut off. A length equal to the thickness of the wire should be left sticking out; it can be snipped or sawn, but it should be filed if snipped to form a flat end. There is a natural tendency to play it safe and to leave too much wire sticking out to form the rivet. This can be just as bad as not leaving enough, so pay close attention as you cut. The work is then held against a surface plate or anvil, and the hammer is used in the same way to form a second rivet head on the end of the wire. Smoothing up is accomplished with increasingly lighter hammer blows, working alternately on both sides of the piece.

This method yields almost flat rivet heads that nearly blend into the surface of the work. For various needs you might want the rivet to stand up higher or to blend in completely, and both results are possible. To make a rounded rivet head, the rivet is struck with a beading tool or, for larger sizes, a carpenter's nail set after it has started to flare out. To preserve the shape of the first rivet when making the second, a beading tool is clamped vertically in a vise and used as a form to hold the tip of the rivet in shape. The same beading tool that was mentioned in connection with prong setting is used, except that the handle is omitted.

Another way to make a large, projecting rivet head is to draw a bead on the end of a piece of wire with the torch. The wire is then slipped into a snug hole in the drawplate so that the bead is all that is seen on the front of the plate. The drawplate is supported on the open jaws of a vise or some similar arrangement, and the bead is flattened by hitting it, forming a nailhead on the tip of the wire that can be used as one end of a rivet. A flat head is made by striking the bead with a planishing hammer. A rounded head can be formed by using a *nail set* or beading tool. The head can be left as is or shaped with files or stamping tools. The balance of the riveting process is the same as described above.

To make a rivet that blends into the surface of the metal being held, a hole is drilled and a matching wire cut to a handy length. The top edge of the hole is then broadened or flared with a file or setting bur. The process is similar to countersinking a screw in wood. The rivet is formed in the usual way, except that, after it has been made, it can be filed flush with the surface without undoing its holding power. If contrasting materials or metals are used, an inlay effect is created. If the same metal is used, the rivet will actually disappear.

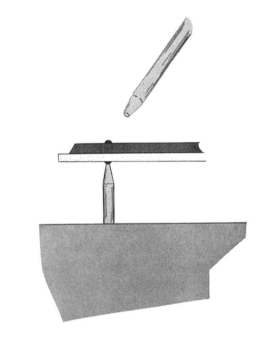

A beading tool or nail set is used to create round-head rivets. To protect the shape of one rivet head while the other is being formed, the concave-tipped punch is gripped vertically in a vise.

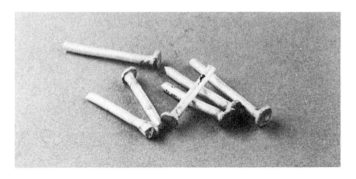

Nail-head rivets, made by flattening the beaded end of a wire, can be used as is or decorated with punches, files, or a saw. If the bead is pressed down with a nail set, the result is a symmetrical dome.

111

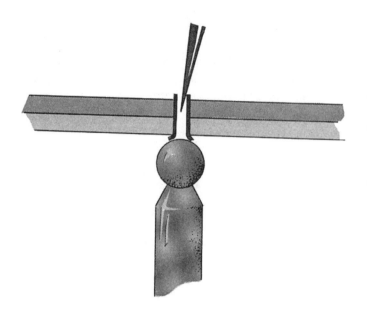

The first step in making a tube rivet is to flare one end by rotating a scribe point in it. The tube is then slid into place, sawn to the correct length, and flared by again inserting the scribe point and rotating it. With one end supported on a dapping block to preserve its shape, the other end of the rivet may be tightened by lightly tapping it with a second dapping tool.

Tubing can also be used to form rivets, which is especially useful if stress is to be minimized, as in the setting of enamels or shells, for instance. As with a solid rivet, a snug fit is needed between the tubing and the hole through the work. A length of tubing that projects only a tiny bit on each side of the work is cut and slid into position. The spreading of the rivet is begun by inserting a scribe point into the tubing and rolling it around with the hand to flare the edge. This is done alternately on both sides or ends of the tube until enough of a flare is formed to hold the rivet in position. The flare may then be broadened by using a small dapping punch or rounded repoussé tool and a light hammer. This will curl the edge of the tube out further and roll it over. Work continues from front to back until the rivet is securely set.

Marc Zimmerman. Belt buckle, copper and brass, 2½″ in diameter.

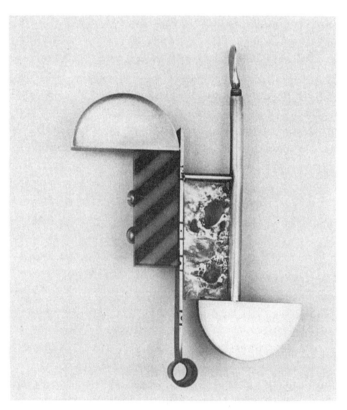

Rick Guido. Pendant, brass, fused sterling, plastic, 5″ high. There are many ways to hold jewelry pieces together, and sometimes the obvious ones are overlooked. In this piece the plastic element is held in place with screws.

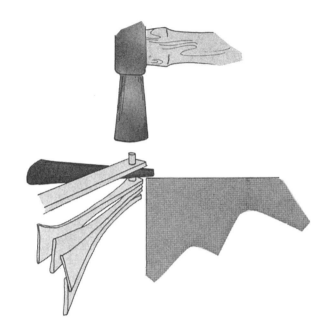

There are some cases in which a rivet pin will bend rather than flare. One solution is to grip with pliers as shown. They can be supported against the bench while the rivet head is formed by a gentle tapping of the rivet hammer.

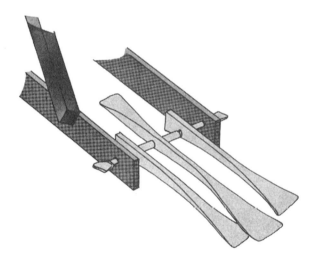

When a rivet head is impossible, a crimped end will often work. This is made by pressing a wire between pieces of steel, usually an anvil or surface plate and a flat-faced punch. Though it is tempting to stamp before cutting the pin to its exact length, this will interfere with the formation of a broad, flat tip. When working in a hard-to-reach place, the anvil support beneath can be replaced by another punch held in a vise.

For a rivet head to be properly formed it is important that the wire be supported all along its length. In this way the weight of a hammer blow forces the metal out to the side instead of just bending the wire. When used to connect two flat materials together, this support is automatically provided by the materials themselves. If the wire is unsupported, as in the case of a length used horizontally to hold dangles, a special need arises. As shown in the drawing, the wire is sometimes grasped with pliers to hold it for riveting. The tip of the pliers can be rested on the workbench for support, and a successful rivet can usually be made. If such a grip is impossible, as in this diagram, *crimping* is an alternative to the rivet. In this process a piece of metal is pinched between a steel plate (such as an anvil) and a flat-faced repoussé tool, which is struck with a hammer. It is necessary for this type of attachment that the wire be at least 20-gauge: anything less will leave a flattened bit of metal that will easily break off. The first end may be formed before the wire is slid in place. For the other end to match the first it must also be struck on the end cf a piece of wire, which means that the wire must be cut to size before stamping.

Like any other technique riveting has its share of tricks. When riveting soft materials such as wood or leather, use washers to provide a better grip. They may be made in the usual round shape, ornamented,

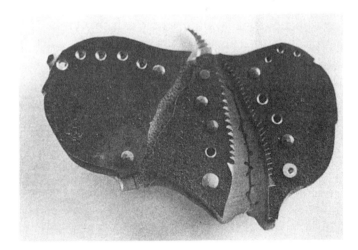

David LaPlantz. Pin, brass, iron, copper, 3″ across. Photo courtesy of the artist.

or made in contrasting metals to contribute to the design of the piece. When a rivet is meant to allow movement, as in the case of a dangle that is to swing from side to side, a piece of thin cardboard such as matchbook-cover material can be included in the riveted layers. After forming the rivet and tightening the unit the cardboard is removed by burning it out or softening it with water to allow the pieces to swing.

In addition to the use of rivets to hold nonmetal materials in place or to secure a dangle holder or hinge pin, several other functions should be mentioned. There are cases in which soldering, though possible, is undesirable, because it might anneal metal that should be left hardened, as in the case of the fibula shown in the photo. Since soldering would remove the springiness essential to the piece, the sections are riveted together. There are similar cases in which the finished assembly would be much more difficult to polish than would the unassembled sections. Since riveting does not dirty the metal as soldering does, it can safely be used to join such pieces together after they have been polished.

Enamels

The use of *enamels* is an ancient and varied art that should be mentioned under the category of nonmetal elements. Enameling is a large field in itself; and, although it is a very workable field for a jeweler to pursue, it is impossible to teach its various methods here. For those who wish to pursue enameling there are many books available on the subject. Since any jeweler should be at least conversant with the process, though, I will describe a few of the terms.

Enamels are pieces of high-quality glass that are ground into fine particles and laid onto a metal surface. When heated to high temperatures—roughly 1400°F to 1550°F (800°C to 850°C)—the glass melts and fuses, forming a thin, colorful layer that is bonded to the metal. Enamels are relatively inexpensive and are furnished preground or in lumps that are ground up with a mortar and pestle as needed. Enamels are made in transparent, translucent, and opaque glass, and a wide color range is available in each.

Because sterling silver darkens at high temperatures, it is not generally appropriate to enameling. Copper is often used, and fine silver and gold lend themselves nicely to the technique. Special high-melting solder, called *IT*, must be used when fabricating pieces to be enameled, since normal solders might come apart at enameling temperatures. For special effects foils of precious metals are used under transparent and translucent enamels to provide a bright surface. They may be applied in large sections or cut in small pieces to accent design areas.

Because each enamel fires at a slightly different temperature and because some turn other colors than expected when under- or overfired, care and research are needed to find a range of enamels that will fire together to provide a desired result. As a rule, enamels are applied in several layers, since each fusing spreads and flattens the glass. Though some enameling is done on an entire jewelry item, it is not unusual for the enamel to be made on a disk or plaque that is then set into a constructed piece with rivets or bezels.

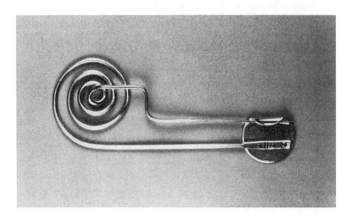

Fibula, sterling, copper rivets, 5″ across. This piece depends on its work-hardened springiness to close well. Since soldering would anneal the metal, the components were riveted together, preserving the temper.

8. Casting

All the techniques described so far can be lumped together under the heading of *fabrication*—they deal with the construction of products from stock shapes of sheet and wire. A similarly broad heading is *casting*, which deals with any method of forming material by pouring it into a mold. Although casting comprises only one chapter in this book, it is a wide field that has many applications to jewelry making. Casting can be used to make delicate earrings or heavy belt buckles; smooth, refined shapes or coarse, primitive forms. It is an ancient art that was raised to a high level of proficiency by the Egyptians and is certainly relevant to the modern world, since probably a third of the objects that we pick up in an average day have been made by this method. The technique is important to any jeweler, since certain forms are inappropriate for any of the fabrication techniques. Casting and fabrication are different enough in fact that students are warned of the difficulty in changing gears. It's hard to design both pieces sawn out of sheet and forms to be cast in the same mental breath. A little patience, however, will suffice to show you the limitations and possibilities of each process, and that point is where the fun begins.

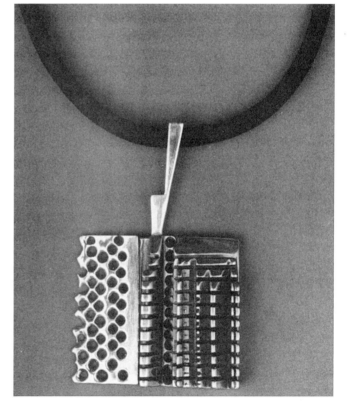

Curtis K. LaFollette. *City Scape #2* (sterling pendant), 1½″ wide. The model for this piece was cut from hard wax, using drills, a saw, and large files.

Terminology

Though casting is not a terribly complex process, it can get a bit confusing, and a firm grip on the terminology is important at the outset.

1. A *model* or *pattern* is an exact replica of the piece that is to be made in metal.

2. The *mold* is the material that contains a negative of the pattern—that is, a hole that is the same shape as the pattern.

3. A *sprue* is a channel that runs from the pattern through the mold to its surface. It is used as an exit hole for melting pattern material and is the tunnel through which the molten metal is poured into the mold. Early in the process the sprue is a solid wire, but later the same word refers to an empty passageway.

4. A *waste mold* refers to a family of casting methods in which the mold is destroyed in the process of casting. The opposite would be a reusable mold. Most of the techniques used by handcrafters use waste molds.

5. A *crucible* is a small ceramic or graphite container in which metal is melted in preparation for casting. Some are designed to be held in tongs, while others fit into specific machines.

6. A *flask* is a cylinder used to contain the mold. It is usually a stainless-steel tube, but other materials can be used.

7. *Burnout* is the process of heating the prepared mold to melt out the pattern.

8. An *investment* is a mold-making material, usually a mixture of silica, crystobalite, and gypsum.

9. A *rubber base* is a disk of hard rubber equipped with ridges, which make a watertight fit with a matching flask.

10. A *biology needle* is a steel needle fixed into the end of a dowel handle. It might be familiar to some as a clay needle.

11. A *button* is the lump of excess metal left attached to a casting. It provides weight to force the metal into the mold and extra metal to allow for shrinkage as the casting cools.

When the Egyptians began casting almost 5,000 years ago, they started with a shape formed out of beeswax. This shape was then covered with a layer of soft clay that was allowed to dry in the sun. A second layer was applied, and a third, and perhaps several more until a solid mold had been created. The clay was put in an oven and allowed to heat up. In the process it became harder, and the wax melted and dripped out. The lump of clay was then quickly pulled out of the oven, and molten metal was poured into the hole left by the wax. With a few wrinkles this is the same process that is followed today. It is called a *lost-wax waste-mold* process.

The Pattern

The largest part of casting is making the pattern, and this is unfortunately a factor that lends itself more readily to experimentation than to formal instruction. Just as it would be silly to tell a child that there is a "right" way to shape a lump of clay, it is incorrect to say that there is a right way to work wax. Each worker has a special trick or two, and perhaps you may develop a style that nobody has ever tried before. At the same time it would be irresponsible for me to pass along to the next step without giving some ideas on how to get started. The point, though, is that perseverance and a willingness to experiment give better results than just following directions.

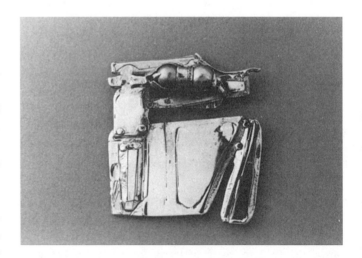

John Heller. Pin, sterling with blue pearls, 3″ across. The basic shape of this piece was made by brushing melted wax over textured clay. The resulting model was then refined and built up with sheet wax. Photo by Robert E. Barrett.

Wax

Hard Wax

Wax is available in two basic consistencies: hard and soft. *Hard* wax is supplied in blocks, tubes, or sheets and is color-coded for three grades of hardness: purple (the hardest), blue, and green. The differences between them are slight, and personal taste is the deciding factor in choosing which to use. Hard wax is about as hard as a bar of hand soap and is shaped with saws, files, and small carving chisels. Regular jeweler's saw blades can be used; but the friction heat of sawing quickly melts the wax along the cut, and the blade can easily get stuck and break. A blade made specifically for wax, called a *spiral saw blade*, removes enough material to keep the cut from sealing itself. It can be bought from jewelry-supply houses and fit into the standard saw frame. Regular jewelry files may be used, but even the coarsest require frequent cleaning. If a Dremel tool or flexible-shaft machine is available, coarse rotary files can be used to great advantage on hard wax. Small chisels or carving tools can be made from any piece of steel (coat-hanger rod works well, for instance) or from dental tools. On your next trip to the dentist ask about used tools—the chances are that he or she has a drawerful just waiting to move on to some other useful existence.

Be careful in carving not to get down to details too quickly in the shaping process. Because wax is so much lighter and more fragile than metal, it's easy to make forms that seem light but will be oversized and heavy when cast. The photo shows some rings that were carved in hard wax and cast in sterling. The four on the left were carved with the flexible-shaft machine and hand files; the right-hand one was shaped with the same tools and then carved with a dental chisel. When the forming is complete, the wax may be softly brushed with fine steel wool (4/0) or a piece of fabric to remove scratches.

When making a ring in wax, an appropriate-size square is cut off the larger block. The finger hole can be drilled, carved out with the saw and hand files, filed out with the flexible-shaft machine and a coarse cylinder bur, or melted out with a hot mandrel. The last method is needed when a perfectly round interior hole is desired. A hole is cut through the wax using any of the methods listed above and left smaller than the desired ring size. A ring mandrel is supported vertically—by clamping it in a vise, for example—and heated with the torch. When it is just too hot to touch, the torch is removed and the wax is slid down the taper. It is allowed to slide only to just above the correct size, which can be marked beforehand with a piece of masking tape (don't apply the flame to the tape: it will burn). The wax is then slid off the mandrel, inverted, and again slid to a point just above the correct size. This flipping is important, since failure to do this will yield a ring with a tapered finger hole that will be uncomfortable to wear. It might be necessary to heat the mandrel several times in the melting process. When finished, there will be a small rim of melted wax around the hole, which can be pulled away. The interior of the hole will show small ridges that are formed as the wax was cooling. These are smoothed with steel wool, removing some wax in the process, which is the reason for stopping before the hole is exactly the right size. As a rule, the ring is completed up to this step before any other shaping is begun.

Rings, sterling. These rings were all carved from wax using the flexible-shaft machine and a cylinder bur. The design on the right was carved with a dental chisel.

117

Soft Wax

Soft wax is shaped in an altogether different way and is used to produce completely different results. A soft wax called *microcrystalline,* mentioned in the repoussé section, is at the soft end of the soft-wax spectrum. It is sold in thick slabs of several square feet and can be softened with body heat. It can be pinched into shapes and will always yield rich textures, since it retains every fingerprint and tool mark. Because it is so soft, however, it can be frustrating to work with. It can be formed with heat, but too much heat makes it gooey and impossible to control. A slightly harder wax that can be bent at room temperature is available in the form of wires that are drawn to B & S gauges. Like sterling wires, this wax is available in round, half-round, square, and other novelty shapes. It is usually blue or green in color and can be bought in short lengths or on a spool, which is more economical. Soft wax that is only slightly harder than these wires (pink-colored) is pressed into flat sheets. Again, these are sold in standard B & S sizes and are available, like the wires, from jewelry- or dental-supply houses. While the

Gail M. Markiewicz. Rings, sterling. The band on the left was formed in soft wax and tooled with a needle. The top section of the other ring was made by pouring wax into a depression pressed into clay. The resulting shape was then combined with sheet wax to make the model for the ring.

wires are easily bent in the fingers, the sheet wax often breaks unless it is warmed slightly. This can be done by breathing on it or by dipping it into a bowl of warm (not hot) water. When warmed slightly, it can be bent, folded, or cut with scissors or a razor blade. Since it is transparent, shapes of sheet wax may be cut by laying the warm wax on top of a design drawing, which will show through.

Soft wax is almost always worked with heat, which is usually provided by an alcohol lamp. This can be purchased from a jewelry supplier or in the science section of a department store. A satisfactory substitute can be made from a small bottle with a tight-fitting metal lid. A hole is punched in the center of the cap from the inside out; a short piece of rope is threaded through it; and alcohol is poured into the bottle. The rope or wick becomes saturated with alcohol by capillary action and holds the flame on its tip. Ethyl alcohol for burning can be bought at a drugstore or a chemical-supply house. Proprietary solvent or duplicator fluid for a ditto machine can be substituted.

Any steel tool can be used to work the wax: a biology needle allows a great deal of versatility and is light enough to be easily manipulated. Wax is supplied to the work in progress by heating the needle and pointing it at the area that needs more material. A wax wire is then touched to the needle midway on its length, and a drop of wax is formed, which runs down the needle and falls off the tip. The trick here is to be able to control the heat of the needle, since the wax will not fall off if the needle is too cool and will flow like water if it is too hot.

Some wax workers prefer to use an electric *wax pencil*. This is a tool that looks like a child's wood-burning gadget, except that the tip is equipped with a reservoir and a hollow nib that automatically feeds hot wax. A more expensive version is available that works like an extruder, pushing warm wax out of the tip as you proceed.

The most common problem in working with hard wax is an oversized model. The most common problem with early projects in soft wax is that they tend to be pieces that can be fabricated directly in the metal.

This is logical, since the starting point is sheet and wire. It is not, however, all that the medium can accomplish. Soft-wax sheet can be warmed in water and formed in the fingers or around objects. It can be pressed, scratched, or folded. Wires can be made thicker and thinner, attached with an organic flow difficult to achieve in direct metalwork, or dripped for a blobby textural effect unlike anything possible by fabrication methods. It is probably a good idea for the beginner to play with soft wax in order to discover some of its possibilities before starting on a specific piece. If the need to avoid a constructed look is kept in mind, I'm sure that you will find other exciting directions.

Making a finger hole in a soft-wax ring is an easier proposition than in hard wax. A short piece of dowel about ⅝″ (12mm) in diameter is used to form the core of the ring. Masking tape is wrapped around one end of it until the correct ring size is achieved. This can be determined by sliding a ring sizer or an existing ring over the tape until it is snug. Wax wires or sheet may be formed directly onto the tape, with care being taken to pry the model loose periodically so that it can be slipped off when completed. When the work is formed in soft wax, it cannot be smoothed with steel wool, since the steel fibers stick to the wax and may remain in the mold and the finished piece.

Though it is tempting to do so, the piece should not be held over the flame to smooth it out, since this can quickly melt the pattern even if you are trying to be careful.

The possibilities presented by waxwork are too far-reaching to be fully discussed here, but you should realize the importance of experimentation. Waxes may be used in conjunction or blended to achieve specific results. They may be poured or pressed into molds or extruded to achieve shapes especially appropriate to your needs. If you find your interests pointing toward casting as a specialty, be willing to spend an afternoon here and there doing nothing but fooling around with some funny ideas: the results will probably warrant the time spent.

Nonwax Materials

Because it can be minutely controlled, wax is the single most common pattern-making material for jewelers. Anything that burns up completely can be used, however, which opens up all kinds of possibilities.

Richly textured, free-form shapes can be formed in *Styrofoam* by working it with a hot needle or holding it directly into the flame of an alcohol lamp.

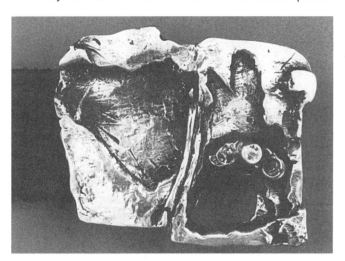

Gail M. Markiewicz. Belt buckle, sterling, 3″ across. A clay depression was used to achieve the coarse textures of this piece.

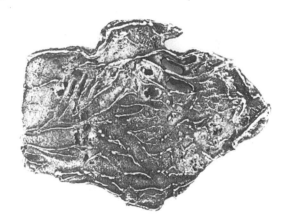

Ellen Israel. Sterling belt buckle, 3″ across. This buckle was cast from a piece of Styrofoam that was textured by working it with a hot needle. Each type of Styrofoam has its own properties: this piece was made from a dense material used in buildings as insulation.

Many types of foam are available, and each has its own textures and melting properties. Since Styrofoam can usually be picked up for free, it's feasible to make a series of models and then to choose those that turn out best. The process is immediate and haphazard but offers a good introduction to casting. Since almost no time and energy are spent in making the model, attention can be devoted to the technical aspects of the process, such as making the mold and throwing the casting.

Chuck Evans. Pin, brass with carnelian bead, 2½" in diameter. This pin was cast from a found object: the bottom of a Styrofoam cup.

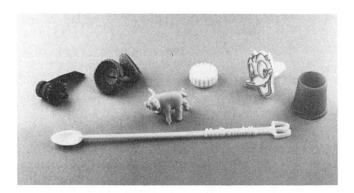

Any material that will burn out completely can be used for a model in lost-wax casting. In addition to the objects shown leaves, flowers, or insects can often be cast.

Organic materials such as leaves, pine cones, twigs, or insects can also be cast. These materials burn up and can thus be treated in just the same way as can a wax model. To test an organic material, hold it in tweezers and heat it with a torch. If it burns up completely, leaving little or no ash, it will probably burn out of the mold. Very delicate objects such as leaves or flower petals should be coated with a thin layer of wax or lacquer before casting. Wax can be painted on with a brush or heated in a pan so that the pattern piece may be dipped in. Spray lacquer is applied according to the directions on the can. Several coats of fixative or hair spray can be substituted.

Plastic items also burn out, opening up a wide variety of shapes. Trinkets from gum-ball machines, parts from a hobbyist's model kit, and the thousands of mechanical parts that we use every day are all raw material for the discerning jeweler.

Any plastic, including Styrofoam, gives off very unpleasant fumes when burned, and they can be unhealthy. Burnout should always be ventilated; but, when using plastics, take extra precautions such as turning on a fan or leaving the room.

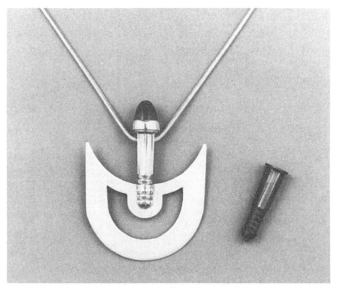

Michael J. Crawford. Pendant, sterling, carnelian, 3" high. Though found objects can sometimes be used by themselves as jewelry pieces, it is more common to incorporate the object in an altogether new way. Here a screw expander (shown at the right) is used as the core of a fabricated pendant.

Spruing

When the wax shape has been completed, it is necessary to attach a *sprue*, or wax rod, that holds the pattern in place during the mold making. Any size of wax rod may be used, but a wire between 8- and 14-gauge is common. A special sprue wax that is made just for this purpose is softer and hardens faster than others, but any wax can be used.

Since the sprue controls the amount and direction of metal as it flows into the mold cavity, its placement is quite important. Intuition and experience are your best friends here, but a few guidelines are in order.

1. Attach the sprue to the thickest part of the pattern.

2. Position the pattern so that the metal can flow smoothly into the piece, with no pinching, undercutting, or backflow.

3. Attach the sprue to an area that can be easily filed—one that has no exotic textures or intricate design.

4. Keep the sprues as short as possible.

Since not all the above rules can be followed at the same time, some common sense is needed to interpret them. The drawing diagrams the problems described below.

The sprues should be attached to the thickest part to allow for shrinkage as the metal cools. The thinnest parts will cool first and contract in the process. Cooling begins on the surface of the form, with the inside remaining molten for a split second longer. As the surface cools and contracts, metal is pulled away from the interior to compensate. If there is no metal to supply what was lost through contraction, spaces will develop within the casting, making it porous. When the piece is sprued at the thickest section (the last to cool), this area will provide metal to allow for the cooling shrinkage around the rest of the piece. As this larger section cools, metal is pulled from the button, which is left porous. If the pattern were sprued at some other point, this porosity would occur in the thickest area of the finished piece.

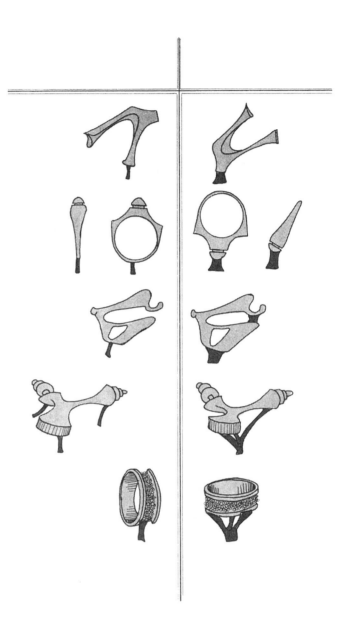

Though it is possible for metal to flow back on itself when properly melted and cast, it is wiser to arrange for it to flow in only one direction. By studying the piece it is possible to determine how the metal will flow and where the rough spots will be. It is important, for instance, that the sprues attach with a slight flare, allowing the metal to fan out as it enters the cavity. It is also a good idea to avoid absolute right angles, since this forces the metal to flow head-on into a mold wall and stalls it a split second. The metal should not be expected to pass through a thin area and then to fill a thick cavity beyond it. In such cases a second sprue is needed on the far side of the thin stretch. As shown in the previous drawing, auxiliary sprues can be used to bridge gaps within the piece. When more than one sprue is used, they should all run from the same point.

After all the wax wires are in place, the pattern is measured to determine the amount of metal needed for casting, a subject that is discussed in the next section. The sprues are then attached to a rubber base with a hot needle and again flared out to allow easy entry for the molten metal. A flask is selected that makes a tight fit with the rubber base being used. It must be tall enough to rise above the height of the pattern by at least ½" (12mm) and large enough in diameter to clear the wax by at least ¼" (6mm). The wax may be invested as is or painted with alcohol or a commercial product called *debubblizer* to reduce surface tension and to eliminate air bubbles that might stick to its surface.

Metal Quantity

There are at least three ways to determine how much metal is needed to fill the mold. One is to make a guess. Some people are better at this than others, and, of course, experience helps. I usually hold the pattern in my hand and imagine how heavy it should feel when it is made in metal. I then pick up the scraps to be used for casting with the other hand until I get the feeling I'm looking for.

A more scientific method is to use water displacement. The pattern is attached to a wire and lowered into a graduated cyclinder that is filled with

water to a specified point. When the wax is submerged, the water level will rise. The high water is noted; the wax is removed; and metal scraps are thrown into the cylinder until the level rises to the same point. This method is more successful with large pieces than with tiny ones.

The most exact method in common use requires a scale. The wax pattern, with sprues attached, is weighed. A ratio between the specific gravity of wax and the metal to be used is then established to determine the correct amount of material. In practice this means that the weight of the wax multiplied by the specific gravity of the metal yields the weight of the finished casting. For instance, the specific gravity of sterling is 10.4; if the weight of the wax were 6 grains, the calculations would run: $10.4 \times 6 = 62.4$ grains, or (since there are 24 grains in a pennyweight) 2.6 pennyweights. The chart below shows the specific gravity of some common nonferrous jewelry metals. Remember that this calculation tells you how much metal is needed for the unit that is weighed: add more to allow for a button. Be sure to keep track of grains, grams, and ounces; it's usually a good idea to double-check your calculations with a commonsense guess.

specific gravity of some nonferrous jewelry metals

18K gold	15.5
14K gold	13.4
10K gold	11.57
silver	10.56
sterling	10.46
platinum	21.45
nickel	8.85
copper	8.93

Investing

The process of *investing* is inherently a messy affair. Some care should be taken to limit the mess; but, since the plasterlike investment becomes hard in only a few minutes, attention should be directed to mold making rather than to neatness. The containers and tools used for investing are made of rubber or soft plastic, so they can be cleaned by flexing after the investment has hardened. Wet investment should never be poured down a sink, since it will clog the pipes.

Investment is basically a mixture of silica, crystobalite, and gypsum. It is available from jewelry- and casting-supply houses and in a pinch and at a slightly higher cost from a dental-lab supplier. Many varieties are manufactured, but the two brands most commonly used by jewelry craftspeople are Crystobalite and Satin Cast.

The mold-making or investing process is a war against bubbles, and there are several ways to fight it. Air bubbles in the investment tend to stick to the surface of the pattern. They appear as negative spaces when the wax has been burned out and are filled with metal when the mold is filled. They form tiny balls or warts on the surface of the completed casting and can actually occur in the hundreds, ruining a design.

Investment is usually mixed with lukewarm water. Put the water in a rubber or plastic bowl; aim for a volume that would fill the flask about two-thirds full. Sprinkle the investment into it. This should be done gently but without taking too much time, since the investment begins to harden as soon as the first particles enter the water. Throughout the mixing process be careful not to splash any water into the container of investment accidentally, since each drop will form a pebble that might interfere with a subsequent mold.

The investment is sprinkled into the water until the mixture seems to be saturated—that is, until the island of powder being formed on the surface of the water no longer sinks. The investment is then massaged with the hand to remove lumps and to ensure that the powder is completely blended. Spoons may be used; but, since it is necessary to feel the consistency of the mix, I prefer to get my hand right into it. Be careful not to stir or agitate the mix violently, since this can decrease the setting strength.

The proper consistency is difficult to describe—it resembles melted ice cream; but, since few people have a working knowledge of what a handful of ice cream feels like, another description is that it is thick enough to resist the hand as it passes through the bowl but thin enough to drip off the fingers when you lift your hand. The investment should pour into the flask with the consistency of cake batter. If it is too watery, the mold is more likely to have bubble problems. If it is too thick, the investment will not coat the model properly, and a distorted casting will result. Thin investment may be thickened if you work fast and are especially careful to massage out lumps. Thick investment may be diluted by adding a small amount of water; again, it is important that the mix be thoroughly reblended.

Hard-core Method

At this point the pattern may be painted with investment, using a soft-bristle brush. The brush should be dragged across the surface of the pattern in such a way that it does not trap air bubbles in pockets. When the pattern has been coated, it is sprinkled with powdered investment to hasten the setting of the inner core of the mold. The flask is then secured onto the rubber base and filled with the remaining investment. The flash should be tilted and the investment allowed to run down the side of the flask so that its weight doesn't knock the pattern loose. Be careful to hold onto the rubber base during this operation, or the investment might spill.

Vibration Method

A small motor with a vibrating table may be bought from a casting supplier and used to remove bubbles from the investment. The rubber bowl with the investment is placed on the vibrating pad and jiggled for no more than half a minute. The investment is then poured into the flask, which is vibrated again. In the process it's a good idea to rap the side of the flask a couple of times with something hard to break the surface tension of the investment and to let the freed bubbles escape.

Vacuum Method

The most effective weapon in the fight against bubbles is the *vacuum invester*, which sucks the air out of the mixed investment. The rubber bowl is placed onto a vacuum table and covered with a bell jar. The vacuum pump is turned on; a second switch is usually required to start pulling air out of the jar. An airtight seal is crucial: it can usually be ensured by wetting the bottom rim of the bell jar. Vacuum pumps made for investing are built to create a vacuum of about 29 pounds per square inch. As the vacuum reaches this point, the investment seems to swell and the surface starts to become frothy, resembling a vanilla milk shake. A few seconds later the investment level will fall back, and the surface will start to "boil" violently, throwing off little splashes of investment. This indicates that the air in the investment has been removed; the motor can be turned off and the vacuum released. The investment is then poured into the flask, again taking care not to pour directly onto the pattern, and the process is repeated with the flask. If the investment has started to set, it is better to omit this step; but, if it was

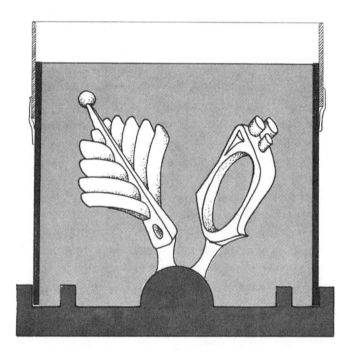

If you could see inside a flask after the investing process, this is what the mold would look like. At least a ¼" separation is needed between models and from the model to the sides and top of the mold. Before placing in the kiln for burnout the rubber base on the bottom and the plastic strip and masking tape around the top would be removed.

properly mixed, there should be time for two vacuuming operations. Because the vacuum process makes the investment rise up in its container, it is often necessary to attach a collar around the top of the flask to prevent overflowing. A strip of plastic can be held in place with masking tape. This should be done before the investment is mixed with water so that you can work quickly and avoid panic.

A flask may be extended slightly to cover patterns that do not fit in any of the flasks on hand; but, since the unsupported section of the investment above the flask is frail, there is a risk that the mold may break open. For tall pieces flasks may be improvised out of tin cans. They are weakened in the burnout process and can be used only once. When doing this, be sure to check before investing to ensure that the can fits into the casting machine. If your sprue base won't fit the can, one can be improvised by using a flat board and wax or clay to build a mound in the center and to make a seal around the base of the can.

Whatever the method of investing, the filled flask is then set to one side where it will not be bumped. In about 15 minutes it will be hard enough to withstand jostling; in about half an hour the rubber base may be removed with a sharp tug; and about an hour after the investing the flask may be put into a kiln.

Burnout

The purpose of the *burnout* is to remove the pattern by melting it and to cure (harden) the investment. This is accomplished by heating the flask in a kiln and requires a certain amount of control over the moisture content of the mold and the rate at which it is heated. Industrial burning out is a sophisticated affair involving the use of expensive equipment that is not usually available to the handcraftsman. If fancy equipment is to be used, I refer you to the booklets that come with the machines. Here I describe my own method for casting, which, while correct and satisfactory, relies on some improvised techniques.

In order to cure the investment correctly, it must be heated slowly. Recent developments in the mold-making industry have yielded an investment that is much more versatile and less demanding than that used ten years ago. The flask still cannot be heated too rapidly, however, since this will weaken and often crack the mold. It is usually sufficient for the handcrafter to arrange a low, medium, and high temperature setting for the particular furnace being used. Some experimentation is needed, but a sample solution would be to prop the door open for the "low" setting, to close the door but leave the peephole uncovered for "medium," and to close it tightly for "high." This is only a suggestion: the size and number of flasks and the speed with which the furnace heats up are determining factors. As a guideline the flask should be heated to 600°F (310°C) for about the first 45 minutes, brought to around 800°F (430°C) for the next hour, and finished at about 1000°F to 1200°F (540°C to 660°C).

Any kiln that reaches 1200°F (660°C) can be used for burnout, but a small electric type is preferred, since it requires no special plumbing, as does a gas-fired kiln. A small kiln made for enameling works well, and it can sometimes be bought second-hand by looking through a newspaper or running an ad in a craft organization's newsletter. Some allowance should be made for the wax that runs out of the mold: a steel grid such as that used in enameling may be placed inside the kiln, or a piece of firebrick or hardened investment may be set into place to prop up the flask. Several flasks may be burned out at once, but it will take longer to reach the proper temperature.

If a mold is put into the kiln before the investment has dried, the moisture in the plaster will become steam, expand, and explode the mold. Check the kiln about 15 minutes after setting the flask into it: if there is water on top of the flask or if steam is rising from it, remove it immediately, let it dry, and try again in about half an hour. Just as it is possible for a flask to be too wet to burn out, it can also be too dry, which results in a fragile mold when heated. If a mold is to be left for more than 24 hours between investing and burnout, it should be wrapped in a damp towel and a piece of plastic in the same way

that clay is stored between workings. An alternate solution is to dunk the flask in water for about a minute before placing it in the kiln. The plaster will soak up the water like a sponge, and the result will be a stronger mold.

During the first stage of burnout the moisture is removed from the investment. At about 800°F (430°C) the wax melts out, dripping through the sprue hole and onto the floor of the kiln, where it will catch fire, flame, and burn up. At this temperature the melted wax leaves a carbon residue that looks like a sooty stain. This will clog the pores of the investment, preventing the air trapped in the mold cavity from escaping. It is necessary to use a higher temperature in order to vaporize this carbon. Since acrylic vapors are released as wax is burned, it is a good idea to keep the burnout area well ventilated.

The burnout is complete when the flask has reached about 1000°F to 1200°F. At this point stainless-steel flasks have a dull red glow when viewed in dim light. The sprue opening should be free of any dark stain, and a slight reddish color should be seen in the sprue in the mold cavity. As the burnout nears completion (for an average jewelry item you can plan on about 2½ to 3 hours), the casting setup should be prepared so that the process can run smoothly.

Casting Technique

Because of its tendency to ball up when heated metal must be forced into the mold with pressure. An ancient method uses centrifugal force to push the metal into the mold. The machine used for this consists of a heavy spring that is contained in a steel canister about the size of a squat coffee can. On top of this and attached to the spring is a steel arm about 1' (30cm) long with a bracket to hold the flask and crucible on one end and counterbalancing weights on the other. The machine should be mounted on a strong object such as a heavy workbench that is bolted to the floor and should be surrounded by a metal wall to protect the user from flying metal. A frequent arrangement is to mount the caster inside a washtub.

The first step in setting up the machine, which is done before the burnout, is to balance the arm. The flask is set into the machine; the nut at the center of the arm is loosened a few turns; and the counter-balance weights are adjusted until the arm is level. I must admit that I don't follow this procedure every time but instead have weights ready for small, medium, and large flasks. This seems to provide a workable balance. If the arm is much heavier at one end than at the other, it will swing with a less even motion and might throw the metal into the mold with a jerk. Lopsided spinning is also hard on the machine. Balancing forces you to check the flask in the machine, which is a good idea, since each machine has limits on the size of the flask that it can hold. Small adjustments can sometimes be made that will allow it to fit, such as scraping some of the investment off the top, and these are much easier to accomplish when the flask is cold.

The machine is wound around to engage the spring. Three turns are usually needed; but, since some machines have more pressure than others, two or four can be used. The idea behind the use of centrifugal force is that pressure be constant and distributed through the flask, not that it be terribly hard. If the metal is thrown into the flask too violently, it will splash against the far side of the mold, recoil, and harden in the throwback position. The ideal speed for centrifugal casting is 300 revolutions per minute; so, if you are really up in the air, you can count the turns that the machine makes to determine how many times to wind it. When the machine is wound, it is held in position with a steel pin that is fitted into a slot on the canister. It is raised until it is only slightly above the arm of the machine, which is allowed to rest against it. The sideways pressure of the arm against the pin is sufficient to hold it in place.

The flask is now set into place using large tongs. It is very important that the mouth of the flask (the funnel shape with the sprue holes) be lined up with the spout of the crucible. To do this, a support of metal called a *cradle* may be needed. It is usually made of sheet metal (steel, brass, copper, etc.) but

can also be made of heavy wire folded into a loop. The metal is bent into the shape of a shallow U and curled over at the ends to rest on the posts that are built into the machine. Cradles are reusable; they should be made for the flasks at hand and stored by the caster. With the hot flask in place, the crucible is slid into its holder and moved adjacent to the flask.

The crucible, when it is new, should be lined with flux to prevent the metal from sticking in it. To do this, the crucible is heated with a torch until it starts to become red, and a pinch of borax is sprinkled in. This is repeated a couple of times until the inside of the crucible, including the spout, is covered with a greenish, glassy surface. This sealing process need be done only once, since the flux used on the metal continues to renew the covering. A separate crucible should be kept for each metal to be cast; and, since it can break easily, it's a good idea to have one or two in reserve.

The metal is placed in the prepared crucible and heated with a reducing flame, which is richer in gas than the usual soldering or welding flame and is recognizable by its yellow, bushy tip and quieter sound. On Prest-o-lite-type torches the air-gas mixture is predetermined and is sufficient for melting. The idea behind this flame is to prevent oxygen from being forced into the metal, since this would result in porous castings. The reducing flame is not as hot as an oxidizing flame, but the extra couple of minutes needed to melt the metal is worth the care. It is also possible to burn the metal—to overheat it until its surface rolls violently, allowing it to combine with oxygen—which should obviously be avoided. To help protect against oxidation, the metal is covered with powdered flux. This is usually done just as the metal starts to melt and again just before throwing the casting. Commercial-quality borax, available at a grocery store, is a common flux, and variations are sold by casting-supply houses. The metal is heated until it melts completely.

When molten, the metal will appear shiny over its entire surface and will roll itself into an oval lump. There should be no sharp edges or rough surfaces; these indicate an incomplete melt. As the metal approaches the molten state, the torch should be played through the crucible spout to preheat it. To throw the casting, get a firm grip on the arm of the machine and wind it sufficiently to take pressure off the pin, which will drop down out of the way. The arm is jiggled up and down to check that the melt is complete. If the metal rolls around the crucible like mercury, the arm is released while the torch is simultaneously lifted out of the way.

Though only the first few seconds are critical in the actual filling of the mold, the casting machine should be allowed to spin freely until it stops, which may take a few minutes. This allows the metal to cool, lessening the risk of destructive thermal shock when the mold is quenched. If you are in a hurry, sterling can be quenched as soon as it has lost its red color; gold should be allowed to cool for several minutes.

When the machine has stopped spinning, the flask is removed with tongs and plunged into a container of water. This container will fill up with used investment and will need to be drained and emptied periodically, so it shouldn't be too large to lift. A scrub bucket works well. The investment will start to break apart in the water; a knife might be needed to help loosen parts of the mold. The casting—that is, the metal article—is located and scrubbed clean with a toothbrush. The flask should be scraped clean and rinsed off, since it will corrode quickly if left in the investment bucket.

The piece is now ready to be cut off the button with a saw or snips. The button should be cleaned to remove all bits of investment so that it can be used again. The work should be pickled, allowing a clearer view of the surface to ensure that the cast is complete and solid. Most castings require some sanding; with some more heavily textured surfaces you may proceed directly to tripoli. The casting is then finished and may be polished, soldered, or colored as with any fabricated piece.

Because casting is a technical process that is usually carried out without the expensive equipment used commercially, it is not impossible for a casting to fail occasionally. In order to learn from your mis-takes, the incomplete casting should be examined to see whether you can determine what went wrong.

The most common problem is probably pitting. It usually occurs in the form of a porous surface that looks all right at a quick glance but resembles a sponge under a magnifying glass. This problem may be caused by overheating the metal, not using enough flux, or heating with an oxidizing (oxygen-rich) flame instead of a reducing flame. The solution is easy enough: use the right flame, add more flux, and throw the casting as soon as the metal is fluid and before the surface starts to spin. If pitting is extreme, the casting should be scrapped, since it can never be made to shine properly. If it occurs in only one area of a casting, it can be camouflaged in this way: lightly planish the area with the ball peen of a chasing hammer, pushing the surface metal over the holes. Continue this action with a burnisher until the surface looks smooth and shiny. The piece can then be lightly buffed—not so hard that the surface metal is removed—opening up the holes again.

Another frustrating problem is the old half-a-cast number. If not enough metal is used, the mold will fill only partway up. This is pretty obvious to spot: it's like pouring 4 ounces of milk into an 8-ounce glass. More confusing is a case in which only the bottom half of the mold is filled. This indicates that the metal was blocked in some way. One possibility is that the pattern did not completely melt out. If you rush the burnout or use an exotic material for the pattern, this would be a likely solution. Another explanation is that the mold cavity might have been filled with air and other gases, occupying the space and preventing the molten metal from entering. In a proper casting these gases are pushed into the mold, which is porous enough to absorb them. If the burnout is not hot enough, however, the carbon residue left by the wax can clog the pores and prevent the gas from escaping. A final explanation is that the pattern may have a thin spot along its length that allows the metal to freeze, creating what amounts to a plug in the cavity at that point. The solution here would be to add a sprue above the thin area.

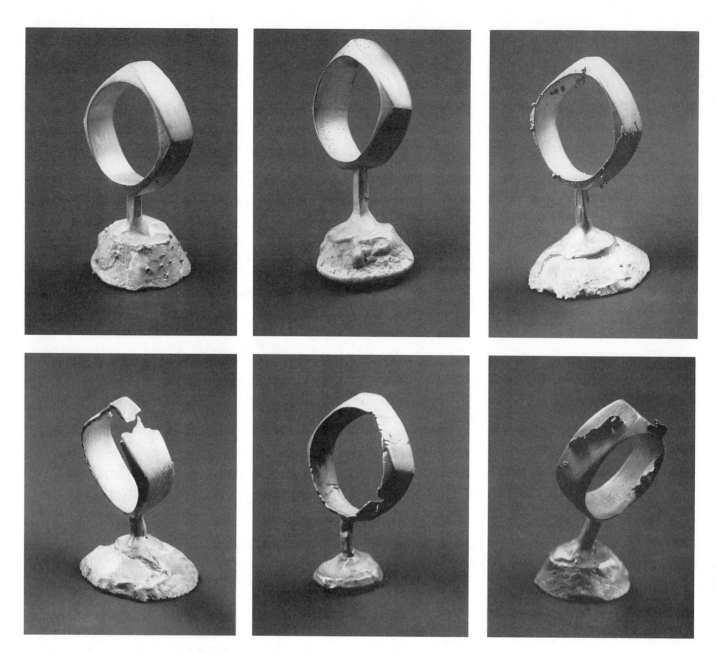

Some typical casting problems. Upper row: a good cast, porosity, bubbles. On the bottom: metal not sufficiently melted, incomplete burnout, flashing.

The metal will occasionally appear to stop right at the top of the sprue, perhaps filling only the tip of the pattern. This would indicate that the sprue became narrower at the point of attachment instead of widening as it is supposed to. It might also mean that the angle of the sprue was too great to allow the metal to flow in, but this is a rare case.

Thin, jagged sheets of metal sometimes seem to have grown out of the surface of a casting. These are called *flash* or *flashing* and are formed by heating the mold too rapidly or too soon or by dropping the mold on the way from the kiln to the casting machine. The solution to these problems is not too difficult: be careful.

Alternate Methods

Vacuum

The *vacuum* method is similar in many ways to the standard lost-wax centrifugal process just described. The same procedure is followed through the burnout with one exception. When filling the flask with investment, it is important that a space about a ¼″ (6mm) deep be left between the top of the investment and the top of the flask. Since a ¼″ (6mm) minimum is also needed between the pattern and the top of the mold, this means that a flask that allows at least ½″ (12mm) between the pattern and the top is needed. Centrifugal force, used to push the molten metal into the mold in the centrifugal process, is replaced in this method by vacuum pressure, which sucks the metal into the cavity from below. All that is required is a vacuum pump like the one needed for vacuum investing (most machines are set up to do double duty) and a suitable stand to direct the vacuum.

When the burnout is complete, the flask is set upside down or with the sprue opening at the top on a heatproof silicon-rubber pad on the vacuum table. The table and pad have a hole in the center, which is situated under the center of the flask. The metal is heated in a pouring crucible, a small ceramic dish on a long steel handle. When the metal is almost molten, the vacuum machine is turned on. The molten metal is then poured with a smooth, quick motion into the mold, where it is pulled into every cranny. After a few seconds the machine is turned off; the metal is allowed to lose its redness and is quenched in water.

To allow the vacuum to permeate the flask with maximum pull, channels can be left around the outside, as shown in the photo. Pins made of any thick wire (in this case a coat hanger) are hooked over the edge of the flask during investing. After the mold has hardened but before burnout, they are pulled out, leaving open shafts around the pattern that spread out the sucking action of the vacuum.

To allow an even distribution of suction when vacuum casting, it is important that there be a space between the investment and the top of the flask. The pulling power of the vacuum is increased if channels are left around the outside of the flask along which the suction can pull. This is done with the pieces of wire shown: in this case pieces of a coat hanger. They are removed after the investment is set.

129

Steam

The *steam* method is attractive for the beginner, since it does not require a casting machine. It is also similar to the standard centrifugal process except for the method of getting the metal into the mold. One other change is necessary here—sprues should be rectangular instead of round for the reasons explained below. They may be made by cutting 14-gauge sheet wax into strips about ¼" (6mm) wide. Other than the shape the spruing is done as usual. Investing and burnout are the same as described in the first section. A steaming handle is needed, which is easily put together as shown in the drawing. The jar lid is about 1" (24mm) larger in diameter than the flask to be used and the newspaper pad should be at least ¼" (6mm) thick.

When the burnout is complete, the flask is removed from the kiln and placed on a soldering pad, with the sprue opening facing up. The pad in the steaming handle is soaked, often by setting the handle in a dish of water. The metal to be cast is placed directly into the funnel shape in the mold and heated with a torch. If the sprues were round, the metal might slide into the holes, where it would harden and block any attempts at filling. Because the sprues are rectangular, however, the surface tension of the metal is sufficient to keep it from running in. When the metal is molten, showing no angular edges or lumps, the steaming handle is

quickly clapped down onto the flask and held there so that it makes a tight contact all around. The heat given off by the flask and hot metal immediately converts the water to steam, which, as it is trapped from above by the handle, forces itself down, pushing the metal into the mold. Once cooled, the casting is quenched as before.

Double Metals

Casting is a process with a thousand tricks; and, though I can't cover all of them here, *double-metal casting* is one that deserves mention. It is used to create a design in which two metals are made into a single piece. One way to achieve this is to make a complete casting in one of the metals and to finish it as usual. Wax may be formed around this casting by dripping or pressing it to fit the contours of the first piece. The wax can then be pulled away from the completed metal piece, carved to its final shape, and cast as usual. This is the process usually used to create rings that nestle together.

Another method that is especially appropriate if small units such as details are to be cast in a second metal is worked in the following way. The largest unit is cast by any method and cleaned to the tripoli stage. Either hard or soft wax (depending on the effect desired) is melted into place where the other metal ornament is to be made. The wax is then carved or shaped in place. This ensures a perfect fit and gives an idea of what the piece will look like when finished. When the carving is completed, the entire unit, including the first casting, is invested as shown in the drawing. It is important that the second metal be in contact with the mold, keeping it locked in place during burnout. Note that the sprue on the left runs to the outside of the sprue base. It is used only to support the weight of the metal piece through the investing process. It will burn out in the same way as any other sprue; but, because it is so far to the side, no metal will flow down it. Investing and casting are the same as usual; any of the methods mentioned can be used.

When burnout is complete, the casting is done and the flask quenched as before. Because the molten metal is slammed into the first casting with such force, it is possible that the two metals will fuse together. It is more likely, however, that they will be tightly interlocked and will appear to be permanently joined but might fall apart when stressed. To prevent this, it's a good idea to solder the new unit in place immediately, before filing and polishing have a chance to ruin the perfect fit left by casting in place.

The same process can be used effectively to include small pieces of metal in a model. Bezels, tubes, and hooks are sometimes easier to make in metal than in wax. If they must blend into the shape of the piece, they can be set into the wax and secured in place with a wax buildup. If they are light enough, the auxiliary sprue mentioned above can be omitted, and casting can proceed just as usual. It makes no difference if the section set into the model

This drawing shows the spruing arrangement for a ring. The lighter section was previously cast in sterling. Wax (the darker area) was then attached and carved in place and is about to be cast in gold. The two dark sprues allow the wax to burn out and a passage for the molten gold to enter. The lighter being invested. This wax will burn out; but, since the connecting point is off to the side, no metal will go down this channel.

is of the same or a contrasting metal. As outlined above, it is important that the included piece have some connection to the investment. If it were completely surrounded by wax, it would fall out of the mold when the wax was burned out.

Multiples

Reusable *rubber molds* are used to create unlimited repetition of a jewelry form. This has an obvious commercial application, since thousands of a single item are often made. For the handcrafter it can be used in the same way to make 10 or 20 copies of a given item or to produce a single item composed of a repeated form, such as a necklace or bracelet. Hobby shops and jewelry suppliers sell a mold-making compound that can be cured in a standard kitchen oven. It might have possibilities for a piece that is to be repeated only a few times, but such a mold will split slightly with each use, making it short-lived and inappropriate for full-scale production.

A mold is made by shaping natural rubber under heat and pressure around an existing article. When cooled, the rubber is cut with a scalpel to create two mold halves that can be pulled away to release the original form. Because the rubber is pliable, it will lift itself away from undercut areas that would be impossible to recreate in a hard mold. The rubber sections are then laid back together and firmly clamped. Melted wax is squirted into the cavity and allowed to harden. When it is solid, the mold halves are separated, the wax is removed, and the process is repeated. The wax thus formed is then cast by any method.

The equipment needed to make rubber molds, notably a vulcanizer and a wax injector, is too expensive for most home workshops. Many schools have it, and students would be well advised to make the most of them while they can. The independent crafter might consult one of the casting houses, which reproduce other people's jewelry. For a charge of between $8 and $15 they will make a rubber mold from a wax or metal model. If you want, they will then return the mold to you. A more common arrangement, however, is one in which the caster keeps the mold in his files and supplies you with the number of items you want in the appropriate metal and form. You are billed a certain casting charge per item (a conventional ring might cost around $1, depending on the size of the order) plus the cost of the metal used by weight. This is a common method for people who make their living at jewelry production; and, though there are some purists who would deny that such an item can be called "handcrafted," I think that, since the original piece and all the subsequent finishing is done by hand, it is a legitimate production method. Be advised, however, that the key to this game is numbers: if you can buy in quantity, your cost will be cut at least in half.

Primitive Methods

The casting methods just described are the ones most commonly used in the modern jewelry shop. They yield the best results in the fastest and most economical way. Some ancient techniques also have a place in the contemporary scene, not because of any nostalgic loyalty but because they can create rich forms and textures. Only three types are described here, but each can be modified, making them a broad avenue of experimentation for the interested student.

Charcoal

One primitive casting method is to carve a form directly in a lump of *charcoal*. If you want to be authentic about it, start a fire, get a log burning nicely, and then cut off its air supply. A more practical starting point is to buy several charcoal blocks from a jewelry-supply house. They are rectangular blocks measuring several inches on a side that are especially treated to resist burning. They are used up in the casting process, however, so you should have at least a couple on hand.

The shape to be cast is carved into the charcoal with any hard tool: knife, nail, or scribe. The form should be at least ½" (12mm) from the edge of the block and a couple of millimeters deep. When the

carving is complete, cut a groove from the pattern hole to the outside of the block: this will serve as a sprue through which the molten metal will enter. Flare out the top of this channel to act as a funnel. In order to allow release vents for the air that will occupy the hole when the metal enters, scratch thin lines outward around the mold. They do not need to be deep but must not be omitted. Excess charcoal dust is blown away, and the block is tied with wire to another block that will make the back of the casting. Some carving can also be done in this piece, but it is difficult to line the two sections up.

Ring, sterling. The bezel, or top element, of this ring was made by casting in charcoal. The pattern was cut into a block of charcoal with a scribe. A blob of silver was melted in the cavity and then pressed into place with a second charcoal block held in the hand. The resulting shape was then trimmed and soldered onto a shank of 10-gauge square wire.

The melting and pouring of the metal can be done in two ways. In the first the charcoal is propped in a suitable container, such as a pumice pan, that can catch any metal that might spill. A pouring crucible—a small ceramic dish clamped into a handle—is loaded with the proper amount of metal (estimate this), which is melted with a torch. During the melt the metal should be lightly fluxed with borax or a commercial preparation to prevent oxidation. As the metal reaches pouring temperature, the crucible is tilted so that the metal is poised right on the edge, and the torch is held directly over it. The mold is then filled with a smooth pouring motion until it fills up and overflows at the top. After a few seconds' delay the charcoal pieces can be opened and the casting examined.

A variation on this method is to carve the shape as above but to squash the metal into place instead of pouring it. In this case the charcoal is laid flat with the mold hole facing up. Metal is melted right in the carved area; and, as it becomes molten, a second block of charcoal, held in the hand and poised for action, is clamped down onto the molten blob to press it into all the cavities of the mold and at the same time to give it a flat back. When trying this last method, be careful to stand back at arm's length, since the force of the block hitting the molten lump can splash hot metal out to the side.

Plaster

Another primitive casting method that is similar to the charcoal technique utilizes *plaster*. Regular plaster from a hardware store can be used, but you might have better luck with investment, which is made to stand up to high temperatures. The process is exactly the same as above: either the pouring or the squashing method will work. The difference is that, instead of buying the charcoal, you begin by making blocks of plaster yourself. It's important that the blocks have perfectly flat planes so that they will make a tight fit. An easy way to ensure this is to pour the plaster onto glass. Strips of wood can be laid on glass and held in place with clay or soft wax. A square or rectangle is formed and then filled with plaster. When the plaster has set (it will feel dry and cold), the wood can be removed and the plaster will slide off. This form is then carved with any hard tool, and the casting is worked in the same way.

A variation on this method is to cast an imprint made by a found object. If a given object is set onto the glass and then covered with plaster, the plaster would take on all the details of that object. In order for the object to lift out of the plaster after it has hardened, it must be something without undercuts. The loosening process would also be aided if the object is coated with Vaseline or talcum powder before the plaster is poured. If the object is so light that it floats to the top of the plaster, it can be glued to the glass.

Cuttlefish

Another mold-making material that is especially exciting because of the texture that it produces is the skeleton of a squidlike mollusk called a *cuttlefish.* This skeleton, which is a white, porous substance, is familiar as material that is put into canary cages. It can be bought in a pet store but is a bit cheaper at a jewelry-supply house. The bone looks like a deflated football and is soft on one side and covered with a thin, plasticlike layer on the other. The first requirement is to establish two flat sides: this can be done by rubbing the soft sides of two of the bones against each other. Do this over a wastebasket, since it will make a bit of a mess. When the flat surfaces have been formed, the design may be carved into the cuttlefish in the same way as in plaster or charcoal.

All these methods lend themselves to objects with flat backs, such as pendants or pins, but it is possible to cast a ring in the cuttlefish technique. A model, which must not have any undercuts, is made of some sturdy material (wood, hard wax, plastic), and the cuttlefish faces flattened as described. Three or four short pins about ½" (12mm) long are made of wood and pushed partway into the bone in a location that will not interfere with the ring pattern. This pattern is then laid into place on one side of the bone; the other half is laid over it; and the two sections are slowly brought together with an even pressure. Be careful to support the cuttlefish along its entire length so that it doesn't crack in two. Continue pushing until the two pieces make a perfectly flush contact. They may now be opened up and the pattern carefully removed. A sprue hole is cut from the pattern to the outside of the mold, where it is flared to allow easy entry of the molten metal. As before, it is a good idea to scratch some small lines to permit air to escape from the mold cavity. The two cuttlefish sections are then put back together, with the pins serving as guides for aligning the halves properly. They are tied with binding wire or masking tape, and metal is heated in a pouring crucible and poured into the mouth of the sprue. The smell of burning bone is not pleasant, so expect a bit of complaining from anyone who is in the room with you. As soon as the metal has lost its red color, the sections can be pulled apart and the casting examined.

The characteristic advantage of cuttlefish casting is the rich texture produced by the growth lines evident in the fish skeleton. This texture can be emphasized by lightly brushing a prepared mold cavity with a soft brush. The bone structure consists of ridges that are slightly harder than the powder between them, and by brushing the powder can be removed, allowing the ridges, or grain structure, to stand up more clearly.

Any of these methods involves some luck and intuition. For the crafter who is willing to persist through some bad castings the results can be very rewarding. But don't get discouraged if the first attempt doesn't turn out. It's in the nature of the process and is probably not your fault.

Of all casting techniques the cuttlefish method probably produces the richest textures. After rubbing two of the soft fish skeletons together to achieve matching flat surfaces the desired shape is cut or pressed into the bone. When a model is being used, short pins for realignment are also set into place. The model is removed, and the two halves of the mold are set into place and held together with tape or wire. Molten metal is poured down the cavity to create the cast object. Note the vent lines: they are cut to allow air in the cavity to escape. If they are omitted (provided that there is a tight fit between the two halves), air might fill the bottom half of the mold and prevent the metal from filling the cavity.

Pendant, sterling, 2″ across. The shape of this piece was carved directly into a cuttlefish bone using a scribe and the end of a small file. The contour of the grain pattern was allowed to dictate the angles of the piece.

9. Findings

The term *findings* is usually used to describe the mechanical attachments needed to make a piece of jewelry wearable—a necklace clasp or earring posts, for example. For the purposes of this chapter I'd like to expand that definition to include all the mechanical devices that are involved in making a piece accomplish its purpose, which would include chains and hinges.

Commercial Findings

There are many dealers in commercial findings, and most sell both high- and low-quality goods. Cheap findings made of inferior materials should be avoided in favor of the sterling or karat-gold variety. Each craftsperson has his or her own favorite style of ear wires, pin backs, and other findings, and it is unnecessary to describe them here. Several suppliers are listed at the back of the book, and a look through their catalogs should be enough to show you the wide range of findings available. In many cases, however, it is more desirable and consistent with your design for the finding to be constructed along with the piece. The rest of this chapter explains how some of the basic types of findings are made. I hope that these examples trigger some ideas of your own.

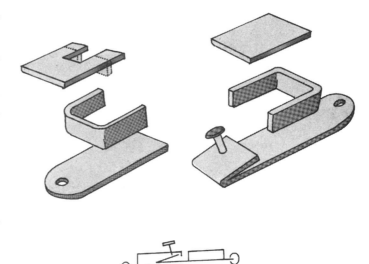

This is called a box clasp and is one of the staples of bracelet and necklace clasps. Its construction requires a bit of care and patience, but its smooth-working mechanics and excellent holding power justify the time spent. There are several methods of assembling a box clasp; in this one the flap on the top piece of the receiving (left) half is folded down. Though this flap is very small, it is the element that makes the clasp work, so it must be of the correct size and shape. The trick is to cut the metal oversize to allow the bend to be accurately made. The excess can then be trimmed off before assembling the box. To preserve temper in the folded gripping mechanism, keep it straight until after polishing. It can then be bent up and tapped into place with a mallet.

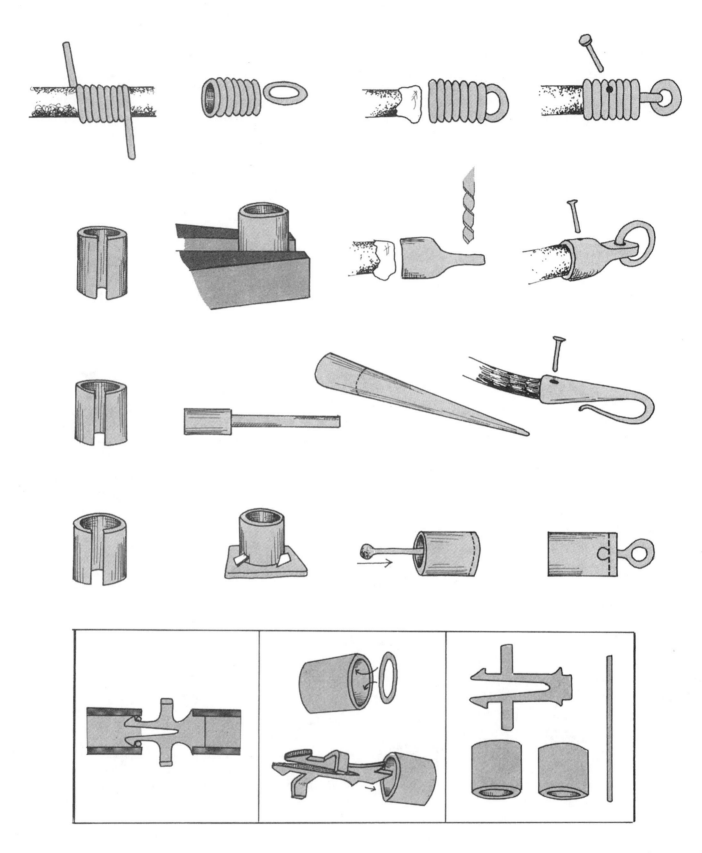

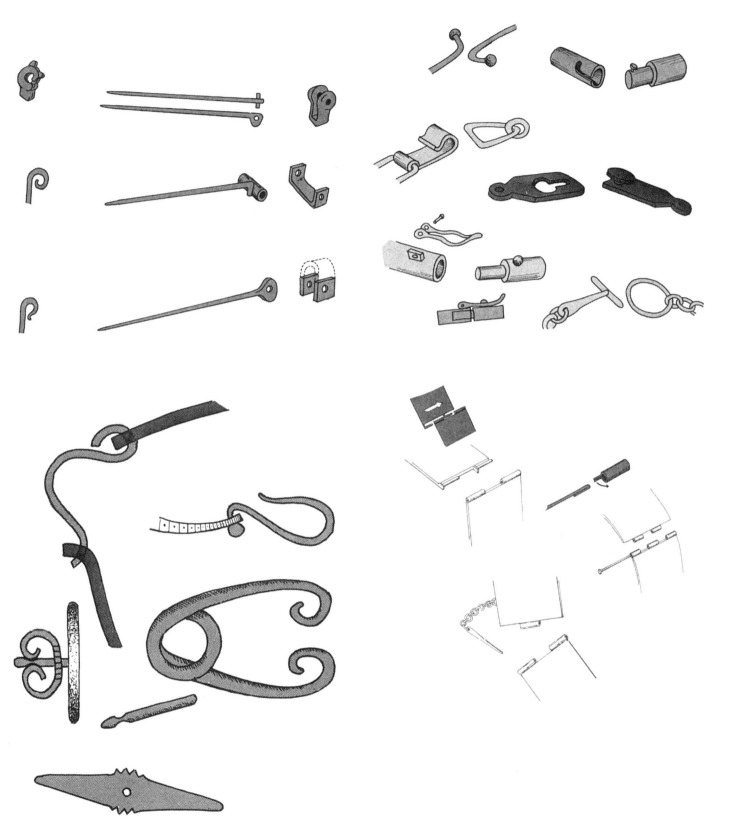

Chains

There are several standard types of *chains*, and each has many variations. Jump-ring links are made as described in chapter 3 and may be combined arbitrarily or in a repeating pattern. Medallion shapes may be made by any method and spaced along the chain. In some cases it is legitimate to leave links unsoldered when the size of the wire is sufficient to guarantee the chain's strength. It is a challenge for the beginning craftsperson, however, to make a chain with soldered links.

It's often a good idea to follow a specific soldering sequence, since this lessens the risk of soldering links together. After making all the links and checking the tips of the wire to be sure that there are no burs that might keep the ring from closing completely, twist half the wires closed and lay them out on the soldering pad. They are fluxed, soldered with hard solder, picked up in pairs, and slid onto a single ring, which is soldered closed with medium solder to create a unit of three rings. Two of these units are then joined with one ring between them to create a

unit of seven rings. The process is continued, with all subsequent soldering utilizing easy solder.

When finished, the piece should be thoroughly pickled and dried. It can be slightly shaped and elongated by gently pulling it through the drawplate. It is also possible at this point to vary the shape of the links by twisting them or pinching them with pliers. Though it is possible to polish chains carefully on the buffing machine, I do not recommend it. The metal may be colored if desired and polished with a hand cloth by holding the cloth around the chain and pulling it along its length.

Roman Chains

An attractive and substantial *Roman chain* can be made by weaving loops together as shown in the drawing. The building block here is a loop, which is soldered closed. It can be any size, but even a fine wire such as 22-gauge will make a hefty chain, so think small. Loops can be of any diameter as long as they are consistent, but I would recommend approximately ½" (12mm). The loops are soldered closed with as small a bit of solder as possible and pickled. Lumps of solder will make the links unusable, so precision is important. Each loop is then elongated by pulling it open over the jaws of round-nose pliers. This performs a second job of weeding out any loops that are imperfectly soldered. Set these aside for resoldering.

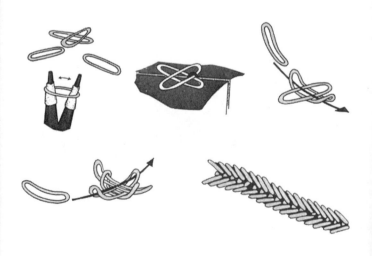

The same chain can be made in several sizes by weaving one chain inside another. A simple chain is made by feeding one loop through the next, folding it, inserting another, and so on. The top chain in the photo is made in this way. The others use this same idea but build more than one strand at a time.

The drawing shows how to make a double strand, as in the second chain in the photo. To start, you will use two loops held in an X; they can be soldered together, soldered to a peg for easier holding, or simply gripped with a scrap wire clamped in a vise as shown. The tips of the lower loop are folded upward so that a new loop can pass through them. It is folded in the middle to hold it in place. The ends of the second starting loop are then folded up, and a new loop passed through them. The weaving continues in this way until the desired length is achieved. To smooth out small lumps, the chain may be pulled through a drawplate or lightly tapped with a mallet while rolling it across an anvil. This will tighten each loop and decrease the chain's flexibility. To regain it, anneal the chain and flex it, pushing it back into itself. Repeat until it shows easy movement.

The larger, more intricate-looking Roman chains shown in the photo are made by weaving three, four, and five chains simultaneously. Start by laying out the desired number of loops symmetrically; three will look like a snowflake, four like an asterisk. The weaving procedure is the same, always feeding the new loop through the lowest loop in the pile. Though this is a simple process, be warned that it is time-consuming, especially to make and solder the loops. When using 22-gauge wire in a ½" (12mm) diameter loop, you will need 11 loops per inch for double weave and 20 per inch for triple.

Rope or Interlocking Chains

The *rope* or *interlocking chain* shown in the photo is more flexible than the Roman chain. It is very difficult to solder each link, since it must be looped through several links before closing, so I would recommend using a wire of a heavy enough gauge so that it doesn't need to be soldered. For a loop with a ¼" (6mm) diameter 16-gauge would be a good size, for example. Links are made by wrapping the wire around a rod. A consistent size and shape must be used. The easiest way to get started is to link one loop into another and to lay both down flat. Place the ring openings on the point of contact and solder them in this position. To hold the unit while building the chain, clamp the end ring into a vise or tie it to something solid with string. Feed a loop through the overlap area and close it. Remember to open and close links by twisting sideways, not by opening out

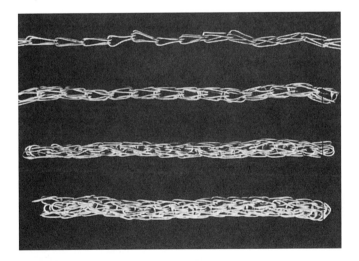

Roman chains, sterling. The top chain uses one series of loops joined together; the second chain uses loops running in two directions; the third has loops running in three directions: and so on. In each case the loops are made of 22-gauge wire in a ½" diameter link. The thickness of the bottom chain is about ¼".

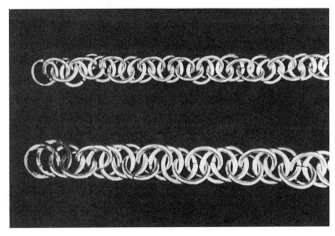

the circle. Feed another loop through the middle and end link and twist it closed. Continue in this way, always linking through the last two loops, until the desired length is achieved. A 16-gauge, ¼" (6mm) loop will need 8 links per inch; an 18-gauge, 3/16" (4mm) loop, 10 links per inch.

Chain-mail Chains

A substantial *chain-mail chain* can be made by forming a tube out of chain mail. This is a rich-looking chain, but be warned that it takes a while to assemble. As before, the starting point is a round jump ring. The rings are left unsoldered, so it is a good idea to toughen the metal by stressing it before forming the rings. The fastest way to do this is to draw the wire down a few gauge sizes and to leave it unannealed. Round jump rings are then formed as described before. Since quite a few loops are needed for 1" (2.4cm) of chain, you should again think small: the use of too large a jump ring will result in a fat cord instead of a wearable chain. Start by making a large quantity of rings. When using 22-gauge wire in rings of ⅛" (3mm) diameter, for example, 80 rings are needed for each 1" (2.4cm) of chain.

As shown in the drawing, the first step is to put together a unit of four closed links that hang on a single loop. They are then connected with another ring, which passes through two loops on one unit and two loops on the next to make the strips shown in the next figure. Four of these strips are connected side by side with more loops, passing this time through single (as opposed to double) rings. The result of this step is to create a piece of "fabric" that is four units wide and as long as can be easily handled. This section is then rolled around to connect the right side with the left side, again using a ring that passes through single loops. These units are then put together lengthwise in logical fashion until the desired length is achieved.

Many variations on this assembly are possible: try using other placements of double and single loops, for instance, or mixing rings made of different metals.

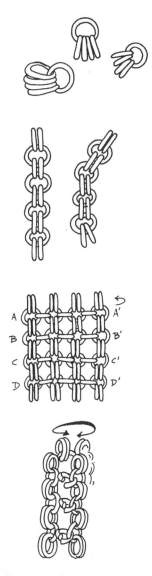

David LaPlantz. Chain-mail chains, iron and copper links. Photo courtesy of the artist.

140

Hinges

Hinges are used to provide movement in metal-work: on box lids, on bracelets, on pendants, and in many other ways. By definition a hinge includes lengths of *tubing* that are fitted together in such a way that a pin, when slid through all the tubing pieces, holds the sections in alignment while allowing them to move.

Tubing can be either bought or made. Sterling and gold tubing is sold through many metal distributors, and copper and brass tubing in small diameters is often found in a hobby shop. Larger sizes are available through a plumbing-supply house. Commercial tubing is *extruded*—that is, formed by pushing molten metal through dies that yield a desired shape. They have no seam and are often thicker-walled than tubing made in the shop. Both these factors are advantages in hinge construction, but extruded sterling and gold tubing is quite expensive, and the homemade variety can be made to work just as well.

Tubes

The first step in making a tube is to procure or roll out a piece of sheet that is quite thin—about 24-gauge or thinner for small tubes—and slightly longer than the tube is to be. To determine the width of the strip needed, the inside diameter desired is multiplied by 3.14 (pi). It is important that this strip have smooth, straight edges, since it is difficult to clean them up after the tube is formed. A point is cut on one end of the strip about 1″ (2.4cm) along its length. The strip should be annealed. It is then crimped to start the tube-making operation. This can be done with a pair of pliers or by setting a round rod along the center of the strip as it is resting either on a sandbag or in a V-groove cut into a block of wood. The rod is hammered down onto the metal strip, bending it into a trough shape. This procedure is continued until the blank fits through the drawplate, where the point is

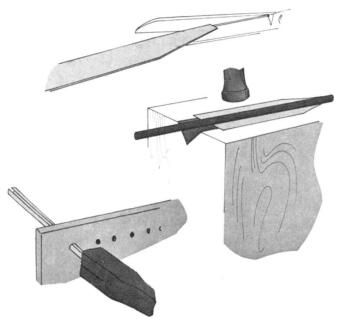

Container ring. Sterling, tourmaline. The fact that this ring opens involves aesthetic as well as practical appeal.

Though commercial tubing can be bought, it is not difficult to make in the shop. Thin-gauge sheet is cut to size with scissors. The strip is then crimped or folded along its length. One way to do this is to pound a steel or wooden rod onto the strip while it rests in a V-groove. The strip is then pulled through the drawplate until the sides of the tube meet. Since the end will be scarred from the drawtongs, be sure to allow extra when measuring the starting blank.

gripped with the drawtongs and pulled through. The blank has a tendency to twist as it is pulled through increasingly smaller holes, which should be minimized by maintaining a backward tension on the tube. Continue pulling until the sides of the tube close up and are burnished into each other. If a specific interior size is needed, a length of wire in that size may be set into the tube in mid-process to form a core to guide the tube into shape. To prevent this wire from sticking, make it longer than the tube and coat it with oil or Vaseline. When the tube is correctly formed, back up two or three holes and insert the core wire through the drawplate. The tube should catch on the plate, allowing the wire to be pulled out with the tongs.

Technique

When the hinge tubing has been made, it can be soldered closed or arranged so that the open seam is soldered in the process of joining it to the work. I personally prefer the former technique, since there is enough to worry about in the assembly process without having to remember to place the seam downwards. The knuckles or sections of a hinge are usually the same length and are used in odd numbers. The correct size can be determined with a ruler and the pieces cut. It is difficult to cut tubing straight enough to yield the square ends that make the hinge look good and work well. A tool called a *tubing cutter* or *joint tool* is used for this purpose. The tool consists of a V-shaped track into which the tubing is set. A wire attached to the tool is pulled over the tube and held down with the thumb to keep the tube from moving. The tube can then be sawn and filed square against the end of the tool. Both ends of each tube section are filed at a slight bevel to keep the solder from joining two of the knuckles. When the knuckles are cut and filed, they are slid along a steel rod that fits inside the tube: nails, pins, or saw blades are handy here.

It is important to prepare a groove or seat into which the knuckles can sit to hold them while soldering. It can often be made by filing a 45° angle on each half of the unit (e.g., the box and the lid) while they

are apart. An alternative method is to use a round, untapered file or a joint file, which is a flat file with teeth only on the edge, which is rounded. When the seat is made, the halves of the piece are tied together with binding wire, and the tube sections (with steel pin in place) are laid into position.

The work is fluxed and a small bit of solder is placed in the middle of each section. The piece is carefully heated until the solder just starts to flow, tacking the tubes into position. The steel pin is then removed; the top and bottom pieces are separated; and the soldering is continued until a proper joint is made. The fit is checked and repaired if necessary. When all is well, the work is polished, and, as a final step, a hinge pin is slid into place and lightly tapped on the ends to form small rivet heads.

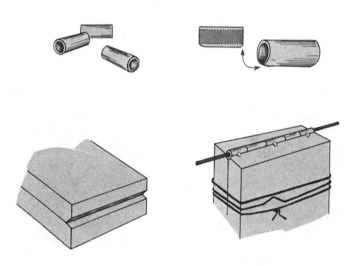

There are as many variations on hinges as there are applications for them. This drawing shows only the most basic sequence of assembly. The knuckles, or hinge sections, are cut to the correct size and filed to a perfectly square end. The underside of each end is then filed away at the point indicated by the arrows. This helps stop the solder from flowing along the hinge area and joining the sections together. A seat is prepared in which the tubing will lie. Care and patience at this step makes the rest of the job easier and neater. The unit that is being connected is then assembled and tied with binding wire. The knuckles are laid into place and held in alignment with a steel pin. Flux is applied and a small bit of solder is set into place. The work is heated carefully, and the torch is removed as soon as the solder has flowed.

A slightly more sophisticated hinge can be made by including two sheets of metal soldered along the edge that is to receive the hinges. These sheets are called *bearers,* and they strengthen the hinge area and keep the lid from opening beyond a certain point. The bearers are soldered into place and filed as shown in the drawing. The hinge sections are made and attached as described above. Delicate filing might be necessary after the sections are in place to trim the bearers and allow exactly the desired opening range.

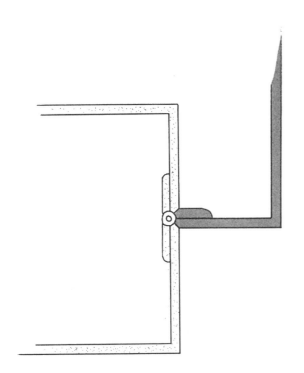

Spring Hinges

A special kind of hinge, built with a *spring* inside, is a handy device to know about and fairly easy to assemble. The spring may be used to hold the units closed or to make them open. In the first case this means that a box can be held closed without a clasp, and in the second that a clasp will hold better, since the spring maintains tension.

The hinge is constructed in the usual way, except that it is made with an even number of knuckles. In this way the last knuckle on one end is soldered to the top, while the other end piece is attached to the bottom. The hinge pin, instead of being made of wire, is made of a flat strip of spring steel. The best source for this is a section of watch or clock mainspring obtained through a watch-repair shop. A word of caution: mainsprings are under tremendous pressure and require a special tool to be removed. Trying to get one out yourself can cause serious injury.

After the article is polished and ready for final assembly, a length of spring that forms a loose fit is slid through the hinge and left flush at one end and projecting at least 1″ (2.4cm) on the other. To grip the spring in place, a wedge is tapped into the flush end. The easiest way to do this is to file a flattened point onto a piece of wire, which is trimmed off later. With one end of the spring held in this way, the projecting end is gripped with pliers and twisted. A twist in one direction will make the box spring open; in the other it will snap shut. After one turn test to see that you are twisting the right way. Depending on the size of the spring, one or several twists are needed to build up the proper tension. When this is done, insert a wedge-ended wire like the first and firmly tap it so that it will keep the spring in place. Snip off excess wire and spring, tap the wedges in as tightly as possible, and smooth off the ends with a file. Such a spring should last for many years if properly made, but it must not be heated since this will remove its temper.

10. Considerations for the Professional

One of the questions I am often asked by students is, "Can I earn a living making jewelry?" Since it seems to be on a lot of minds, let me answer that question once and for all: yes and no. If the questioner is asking, "Can I make a lot of money by selling my crafts?" the answer is no. Though it's possible, I can say almost certainly that those people who are making a good living at crafts today did not start out by looking for a fast buck. If the question is, "Can I really do what I enjoy and make enough to get by?" then I would say the answer is probably yes.

Anyone who makes jewelry is soon faced with the opportunity to sell a piece of work. This is good, both financially and psychologically. This chapter deals not with that kind of sale but with the concept of setting oneself up in business—saying to the world that this is who you are, what you do. For the student involved in the early stages of setting up a business there are several how-to books as well as federal publications available. It is the intent of this chapter to ask some questions that should be planted in the craftsperson's mind early and to offer some tentative suggestions. Instead of specifics I'm interested in showing the *kinds* of factors that are involved in a crafts business: if the next few pages seem foreign and forbidding, you may not be cut out for the crafting trade.

Business Practices

The first thing that impresses most people who are making their living from a crafts business is just how businesslike it is. Before long you'll find yourself using terms such as test marketing, production schedule, and shipping invoice. This is not automatically bad and it can provide an agreeable challenge, but it should not catch you unaware. Make up your mind that the silent craftsman living in his or her own world with no involvement in the marketplace is an image of the past.

Certain factors are immediately obvious but bear quick mention. You must be concerned with *markets*—that is, where you can sell your work. This is less of a consideration for jewelers than for other craftspeople, since it is feasible to send work far away if necessary. The point is still true, however, that you need to find people who want to buy what you want to make. If you want to make something outlandish such as a sterling toothbrush, you have to look harder for your market than if you make a more common item. You'll have to be concerned with the laws of *supply* and *demand*. If a dozen people in your part of the country are making silver toothbrushes, it's going to be rough going for you. Many people are making jewelry today; and, unless you can find something that is different and sets your work apart, there's a good chance that you will be plowed under by somebody who can make it faster and sell it cheaper. You have to decide whether to fit youself to a market or to find a market waiting for your special talents.

Overhead—how much it costs you to live—is another basic factor. If you can get by in a cheap place that has room for you to work, you'll stand a better chance of showing a profit than if you live in a fancy penthouse downtown and rent a studio in a prime location. Another aspect of overhead is your tools. Can you get by with secondhand or jerry-rigged equipment? Can you make and repair tools? Are you willing to spend time on this sort of chore?

Another commonsense factor that is too often overlooked is this: are you the type of person who can take the slings and arrows of outrageous fortune? Not everybody is cut out to make his or her living in the crafts; and, if you don't think you can make it, there is no point in getting started. As rewarding as it may be, I think that any craftsman will agree that every once in a while the life can get miserable. To make a go of it, it is necessary for you to shrug off some disappointments and to have faith in yourself and your work. As your work becomes well known, crafts can be a genuine ego booster, but in the early years they most definitely are not, no matter how good your work may be, and you should be prepared for this.

The Product

One of the factors that determines whether or not you will succeed in business is just what it is that you have to sell. In general terms I would advise a craftsperson to find a niche and stay in it at least for a while. To make this clearer, think of a continuum running from simple jewelry on one end to more complex work on the other. Simple work—bent-wire earrings, plain band rings—sells at a lower price and yields less profit per piece. It is necessary to sell a large quantity in order to make a living. You are also competing with the greatest number of jewelers in this category, since this is where everybody starts and no one has dropped out yet. Because it is sim-

ple, this kind of work can be quickly made; and, because it is cheap, people can buy it without much deliberation. Work on the other end of the scale is harder to sell, especially since the price has to be higher due to lower volume, more expensive materials, and increased time, but there is a market for this category as well. It is a matter of selling Coca Cola or Cadillacs—people are making money at both, but their approach to business is different. I find that the beginning jeweler who is confident enough to make a stand at some point on this continuum has a better chance of succeeding than does someone who makes a jumble of goods and hopes for the best.

The factors that determine the location on the continuum at which you ought to start (and this does not mean that you will be here forever) are interrelated and therefore a bit confusing at first glance. Have a heart-to-heart discussion with yourself, pick these factors apart, and deal with each as objectively as possible.

Goals

Do you want to get rich, do you want to live in the woods, or do you want to end up teaching or managing a store? It's not necessary to write a specific plan for the rest of your life, but some decisions here will help the rest of your business fall into place.

Personality

I think that this factor is too often overlooked. What kind of person are you? Can you stand the routine of working at a buffing wheel for several hours every afternoon? Do you have enough nerve to present your work to a store buyer? Not each of us is meant to be a Henry Ford, and the sooner you realize your skills and lacks, the better off you'll be. If you know, for instance, that you can charm the fur off a bear, your approach to business will follow logically. If you feel tongue-tied and dislike dealing with people, certain decisions about your business will again fall into place naturally. If you think that a lot of personal evaluation is needed, you're right. If you are constantly fooling yourself, thinking that you can be someone you aren't, your business career will move ahead in spurts, with high highs and low lows.

Finances

It takes money to make money even in a simple one-person business. If you can afford to stockpile goods and materials, your business can take a different direction from that of someone who is living from hand to mouth. Related to this factor is the amount of equipment that you own or have access to. If you have a pair of pliers and a file, the kind of work that you can do is obviously predetermined. If you have more tools, not only can you do different kinds of work but you can probably do it faster. Though it's a big step, you might consider taking out a bank loan to start your business. Short of that, get a regular job to build up some capital before starting your own business.

Skills

When you go to work for a big company, there is usually someone else to make up for the areas in which you are weak. There is also a breaking-in period when you can learn new skills as you work. In a crafts business these are rare luxuries. You are only as good as your work, and it is right up front for the world to see. Of course, you learn as you are working; but, unlike conditions in a big company, you will be too busy learning the ropes of marketing and production to advance yourself in your craft. This is not automatically frustrating but should be noted if you are thinking that you can graduate from bent-wire earrings to cast pendants in the first six months. Anything that you can do to distinguish yourself from other jewelers in the marketplace is to your advantage, and one obvious direction is to know more than they do. I don't mean to say that schooling will automatically make you succeed or that you are doomed to failure without it. But you should be aware that production work offers little time for personal growth, so do your growing before getting into business.

Methods of Selling

Many of the decisions that you make are intuitive, but the type of selling is especially so. Each method of selling has its pros and cons, and only a delicate interaction among a lot of factors can determine which is right for you.

Consignment

Consignment sales is a system in which you leave your work with a shop on the condition that, if a piece is sold, they take a certain percentage and give you the rest. It is not an especially good arrangement for the craftsperson for several reasons. You must bear the brunt of the investment: that is, your money is tied up in the silver and gold that is sitting on the store's shelf. Especially in the case of jewelry, which takes up comparatively little display room, the shop owner has little to lose by showing your work. The owner might think, for instance, that your work is in too high a price range for his customers but will agree to take it on consignment because it adds a bit of class to the store. In this case you are donating free advertising to his shop. Because the work is not theirs, consignment shops might not take good care of it; they may display it badly, allow it to tarnish, or even keep it in the back room for months in order to rotate their goods. At the same time some very good shops simply do not have the working capital to go out and buy a storeful of top-quality crafts, and they are forced to operate on a consignment basis.

To check out a shop, which is especially necessary for consignment sales, go in and have a look around. A good shop owner is sympathetic to your situation and will not mind your examination. If the cases are a jumble and there are cobwebs on the door, you should obviously pass the store by, even if it belongs to a friend. If the work is well displayed in clean surroundings and if the store seems to be doing a good business while you are there, it might be worth the risk.

Most consignment shops have a standard contract for you to sign. Pay close attention, because it is more to your benefit than to theirs. The owners are most concerned that you don't come in the week before Christmas and take all your work back, and, of course, they have a legitimate right to expect some continuity. You should expect that the work be insured and that you can retrieve it by giving reasonable notice—say, 30 days. You have a right to be paid (assuming that they are selling your goods) on a regular basis, usually once a month. The contract will also stipulate the amount of the cut that the shop will take—30% is standard, but finer shops may take up to 40%.

Wholesale

In *wholesale* marketing you sell your work to a shop, get your money, and go to the bank. Selling the work is the store's responsibility; it takes the risk of theft; it is in its interest to display the work well. Because you avoid these problems, you cannot expect to make as much profit on each piece. The idea is that you make less profit per piece; but, because you have the money in hand, you can go about your business and make more jewelry. Some of the consignment hassles are avoided by dealing on a wholesale basis. A buyer is much more conscientious about what is going to sell, since it is the store's money that is invested. Since you have your money, you don't have to worry too much about the appearance of the shop. It is a good idea, however, to exercise some discretion in this area, since your reputation, like it or not, is influenced by their presentation. This is not as crucial a factor in wholesaleing, though, since you can always refuse to sell any more merchandise to a customer.

There are some standard business practices that you should be aware of before approaching a wholesale buyer. Be clear about what you are selling and how much it is worth. Determine a price for your work and stand behind it. A buyer does not want to hear you say that a piece can be sold for a cheaper price than it is marked. This means that it was overpriced in the first place or that you are desperate for money—indicating that your work must not be too popular. An item should be sold for the same price, whether it is handled on consignment or wholesale. A common practice is to price your work at the final retail selling price; a wholesale buyer will expect to pay half that amount. Because you are getting less profit per piece, you have a right to expect substantial orders. You can set a minimum order, which should also be adhered to. The amount of your minimum can increase as your reputation spreads; it is much more becoming to raise the minimum later than to have to lower it because it is scaring people off.

It's important that you establish terms of sale and keep them consistent from one buyer to another. They are determined by your nature and experience: a common practice is to receive half the money with the first order, with the balance to be paid upon delivery of the goods. Once an account (or customer) is established in this way, a customary courtesy is to extend 30 days' credit from the date on which goods are received. Don't be afraid to send out bills: they are not complaints but reminders that money is due. Some shopkeepers immediately forget what is due and expect to be reminded. You will not benefit in their eyes from neglecting to ask for your money. Of course, all things in moderation. Don't attach your bill to a rock and deliver it through the window! In all ways be businesslike. A buyer carries a lot of responsibility and cannot be chummy and relaxed until he or she knows that you've got a good product that is consistent in quality, delivered promptly, and kept at a reasonable price. When these matters are settled, you can let your hair down and will find that the buyers will be much easier to talk with as well.

The biggest disadvantage of selling crafts wholesale is the money. An item that sells to the public for $10, for instance, has to wholesale for $5. After deducting materials, shipping, and overhead you might get $1 or $2 for your work and creativity. To the craftsperson who wants to live in the woods and not to deal with the pressures of the marketplace, this might be a bargain. To others it might seem like a ripoff. In such cases the obvious solution is to open a retail business.

Retail

A *retail* business is a shop that deals directly with the public. It can be just a step up from spreading your wares on a blanket along the curb or can include other work in addition to your own, which can be handled on consignment, wholesale, or in a cooperative arrangement. The ideal situation for a craftsperson is to own a house on a well-traveled street with good access and parking where you can set up your shop and work while tending the store. The factors that determine location are crucial and too complex to be dealt with here. Suffice it to say that, if you are flexible enough to go where the crowds are, you will have better luck with retailing than will someone who is determined to live at the end of a dirt road.

Retailing involves certain complexities. You will have to spend time being a shopkeeper: building display cases, attaching price tags, waiting on customers, taking inventory, and carrying all your profit to the bank. This is time that you won't be able to spend making jewelry, and only you can tell if it will be a welcome diversion or a frustrating interruption. Operating a retail shop does tie you down, since it is necessary to keep more or less regular hours. You might want to hire some help to work in the store, which gets you into interviewing, hiring, firing, and paying wages. You will have to deal with some sophisticated money matters—collecting sales tax, paying income tax and social security, for example—and might consider hiring an accountant to handle your books. This is not to say that, when you open a shop, you put down your hammer and put on your fanciest clothes to meet the public. Many shop owners find retailing a refreshing chance to meet people and to make the most profit on their work at the same time. It is important, however, to have some idea about what you are getting into.

Cooperative shops are popular and make a lot of sense for some groups. They are set up by a handful of craftspeople, and everybody shares the selling and shopkeeping duties. It would not be uncommon for all the members to contribute some money to get the business started and to share any losses as well.

Beware of large cooperatives that have many members and ask you to contribute a percentage of sales instead of helping with the selling. This is consignment selling under another name; and, because the shop is run by a large group, internal hassles can develop and make it fold quickly.

Image

A handcrafter wants his or her work to make a splash in the world all by itself, but it is unrealistic to count on this in such a competitive market. There is no question that your work must be good. Pendants must hang straight; solder seams should not show. But before a customer has a chance to notice these details, he has to single your work out from the rest. I hasten to say that this is not a con job. The idea is not to misrepresent yourself, which can result from overzealousness: fooling people into thinking that you know more than you do will inevitably get you into trouble. It is another matter, however, to engineer a professional program that will make your work stand out so that it can be assessed on its own merits.

A *hallmark* or *maker's mark* is a symbol that designates your work. It can be a symbolic logo, a geometric pattern, a monogram, or your signature. It makes your work easily recognizable and serves as a handle for customers who want to remember you. The use of a hallmark indicates that you are proud of your work. It also offers a fast way for you to present an image of yourself, since a well-designed hallmark reflects something of the maker. If your mark is a cute duck, for instance, its image will differ from that of someone whose mark is a coat of arms. Though a logo, or actual design, may be used for many things, a hallmark is by definition a pattern stamped into metal to designate the maker. Some simple hallmarks can be made in the shop—see the section on toolmaking in chapter 5. More complicated designs can be made to order; and, since these stamps will last many years, the cost should be considered a worthy investment.

Hallmarking is done somewhere around the sandpaper stage and consists of a single sharp rap with the chasing hammer while the work is supported on a smooth steel plate. At the same time it is a good idea to mark the metal content with a stamp that says "STERLING" or "14K," for instance. Though I've never heard of a craftsperson going to jail for this, the law states that any piece that is to be sold commercially must clearly show the maker's mark and the metal content if it is to be represented as a precious metal. The list of suppliers includes companies that manufacture custom stamps.

To a certain extent you are as famous as you make yourself appear. If you have business cards, stationery, and handbills or catalogs printed up, you will present an image of sophistication that can make you stand out in a crowd. Of course, the obvious place to start is with your hallmark logo, which should appear on everything connected with your business. Many people are surprised to find out how cheaply cards and stationery can be printed. Of course, it will require some investment, but, in comparison to the image presented, I think that it is worth the price. Printing costs can be reduced by doing your own layout—that is, by making an exact copy of what you want printed that can be photographed and offset. If you're at all handy at this and take the time to obtain press type and a good pen, professional results are not out of the question. Don't be afraid to shop around, since printer's rates vary considerably. Again, your layout and color choices have a lot to do with the image you present. If your business card is pink and in the shape of a heart, the customers that you attract will have an idea of the sort of feeling to be found in your work.

Many variations on the printed word are possible. T-shirts can be silkscreened and sold or given away. Balloons, bags, matchbooks, and bumper stickers are all possibilities for the aggressive craftsperson.

Craft Organizations

One of the first social organizations in our culture was the crafts guild, which dates back to the Middle Ages. As factories became common, they evolved into unions, and it is only in recent years that organizations of craftspeople have begun to reform themselves and to become active forces in society. Some craft organizations are little more than social clubs where the members meet to exchange gossip and voice complaints. Other organizations, however, are very beneficial and worth the membership dues and time needed to sustain them. It is difficult to tell from the outside which category a given organization falls into. Words such as "club," "social," and "get together" indicate the former. Organizations that cover a large geographical region (for example, statewide), publish a newsletter, and require at least a $10 membership fee are more likely to be the kind that get things done.

One advantage of a guild is the exchange of information. Through a guild you should be able to find out about shows, used equipment for sale, shops about to open, and special workshops and seminars. A guild can lobby for legislation that will benefit craftspeople. It can also have clout in the form of boycotts of customers with overdue bills. The threat of a boycott by all members of an active guild is a serious weapon against a delinquent shopowner. Guilds are often able to finance seminars and research that would be beyond the reach of an individual.

To get acquainted with local organizations, you might talk to local craftspeople or a librarian. Many states conduct their relations with the crafts through their state department of education, and a card to that department in the capital city should get you started with some addresses. A reference book listing organizations, called *Contemporary Crafts Marketplace,* is published by the American Crafts Council each year. It might be in the local library or can be bought from the ACC.

Appendix 1. Weights

24 grains	=	1 pennyweight (dwt)
20 dwt	=	1 troy ounce
12 ounces	=	1 troy pound
1.555 grams	=	dwt
31.1 grams	=	1 troy ounce

Appendix 2. Drill Sizes

B & S gauge	diameter (in thousandths of an inch)	diameter (in millimeters)	wire		sheet	
			ounces per foot	length per ounce	ounces per square inch	square inches in 1 ounce (approx.)
0	.325	8.255	5.30	2.3″	1.76	.6
2	.257	6.502	3.43	3.5″	1.41	.7
4	.204	5.156	2.14	5″	1.12	1
6	.162	4.064	1.35	9″	.884	1.2
8	.128	3.251	.852	15″	.704	1.5
10	.102	2.591	.536	2′	.558	2
12	.081	2.032	.337	3′	.443	2.5
14	.064	1.626	.212	5′	.351	3
16	.051	1.295	.133	7.5′	.278	3.6
18	.040	1.016	.084	12′	.221	4.5
20	.032	.813	.053	19′	.175	6
22	.025	.635	.033	30′	.139	8.2
24	.020	.508	.021	49′	.110	9
26	.016	.417	.013	78′	.088	12
28	.013	.315	.008	139′	.070	15
30	.010	.254	.005	200′	.055	19.5
32	.008	.203	.003	350′	.041	24
34	.006	.152	.002	500′	.029	35
36	.004	.127	.001	1000′	.019	53

B & S gauge			drill number	diameter *
4	▬	●	6	.204
6	▬	●	20	.161
8	▬	●	30	.128
10	▬	●	38	.102
12	▬	●	46	.081
14	▬	•	52	.063
16	▬	•	55	.052
18	▬	•	60	.040
20	▬	•	67	.032
22	▬	•	72	.025
24	▬	•	76	.020
26	▬	•	78	.016
28	▬	•	80	.014

*(in thousandths of an inch)

Appendix 3. Buying Precious Metals

Buying precious metals is not only expensive—it's confusing. Of course, everyone figures it out eventually, but in the hope of eliminating some frustration I've included below some answers to the questions most frequently asked by people starting out in jewelry making.

Silver is an international commodity, subject to daily market changes. Because of this few suppliers quote prices in a catalog. Some do, but they tend to be a bit more expensive than others. For convenience these suppliers average out the cost of sterling over a predictable time period. They then set a price that guarantees them a fair profit. If the market goes down, you lose, since they will be making more on your sale than expected. If the market goes up, they will raise their prices.

As in this case, it is generally true that the easier the buying is for you, the more you will have to pay. If a hobby shop down the street is willing to cut any size sheet that you need, they expect to make some money for their trouble. By doing some calculating and waiting for mail delivery you will probably save.

Sterling is sold by the troy ounce. Some dealers discuss it only in these terms, while others use linear measurement. To determine your cost, you need to know both. The chart gives the weight of given sizes of metal and the size of given weights. For some orders you'll want to know how much sheet $10 will buy; for others you might need 20″ (61m) of wire and want to know how much it will cost.

Almost all dealers offer quantity discounts. This is usually stated in the form of *add-ons*. The dealer bases his or her price on the daily market price of sterling. A certain dollar amount is added onto this figure for the dealer's profit. When buying a small quantity, the add-on is high; as the size of your order goes up, the amount of add-on goes down.

Another factor determining price is what is called an *item bracket*. Each dealer specifies what is to be considered as an item for a price break. Some companies let you combine items, which means that 20 ounces of assorted sheet and wire are priced in the 20-ounce category. On the same order another company might say, "An Item is a single shape," which means that 5 ounces of round wire would be priced at the 5-ounce rate; 4 ounces of 18-gauge sheet would be priced at the 4-ounce rate, and so on.

All sterling is of equal quality. It is usually furnished in the annealed state ("dead soft"). Since the standard form of sheet is in rolls that are 6″ (15cm) wide, it is often to your advantage to buy sheet with one 6″ (15cm) measurement. If you buy 5″ (14.5cm), you will be charged extra for the cutting fee, so the extra inch is, in effect, half price.

The daily market price of fine silver is quoted on the stock-market page of the *Wall Street Journal*, the *New York Times*, and similar large newspapers. You'll find it in an obscure column called "Commodities." The price is a three-decimal number, which can be confusing: read 4.752 as $4.75. By using this price, the chart, and the supplier's add-on charges you can figure out how much metal your money will buy. But the trouble isn't over yet.

Because prices fluctuate, it is difficult to actually

pay for your order. Even if you've figured the amount to the penny, you can't sent a check to the dealer, since the prices will probably have changed by the time it gets there. One solution is to charge your order either on the company's account or with a national credit card. This is the fastest way, since your order can be shipped directly, with the billing determined later. Another method is to figure the amount as closely as you can and then to add about 15% more to cover possible market fluctuations and shipping. Some dealers will refund or credit you with the amount of the overpayment, while others prefer to add silver to balance. Some companies state their preference in their literature; if not, you should write for suggestions.

The buying of fine silver and gold follow the above rules, except that gold is sold by the pennyweight instead of the ounce. When ordering gold, remember to specify both karat and color.

Appendix 4. Gemstones

Just about everybody likes polished stones; just about every jeweler likes to use them. Stones have a mythology, a beauty, and a monetary value that enable them to add special power to the jewelry piece into which they are set. There are many books available describing the historic and physical properties of gems and others that tell how stones are cut. I would never attempt to offer a detailed explanation of any of these aspects of lapidary; but, since there seems to be a need for some basic information, perhaps I can offer it.

One of the important characteristics of gemstones is their *hardness*: a stone that shines well is not much good if it dulls in wearing. A scale from 1 to 10, called the *Mohs' scale*, is used to describe the hardness of minerals. It is given for a few of the more familiar materials of the jewelry shop in Appendix 5.

Almost all stones are measured in millimeters. Calibrated stones are machine-cut to exact size; they are made to fit mass-produced settings. They are always regular shapes, with round and oval predominant. Individually cut stones are designed to make the best use of the material at hand. They may be regular in shape or follow the contour of the stone pattern. Calibrated stones can be of any quality, while only better-quality *rough* (raw material) is used for individually cut stones.

There are no hard rules for stone setting, but a few general principles are worth mentioning. Opal, elat stone, lapis lazuli, malachite, and turquoise are soft stones and are generally not recommended for jewelry that will get a lot of hard wear. When using these stones, it is often a good idea to design a setting that provides some sort of protective ridge to guard against knocks. Malachite is especially sensitive, and can be bleached out by ammonia or pickle. Silicon carbide, the material used on sandpaper, is very hard. Files, with a hardness of 7 on the scale, are equal to or softer than many stones and should therefore be used instead of sandpaper when cleaning up around a bezel or prongs.

One of the biggest families of stones is quartz. It includes agate, amethyst, aventurine, bloodstone, carnelian, chalcedony, jasper, onyx, and sardonyx. Each of these is available in a range of colors, but the most diverse spectrum lies with the agates. These are made of an aggregate of various forms of silica, often laid down in layers. By treating them with various chemicals these layers take on permanent colors, resulting in a banded or striped agate. A black onyx is produced by soaking the stone in a warm sugar solution for about three weeks and then dipping it in dilute sulfuric acid. Impermeable layers are left white, creating the banded effect. An agate soaked in an iron salt produces a blue color and is called Swiss lapis. It is not to be confused with lapis lazuli, an altogether different stone. Agates may be stained green, red, orange, brown, and many hues in between.

How do you know what price to pay for a stone? This is a good question and one that's often asked. Perhaps the best solution is to find a trustworthy supplier and to stay with him. It is very easy to make a mistake in dealing with stones: a supposed ruby in the Imperial Crown of England has turned out to be a spinel! At the risk of being too subjective, here are a few considerations for buying stones. In the end buy what you like: the visual effect is more important than the cash value.

Inclusions, or feathery lines inside a stone, are inevitable in some stones but a sign of poor quality in others. Absolutely clear emeralds, tourmalines, rubies, and sapphires do exist but are rare enough to be very expensive. A rich color with few inclusions is a guide for these stones. Diamonds, amethysts, garnets, and topaz should have few if any inclusions in order to be considered of good quality.

When buying opaque cabochons, let your eyes be your guide. There is no cost or strength difference between a deep red and a pale orange carnelian, for instance. Buy what looks good to you. Of more importance is the quality of the cut. When rolling the stone in your fingers, you should not be able to see any facets or planes. If the stone is a regular shape such as a circle, you should expect it to be perfectly round. The edge of the stone where the top curves down to meet the base should form a sharp angle. A sloppy, rounded corner requires a higher bezel to hold the stone.

When buying opals, your taste should again be your guide. Bright colors indicate a quality stone. Look closely for any cracks along the surface of the stone: these indicate a breaking point. The stone may have internal fissures that don't show up on the surface, however, so buying from a reputable dealer is especially important here.

It is not uncommon for tourists traveling overseas to look for a deal on precious stones. I don't recommend it. Gems are small enough to be easily shipped; it is common practice to have a stone mined in one country, rough-cut in another, polished in another, and sold in a fourth. The stone that you buy from a street vendor in Calcutta might have originated in South America and have been cut in Germany. You can buy it just as easily from an established dealer when you need it. Of course, there are exceptions, but unless you know exactly what to look for, you might be the victim of a con.

And one last tip. There is no reason for a stone to be marred in setting, but accidents do happen. If a stone has been scratched with sandpaper or a steel tool, the scratch can sometimes be removed while the stone is in place. Use a piece of leather glued onto a stick and a mixture of tin oxide and water. Tin oxide is a fine abrasive; it is sold by lapidary suppliers and, since it is used in glazes, can also be found at ceramic suppliers. Buff the stone with the tin-oxide slurry until the scratch is removed. It might take time but is better than destroying the beauty of a polished stone.

Appendix 5.
Hardness of Minerals

The hardness of minerals is calibrated from 1 to 10 in a system called the *Mohs' scale*. Some popular stones and common shop tools are shown below with their Mohs' numbers.

2½	human skin
	fingernail
	fine gold and silver
	lead
3	copper
2–4	chrysocolla
3½–4	coral
4	pearl
	malachite
	azurite
	rhodochrosite
5½	window glass
5½–6½	rhodonite
	opal
6	moonstone
	labradorite (spectrolite)
6–7	epidote
6½	steel file
7	quartz
	garnet
	tourmaline
7½–8	aquamarine
	zircon
8	topaz
	spinel
8½	emerald
9	silicon carbide
10	diamond

Bibliography

Armstrong, Roger. *Beginning Jewelry Notebook.* Dubuque, Iowa: Kendall/Hunt, 1977
pany, 1977

Baxter, William T. *Jewelry, Gemcutting, and Metalcraft.* New York: McGraw-Hill, 1950

Bovin, Murray. *Jewelry Making for Schools, Tradesmen, Craftsmen.* Forest Hills, New York: Bovin, 1973

Coyne, John (editor). *The Penland School of Crafts Book of Jewelry Making.* Indianapolis: Bobbs-Merrill, 1975

Fisch, Arline M. *Textile Techniques in Metal.* New York: Van Nostrand Reinhold, 1975

Kronquist, Emil F. *Metalwork for Craftsmen.* New York: Dover, 1972

Long, Frank W. *The Creative Lapidary.* New York: Van Nostrand Reinhold, 1976

Maryon, Herbert. *Metalwork and Enameling.* New York: Dover 1971

Morton, Philip. *Contemporary Jewelry.* New York: Holt, Rinehart, & Winston, 1970, revised 1976

O'Connor, Harold. *The Jewelers Bench Reference.* Crested Butte, Colorado: Dunconor, 1975

Rose, Augustus F., and Antonio Cirino. *Jewelry Making and Design.* Rev. Ed. New York: Dover, 1967

Untracht, Oppi. *Metal Techniques for Craftsmen.* New York: Doubleday, 1968

Von Neumann, Robert. *The Design and Creation of Jewelry.* Radnor, Pennsylvania: Chilton, 1972

Suppliers

Jewelry Supplies

Allcraft Jewelry Supply
135 W 29th St. Room 402
New York, NY 10001

800-645-7124
212-279-7077
212-279-6886 fax

Contenti
123 Stewart St.
Providence, RI 02903
contenti.com

800-343-3364
800-651-1887 fax
401-421-4040

Gesswein
255 Hancock Ave.
PO Box 3998
Bridgeport, CT 06605
gesswein.com

800-243-4466
888-454-4377 fax
203-366-5400
203-366-3953 fax

Frei & Borel
PO Box 796
126 Second St.
Oakland, CA 94607
ofrei.com

800-772-3456
800-900-3734 fax
510-832-0355
510-834-6217 fax

Indian Jewelers Supply Co.
601 East Coal Ave.
Gallup, NM 87302
ijsinc.com

800-545-6540
888-722-4172 fax
505-722-4451
505-722-4172 fax

Metalliferous
34 West 46th St.
New York, NY 10036
metalliferous.com

888-944-0909
212-944-0909
212-944-0644 fax

Rio Grande
7500 Bluewater Road NW
Albuquerque, NM 87121
riogrande.com

800-545-6566
800-965-2329 fax
505-839-3300
505-839-3310 fax

William Dixon
750 Washington Ave.
Carlstadt, NJ 07072
grobetusa.com

800-847-4188
800-243-2432 fax
201-935-0100

Precious Metals

David H. Fell & Co Inc
6009 Bandini Blvd.
City of Commerce, CA 90040
dhfco.com

800-822-1996
323-722-6567
323-722-9992 fax

Hauser & Miller Co
Box 500700
St Louis, MO 63150
hauserandmiller.com

800-462-7447
800-535-3829 fax
314-487-1311

Hoover & Strong
10700 Trade Road
Richmond, VA 23236
hooverandstrong.com

800-759-9997 phone & fax
804-794-3700
804-794-5687 fax

Myron Toback
25 West 47th St.
New York, NY 10036
myrontoback.com

800-223-7550
212-398-8300
212-869-0808 fax

United Precious Metal
2781 Townline Road
Alden, NY 14004
unitedpmr.com

800-999-3463
800-533-6657 fax

Index